T0305451

Managing Currency Risk

Managing Currency Risk
How Japanese Firms Choose Invoicing Currency

Takatoshi Ito

Professor, School of International and Public Affairs, Columbia University, USA; Senior Professor, National Graduate Institute for Public Studies, Japan; and RIETI

Satoshi Koibuchi

Professor, Faculty of Commerce, Chuo University, Japan; and RIETI

Kiyotaka Sato

Professor, Department of Economics, Yokohama National University, Japan; Adjunct Professor, School of Business and Law, Edith Cowan University, Australia; and RIETI

Junko Shimizu

Professor, Faculty of Economics, Gakushuin University, Japan; and RIETI

 Edward Elgar
PUBLISHING

Cheltenham, UK • Northampton, MA, USA

Published by
Edward Elgar Publishing Limited
The Lypiatts
15 Lansdown Road
Cheltenham
Glos GL50 2JA
UK

Edward Elgar Publishing, Inc.
William Pratt House
9 Dewey Court
Northampton
Massachusetts 01060
USA

A catalogue record for this book
is available from the British Library

Library of Congress Control Number: 2018931747

This book is available electronically in the **Elgar**online
Economics subject collection
DOI 10.4337/9781785360138

ISBN 978 1 78536 012 1 (cased)
ISBN 978 1 78536 013 8 (eBook)

Typeset by Servis Filmsetting Ltd, Stockport, Cheshire

Printed and bound by CPI Group (UK) Ltd, Croydon, CR0 4YY

Contents

Preface

This book is a result of almost 10 years' collaborative work by four researchers: Takatoshi Ito, Satoshi Koibuchi, Kiyotaka Sato and Junko Shimizu (in alphabetical order). The joint project on pass-through research started when Takatoshi Ito, then Professor at the University of Tokyo, created a research group at the Research Institute of Economy, Trade and Industry (RIETI). In the beginning the group traced an existing study using macro data that are publicly available from ministries. We presumed that invoicing in the yen would be increasing as capital controls are dismantled and competitive Japanese exporters would benefit from insisting on invoicing in yen, at least when they exported to Asian countries. However, we could not see a significant increase in yen invoicing.

We wanted to use micro data to understand how invoicing currency was chosen. However, it turned out that micro data at customs were not available for academic purposes in Japan. Soon after we discovered this data problem, we decided to conduct some interviews at representative Japanese exporters. Samples would be small and we were not sure whether we would be able to gain any interesting insight, let alone data for analysis. However, the interviews provided us with quite interesting results. Those in charge of export contracts (in many cases in the treasury department of a company) were able to explain why they chose a particular currency for invoicing depending on trading partners, destinations and products. One observation we obtained at an early stage was that they tend to use the US dollar for exports to Asia because they are exporting parts and components to their production subsidiaries that assemble goods (say, digital cameras) and export to the US. Exports to the US are invoiced in US dollars, and given that, exports from the Japanese head office (or mother plant) to subsidiaries in Asia are also invoiced in US dollars to avoid subsidiaries suffering from a currency mismatch of inputs and outputs. Another observation we made was that multinational companies had to manage currency risk of various currencies and it makes sense for them to consolidate it in their own global treasury company. In this case, it does not matter whether they trade in the yen or the US dollar, but they can manage world-wide currency risks by using their multi-currency cash pooling system.

The interviews with large companies were very helpful to us in understanding the determinants in choosing invoice currency. But the number of samples would have been quite limited if we had stuck to face-to-face interviews. We decided to opt for sending a questionnaire to a large number of companies. We were keenly aware of the drawbacks of such a survey – a low response rate, a sampling bias and unreliability of answers – but we thought the benefits would outweigh these disadvantages. We were careful not to cause a sampling bias by setting objective criteria regarding to whom the questionnaires should be sent. We also made efforts to raise the response rate.

We were fully aware that a research method based on questionnaires is off-the-mainstream in economics. However, when important information is not available from publicly available sources, this is the second best method and it should be respected. Fortunately, there were two earlier papers based on questionnaires in the literature on pass-through.

We conducted four questionnaire surveys, twice to Japanese headquarters, in 2009 and 2013, and twice to their subsidiaries in the world, in 2010 and 2014. We obtained a large enough number of responses to conduct regression analyses. We are confident that our questionnaire surveys provide very important and interesting insights on the invoicing currency behaviour of Japanese exporters.

We have written journal articles and working papers on each of the questionnaire surveys. We have received a great deal of encouragement and praise for our work. We soon realized that analysing all the surveys in one volume would be quite important for academic research for policy makers in Japan and other countries. So, this book is a result of our hard work with a research method that was not quite mainstream. We think we have gained a great deal of important insight that would not even have been obtained using micro data collected by the customs authorities. We are now hoping that prejudice against the questionnaire method may be dispelled after this work.

Acknowledgements

This book is a product of our collaborative research over the past 10 years. In our earlier research we realized the limit to what we could learn about invoicing currency from publicly available macro data. We shifted to a different research method: interviews and questionnaires to exporting firms themselves. Our first interview was conducted with a large electronics company in 2007, as a pilot study. Through this interview, we were convinced of the research value of hearing answers to our questions directly from firms. We then started to carry out a large number of interviews and several questionnaire surveys with firms in order to investigate the determinants of the invoice currency choice.

First of all, we have to express our great appreciation to all the firms we have interviewed. During this period, we have been helped and encouraged by comments from many of our colleagues.

As we mentioned above, the core part and novelty of our research is designing and conducting a survey among Japanese exporting firms. In total we conducted four large size questionnaire surveys, in addition to follow-up, face-to-face interviews. Details of our interviews and surveys are as follows:

Interviews with headquarters of major Japanese exporters

Year	2007/2008	2013
Number of firms interviewed	23	10

Questionnaire surveys at headquarters and at foreign subsidiaries of Japanese manufacturers

Year	2009	2010	2013	2014
Sent to	Head-quarters	Subsidiaries located abroad	Head-quarters	Subsidiaries located abroad
Number of firms that questionnaires were sent to	920	16020	962	18932

(continued)

Year	2009	2010	2013	2014
Number of responses	227	1479	185	1640
(Response rate, %)	(24.7)	(9.2)	(19.2)	(8.6)

We would like to thank the Research Institute of Economy, Trade and Industry (RIETI) for its continuing financial support of our project, in particular the cost of sending out questionnaires, as well as supporting regular research meetings. Our special gratitude goes to Dr Masahisa Fujita (Former President and CRO), Mr Atsushi Nakajima (Chairman), Dr Masayuki Morikawa (Vice President), Mr Masahiko Ozaki (Former Senior Fellow), Mr Hiroshi Ikari (Senior Fellow), Dr Willem Thorbecke (Senior Fellow) and Ms Reiko Yajima (Staff).

In RIETI, we belonged to a research group where we presented ideas and preliminary drafts, followed by lively discussions. The group members included: Professors Eiji Ogawa, Fukunari Kimura, Yuri Sasaki, Etsuro Shioji, Yushi Yoshida, Kentaro Kawasaki, Taiyo Yoshimi, Michiru Sakane Kosaka and Kazunobu Hayakawa.

We have presented preliminary drafts of chapters at various opportunities and received valuable comments. We give our special thanks to our discussants in these meetings, including Professors Joshua Aizenman, Masahiro Enya, Taro Esaka, Hiroshi Fujiki, Keiko Ito, Masanori Ono, Seiichi Nakajo, Katheryn Russ, Satoshi Shimizu and Hidefumi Yamagami.

We are also grateful to Doctors Linda Goldberg, David Weinstein, Rebecca Hellerstein, Paolo Pesenti, Hugh Patrick, Shin-ichi Fukuda, Yuko Hashimoto, Robert Dekle, Paul De Grauwe, Akira Kohsaka, Zhaoyong Zhang, Chan-Hyun Sohn, Craig Parsons and Zhang Zhiwei for their helpful comments on an earlier version of the chapters.

The authors are also indebted to the Japan Society for the Promotion of Science (JSPS) Grant-in-Aid for Scientific Research KAKENHI Grants. In the past ten years, Ito received (A) 17H00995 (2017–), (A) 25245044 (2013–2016), (A) 20100308 (2008–2012); Koibuchi received (B) 21730259 (FY2009–2010), (B) 23730307 (FY2011–2013), and (C) 15K03553 (FY2015–2017); Sato received (B) 18730187 (2006–2008), (B) 21330074 (2009–2011), (B) 24330101 (2012–2014), (B) 16H03638 (2016–2018), (B) 16K13374 (2016–2017), 17KT0032 (2017–2020), (A) 24243041 (2012–2015) and (B) 16H03627 (2016–2018); and Shimizu received (C) 21530312 (FY2009–FY2011), (C) 24530362 (FY2012–FY2014), and 15K03548 (FY2015–FY2017).

1. Introduction

This book aims to investigate how Japanese exporting firms have managed currency risk. A long-term trend of yen appreciation has been a major problem for Japanese exporting firms since the end of the Bretton Woods regime in 1971. The yen appreciated from 360 yen/dollar in July 1971 to 75 yen/dollar in October 2011, with a large fluctuation around the trend. In each rapid appreciation phase, such as in 1986–87, 1994–95 and 2009–11, Japanese exporters suffered from a large decline in overseas sales and profit. Often a recession follows the yen appreciation phase. One might wonder why Japanese exporters are not able to shield themselves from exchange rate risk by adopting yen invoicing, given that they have a strong presence in global markets. After liberalization in capital account transactions in the 1980s, the yen has become one of the freely traded major currencies. Why couldn't Japanese exporters adopt yen invoicing widely, especially for trades with Asian countries? This will be a recurring question throughout this book.

Exchange rate fluctuations have been considered a significant risk to Japanese exporting firms. Many Japanese manufacturing companies report 'sensitivity to the exchange rate fluctuation' at the time of their regular earnings report, and this sensitivity is carried by the media. For example, companies report how much they lose when the yen appreciates by one yen vis-à-vis the US dollar. Although this is a crude measure, without referring to the total sales or revenue, on 5 June 2012, for example, at the end of the yen appreciation wave after the collapse of Lehman Brothers, Nikkei reported that a one-yen appreciation vis-à-vis the US dollar would reduce Toyota's consolidated profits by 35 billion yen and Honda's by 17 billion yen.[1] The latest reports in May 2017 indicated that Toyota's sensitivity increased to 45 billion yen, while Honda's sensitivity decreased to 12.7 billion yen.[2] Among the electronics companies, Panasonic announced in February 2017 that appreciation by one yen reduces sales by 35 billion yen and operating profits by 3.2 billion yen.[3] Admittedly, these figures are rather anecdotal for representative firms.

---

[1] Nikkei (https://www.nikkei.com/article/DGXNASGD0404N_U2A600C1DT0000/).
[2] The Kabushiki Shinbun (http://kabushiki.jp/gentei/2017/0512.html).
[3] Reuters, technology report, 2 February 2017 (http://jp.reuters.com/article/panasonic -fcpa-idJPKBN15H0QX).

Figure 1.1   *REER vs. real operating income (manufacturing)*

Hanagaki and Hori (2015) used a large corporate panel data set, with
45 000 firms in Japan, and estimated the effects of exchange rate changes
on the performance of firms in FY1994 to FY2013.[4] Of course, corporate
performances are influenced by factors other than the exchange rate. As
control variables, they include the annual growth rates of domestic private
demand, domestic public demand, the US and European economies, and
Asian economies, as well as rate of change of the oil price. They confirmed
that both the sales and Return on Assets of Japanese firms increase
significantly when the yen depreciates.[5]

We examine whether the high correlation between the exchange rate
and aggregate corporate operating profits can be seen in macro data as
well as in corporate-level data. Figure 1.1 shows the relation between the
operating income of the manufacturing sector (deflated by CPI index)
and the real effective exchange rate (REER) from 1985:Q1 to 2017:Q2.
When the yen appreciates (pointing downward), the operating income
tends to go down. This is a very rough measure, because operating income

---

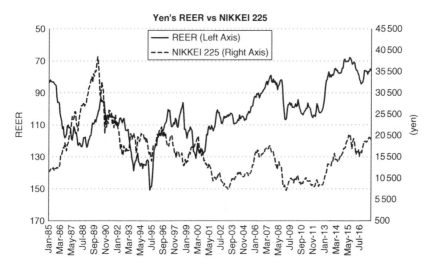

Source: Bank of Japan, NIKKEI.

Figure 1.2   Yen's REER vs. NIKKEI 225

is influenced by domestic income (a boom or a recession in Japan) and foreign income (a boom or a recession in the United States), and oil prices, in addition to the exchange rate. However, the figure suggests that the operating income of the Japanese manufacturing sector has a high correlation with the exchange rate. There were a few sharp yen appreciation episodes – the 1999–2000 period (the euro introduction) and 2009 (global financial crisis) – which coincided with a decline in operating income. There were also depreciation episodes. A long depreciation from 2000 to 2007 coincided with a sustained increase in operating income of the Japanese manufacturing sector. Also, a sharp depreciation in 2013–15 – associated with the Bank of Japan's quantitative and qualitative easing – was associated with a sharp increase in the operating income. Based on the above observations, we think that the Japanese manufacturing sector is still exposed to exchange rate risk, despite efforts over many years to manage the risk.

As corporate profits are affected, stock prices are also affected by the exchange rate fluctuation. Depreciation (appreciation) of the yen leads to a rise (decline, respectively) in stock prices in Japan. Figure 1.2 shows the relationship between the REER and Nikkei 225 from January 1985 to July 2017. The correlation is as prominent as the correlation in the operating income in Figure 1.1.

When the yen appreciation drives down corporate profits, companies may demand a macroeconomic stimulus package. The yen's appreciation was once dubbed the Achilles heel of the Japanese economy. At the height of the US–Japan trade conflict, in 1993–95, it was said that the United States often talked down the dollar, causing the yen appreciation, in order to put pressure on Japan for the particular trade agenda.

Faced with a long-run trend of yen appreciation, and the large fluctuations around this trend, Japanese exporting firms have taken many countermeasures in an attempt to lessen the impact of the exchange rate on their sales and profits. When Japanese export firms did not have much competitiveness in terms of product quality, brand names or design, they had to export from Japan with export prices invoiced in US dollars. This was to keep the dollar prices in the US retail market unchanged despite the yen's appreciation trend and associated fluctuations. As prices are adjusted to the market (pricing-to-market (PTM)), sales are unaffected. However, this strategy could easily make the production costs in the yen exceed the revenues from exports (as profits had to be converted from US dollars to yen), when the yen sharply appreciates.

In the 1980s Japanese automobile industries started to build factories in North America so that both production costs and sales would be in US dollars. This is a natural hedge against exchange rate fluctuations. The profits from US sales measured in US dollars will be stabilized, although yen-denominated profits still fluctuate. Japanese auto makers gradually expanded direct investment in North America and in Europe throughout the 1980s and 1990s.

In order to describe the Japanese exporters' problem, let us describe the relation among invoicing, export price adjustments, sales price, profits and exchange rate. Suppose a Japanese auto maker exports its products to the US. Denote the Japanese exporter's production cost of one unit of exports (say, one automobile) by C (in yen) and profit margin by m^E. The export price in yen becomes $P^E = (1 + m^E)C$ in yen. The export price in the US dollar is derived by dividing the export price by the exchange rate S (yen per dollar): $P^I = (1 + m^E)C/S$.

The exporting company has to decide whether the export should be invoiced in the yen (producer's currency pricing) or in the dollar (consumer's or local currency pricing). Invoicing in the currency of exporters (or yen invoicing in this case) is sometimes called 'producer's currency pricing', and invoicing in the currency of destination market (or dollar invoicing in this case) is sometimes called 'consumer's currency pricing' or 'local currency pricing'.

Invoicing in the yen means the export price P^E is fixed, and denoted by $\overline{P}^E$; and invoicing in the dollar means the dollar price of the export

P^I is fixed, and denoted by $\overline{P}^I$. In the case of invoicing in the dollar, the change in the exchange rate is offset by the one-to-one change in profit margin.

If denominated in US dollars, the firm's export income measured in yen is not determined until US dollar payments are received and converted into yen. As the exchange rate fluctuates between the time of signing the export contract and the time of receiving payment from customers, the firm's income and profit can vary substantially when converted into yen, either adversely or favourably. As most production costs – wages, material costs, capital costs and inventory carrying costs – are denominated in yen, a firm's profits fluctuate with the currency fluctuations. Export prices, if in US dollars, are determined using exchange rate movement forecasts for the near future. However, a sudden yen appreciation could wipe out profits if the exports are invoiced in US dollars.

Suppose that the total amount of international transportation costs and tariff is denoted by t, and that it is added proportionately to export price. Thus, the price, which importers face at the dock side, denoted by P^M, in the case of yen invoicing is defined as (producer's pricing) $P^M = (1 + t)\,\overline{P}^E / S$ and in the case of dollar invoicing (consumer's or local pricing) $P^M = (1 + t)\,\overline{P}^I$.

When the exchange rate fluctuates, an exporting firm can increase or decrease prices in the export market. If exports are invoiced in yen, the import price in US dollars at the dockside of American ports increases if the yen appreciates vis-à-vis the US dollar (between time of contract and time of delivery). This is an automatic process. Invoicing in yen means US dollar prices at the import point change as the exchange rate changes. If exports are invoiced in US dollars, the dockside import prices in US dollars do not fluctuate with the exchange rate.

Put differently, the importers bear the exchange rate risk when yen invoicing is chosen, and the producers bear the exchange rate risk when dollar invoicing is chosen.

The retail price, denoted by P^R, is determined by importer's profit margin m^M and domestic distribution (transportation) costs d^M as well as importer's dock price, P^M.

$$P^R = P^M (1 + m^M) + d^M$$

where
$$P^M = \frac{(1 + t)\,\overline{P}^E}{S} \qquad \text{(yen invoicing)}$$
$$P^M = (1 + t)\,\overline{P}^I \qquad \text{(dollar invoicing)}$$

A pass-through rate is measured as a change in retail price in response to a change in the exchange rate, $\mathrm{d}(\log(P^M))/\mathrm{d}(\log(S))$. *By construction, the* pass-through rate is −1 in the case of yen invoicing and 0 in the case of dollar invoicing.

The case where Japanese products in the US see their prices change one-to-one with the yen–dollar exchange rate changes is said to have a 'pass-through' rate equal to one; the case where prices in the US do not change when the yen–dollar exchange rate changes is the case of zero 'pass-through'.

When the dollar retail price of Japanese imports changes at the same rate as the exchange rate, the 'pass-through' is said to be complete. For example, when the yen appreciates by 1 per cent vis-à-vis the US dollar, dollar-denominated retail prices increase by 1 per cent in the case of complete pass-through. In general, the pass-through is incomplete in that dollar price changes are more than zero but less than the percentage of appreciation.

Yen invoicing will shift the exchange rate risk to importers, and when other parameters such as the importer's profit margin stay the same, the retail price will fluctuate with the exchange rate. The demand function for the imported goods in the destination market is a downward-sloping function of the retail price, $D(P^R)$, with $D' < 0$. When the yen appreciates and the retail price of the yen-invoiced goods rises, the demand will decline. Therefore, the exporters will not suffer from yen appreciation in unit price of exported goods, but will eventually suffer from the decline in export volumes.

In the case of dollar invoicing, exporters incorporate the exchange rate risk in the unit price of exports. Since the pass-through is zero, the retail price does not change with the exchange rate fluctuation. Hence, the sales volume will not change. Export revenue fluctuations come from the change in the unit price converted in yen.

In either case, the exporter's revenues fluctuate with the exchange rate, either through the unit price or the sales volume.

If the exporters consider it important to keep their sales volume stable for some reason – maintaining their market share, distribution network and customer reputation for price stability – then local currency pricing will be chosen. A more rigorous analysis requires a model to be built specifying the demand function. This is done in Chapter 2.

As a summary, Figure 1.3 shows the relation among export prices, import prices and retail prices. First, Japanese exporters choose the export price and its currency denomination. When the export price is denominated in US dollars, the export price plus transportation costs becomes the import price in the destination market. When the export price is denominated in yen, then the export price divided by the yen exchange rate plus transportation costs becomes the import price in the destination

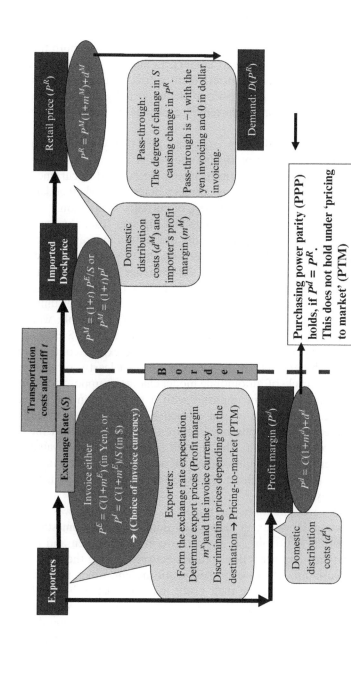

Figure 1.3 Relation among export prices, import prices and retail prices

7

market. Second, the import price (or dockside price) will be inflated by the profit margin of the importer and the distributer. The price will be further increased by local inputs such as assembly, packaging, transportation, handling and advertising. Some additional costs come from both tradable and non-tradable inputs (such as labour). In summary, a long chain of pipelines stretches from the exporter's factory price to the retail price in the destination market. The retail price of the imported goods is the sum of the export price (in exporter's currency), exchange rate, profit margin and costs of local inputs.

If exports are invoiced in yen, exporters' profits in yen are determined with certainty at the point of signing the export contract. If exports are invoiced in dollars, exporters' profits in yen are exposed to currency risk. Therefore, the choice of invoicing currency determines whether Japanese exporters or US importers bear the risk of currency fluctuation.

Invoicing currency matters through the pipeline from the exporter's factory price to the import prices in the destination market. In the short run, the pass-through of the exchange rate changes has two aspects: (1) import price changes in response to the exchange rate changes; and (2) profit margin and local input prices change in the export destination market in response to the exchange rate changes. This book examines the former issue from Japanese exporters' viewpoint. For example, when the yen appreciates, how will prices of Japanese exports in the US change?

So far, the explanation has ignored details of export contracts and renewal of such contracts in the medium run – at least several months and at most the cycle of automobile model changes. Suppose a Japanese exporter contracts with an importer with a specific number of autos and the price. In the case of yen invoicing, the contracted price is in yen. The agreement was contracted before the exchange rate at the time of payment became known. The amount of exporter's sales value, that is, the number of autos multiplied by the unit price, is determined with certainty. For this sales contract, the exporter can avoid the exchange rate risk completely.

In the above explanation, the importer's profit margin was assumed to be the same. However, in general, an adjustment of domestic mark-up by importers is possible. If imports are invoiced in yen and the yen appreciates, then importers face a choice between raising the retail prices (complete pass-through) to keep their profit margin, which may result in declining sales, and lowering their profit margin to keep the retail price constant, which would avoid declining sales. In either case, yen invoicing exposes the importers' profits to currency risk. If the volume declines, the exporter's profits are also affected. In either case, the importer suffers a loss from yen appreciation. Then most likely, the importer will either demand the export price in yen be lowered, or that the export volume be lowered.

So, in the next contract, the exporter faces a demand from the importer for a lower price and/or for a lower number of sales. In this sense, even in the case of yen invoicing, the exporter is not immune from exchange rate fluctuation in the medium run.

When the export contract uses dollar invoicing, the importer's price to pay is not affected by the exchange rate change. The retail price in the US will not change and the sales will not change when the exchange rate fluctuates. But, the exporter's profits suffer when the yen appreciates. However, when the time comes to negotiate the next contract, the exporter may demand higher prices in yen to make up the loss in yen receipts. Thus, in the medium run, the yen-invoiced price may change.

In the medium run, the Japanese exporter may adjust export prices to maintain sales in the US retail market. Hence, invoicing in yen or dollars will not matter in the medium run if Japanese exporters want to keep US retail prices stable. This is the origin of 'pricing-to-market' (PTM) behaviour. PTM is automatic if the exports are dollar invoiced, but, in the medium run, yen invoicing does not necessarily lead to the violation of the PTM.

This brief description of currency risk invites three obvious questions:

1. *If the currency risk is substantial, why does the Japanese firm not insist on denominating export prices in yen?* Exporters may face reluctance and complaints from US customers who would thus be exposed to the currency risk. The import price in US dollars may be uncertain until the delivery of goods and payment. The importer may insist on a US dollar denomination, saying, for example, that there are comparable (in terms of price and quality) made-in-USA automobiles denominated in US dollars. Thus, whether the exporting price is denominated in the exporter's or importer's currency depends on the relative negotiating power between exporter and importer. Such negotiation power may be related to the ability to manage currency risk as well as the competition, or lack thereof, in the retail market.

2. *In the age of financial innovation, why does the Japanese firm (or importer) not use a forward contract (with a bank) to hedge the currency risk?* A simple answer is that hedging with a financial instrument, such as forward contracts, is not costless. Hedging costs may add to production costs if borne by exporters, and to import costs if borne by importers. This may also be a point of negotiation between exporters and importers. The cost can be borne by the exporter if the hedging cost is cheaper for the exporter than for the importer, depending on relative costs. If the exporter is a large, multinational firm, then it will

have smaller hedge costs as it has a strong negotiation power with the bank handling exporters' payments and portfolio management. Accordingly, which currency is used can be translated into a question of relative hedging costs.

3. *Even if the importer's currency is chosen as the invoice currency, shouldn't export prices be adjusted to reflect currency fluctuations?* A sceptic may insist that the invoice-currency question can be framed as part of a bigger question of exporting firms' pricing strategies. If the contract is written in terms of US dollars, then an export firm can change the export price in yen when the exchange rate changes to make up the loss to stabilize yen receipts. The negotiation cost of price revision – broadly dubbed the 'menu cost' in the literature – may be substantial. However, export prices can be revised only occasionally, say at the time of a model change for autos. Hence, at least in the time horizon of six months to one year, the choice of invoice currency may not be so important.

If the currency choice is a result of rational decisions by firms, then the government may not worry about which currency is used in exports and imports – that is, one of several criteria for the 'internationalization' of the currency. Japan once promoted internationalization of the yen, but use of the yen in trade denomination as well as the yen's ratio in foreign reserve assets of central banks other than the Bank of Japan have not changed much in the last 10–20 years. Some have lamented this as a failure of the initiative to internationalize the yen, but it may be a rational result, at least in terms of the trade denomination criterion.

To academically examine the question of currency denomination and pass-through of exchange rate changes to domestic prices, collecting data on exporters' choice of currency denomination is important. Aggregate data on currency choices of Japanese exporters are released by the Ministry of Finance but are not disaggregated to answer most of the important questions at the firm level.

An innovative feature of our research method is as follows. We wanted to have first-hand, direct evidence, so we undertook to collect it ourselves. We conducted interviews with large exporting firms, sent questionnaires to many exporting firms and to a large number of subsidiaries abroad. We know that the survey method is not standard in the field of international finance. However, information at the individual firm level is essential in order to obtain convincing findings.

The interaction between the exchange rate and domestic prices has been a focus of many branches of macroeconomics and international finance. *Understanding firms' behaviour – microeconomic questions – is key to answering some important questions, such as pass-through and PTM behaviour and J-curves, in macroeconomics and international finance.*

An implication of the micro behaviour of choosing an invoice currency and pass-through on a macro phenomenon of trade surpluses can be understood as follows. When the exchange rate suddenly undergoes a substantial change, it should affect export prices, volumes and values. When the yen suddenly appreciates, export values (in dollars) may not change when the export contract price is denominated in dollars, but the export values (in dollars) will decline immediately when export contract prices are denominated in yen. However, in the former case, sales at the destination market may decline, along with export volumes. In the latter case, sales and export volumes may not decline due to demand-side reasons, but in the medium run, export volumes may decline due to smaller profits for exporters. The trade balance eventually adjusts in the right direction, but the speed of adjustment may be different, depending on the currency denomination of exports.

Japanese trade surpluses were supported by ever-increasing exports from Japan in the 1970s and 2000s, despite a sharp appreciation of the yen. Some doubted the validity of the exchange rate's role in adjusting current accounts. In the long run, the yen's appreciation did not seem to hurt exports. Moreover, some argued that Japanese exporters were keeping prices in the destination market constant so that export volumes would not change. If the suspicion was true, then changes in the exchange rate (in this case, appreciation) did not 'pass-through' to domestic prices in the destination market. *Invoicing exports in the destination market's currency means a lack of pass-through, at least in the short run.* In the medium run, the yen's appreciation squeezes the profits of Japanese exporters, leading them to raise export prices in yen, thus resulting in a decrease in volume. If the productivity gains are substantial, even in the medium run, export prices in dollars may be maintained with lower export prices in yen. This may have been the case in the 1970s and 1980s. In this case, pass-through of exchange rate changes into destination-market prices will not occur and export values will not change in US dollars. However, export values measured in yen will still decline due to the yen's appreciation.

When a Japanese auto maker sells very similar, if not the same, models to different markets, say the US, Japan, Europe and Asia, the exporter may consider the local market condition, in particular the price elasticity, in its pricing decision for each destination market. The exporter tends to set different prices in different markets. If the destination market is crowded with locally manufactured cars, then exporters may keep prices constant to avoid losing market share – this is called PTM behaviour – and if the exported car is quite monopolistic in the destination market, the exporter may not fear raising prices when costs, including the exchange rate, change.

A lack of pass-through as well as the presence of PTM behaviour reduce the speed of trade account (measured in US dollars) adjustment, contributing to persistent surpluses in the trade account. These examples show the macro implications of individual firms' behaviour in response to exchange rate changes.

This book also has important suggestions for firms aspiring to become active globally. The issue of how to manage currency risk is very important when a firm decides to expand its export or import business activities. Some patterns for managing risk – from natural hedge (production near consumers) to use of financial derivatives in currency risk management – are found in our study. They provide a clue regarding the strategy that might be employed by a firm contemplating overseas operations.

The following chapters are organized as follows. Chapter 2 surveys recent developments in theoretical and empirical studies on invoice currency choice. We review key concepts of invoice currencies and their relation with the exchange rate pass-through (ERPT) and PTM. Possible determinants of the invoice currency choice are discussed in detail. By observing the officially published data on invoice currency choice, it is shown that the Japanese invoicing-currency pattern violates well-known stylized facts. Previous studies show the following empirical regularities of the invoice currency choice: (1) trade in manufactured products between advanced countries tends to be invoiced in the exporter's currency; (2) trade in manufactured products between advanced and developing countries tends to be invoiced in the advanced country's currency; and (3) differentiated products, such as machinery products, tend to be invoiced in the exporter's currency. More homogeneous products, such as crude oil and primary commodities, are typically invoiced in an international currency such as the US dollar.

Chapter 2 presents two puzzles observed in invoice currency choice in Japanese trade. The first puzzle is that Japanese exports to advanced countries tend to be invoiced in the importer's currency, and the second puzzle is that the share of US dollar invoicing is higher than that of yen invoicing in trade with Asia, even though Japanese firms have built regional production and sales networks where goods are traded between group companies (intra-firm trade). To solve these puzzles, subsequent chapters investigate firm-level data on invoice currency choices that were obtained through interviews and questionnaire surveys.

Chapter 2 investigates the industry/commodity-level data on invoice currency choice in detail. The Bank of Japan (BOJ) publishes data on the invoice currency choice by industry but disaggregated commodity-level data are not available. We develop a new estimation approach to invoice currency choice at the commodity level by using the BOJ export and import price indices and present the estimated share of invoice currency over the sample period from 2000 to 2015. We demonstrate that in Japanese exports, major parts and production equipment tend to be invoiced in yen, which is consistent with the stylized fact that differentiated export products are typically invoiced in the exporter's currency. Automobiles and electronics products are invoiced largely in US dollars or the destination currency, which conforms to the PTM behaviour in the literature. For Japanese imports, natural resources and less differentiated goods tend to be invoiced in US dollars. However, for Japanese imports of machinery products, the share invoiced in yen is relatively high, probably reflecting an increase in intra-firm trade between Japan and Asia. The choice of invoice currency in intra-firm trade will be examined in subsequent chapters.

Chapter 3 examines a new data set based on interviews with globally operating Japanese firms regarding their choice of invoice currency and management of currency risk. In the preceding chapter, we conducted a literature survey on invoicing-currency behaviour and pointed out how the stylized facts discussed in the existing literature fail to explain the invoicing-currency pattern of Japanese exporters who expand their production network to a global level. To solve these puzzles on the invoicing-currency behaviour of Japanese firms, this chapter and the next chapters empirically examine firm-level invoicing behaviour of Japanese exports using unique data sets obtained through the interview surveys with Japanese major exporters and then propose new determinants of invoicing decisions and present new evidence on both traditional and newly proposed determinants.

For this chapter, we interviewed 23 representative Japanese exporting firms to collect information on their invoicing-currency behaviour as well as their explicit policy/strategy for choosing their invoice currency. Through interviews, we found that Japanese electronics and automobile companies have a strong tendency to invoice in importer's currency for exports to advanced countries, while US-dollar invoicing is largely used when exporting to Asian countries, especially when exporting electronics products. Such an invoicing strategy aims at stabilizing the local currency (US-dollar) price of their export products in local markets, which conforms to the PTM behaviour discussed in the literature.

We also propose new determinants of invoice currency together with related hypotheses. We then test those hypotheses using a newly constructed firm-level data set. Our novel findings are three-fold. First, invoicing in the importer's currency is prevalent in Japanese exports to advanced countries because most of their exports are destined for local subsidiaries that face severe competition in their local markets. In this case, Japanese parent firms have a strong tendency to take an exchange rate risk by invoicing in the importer's currency, which is consistent with the PTM behaviour discussed in the literature. It also makes sense to concentrate currency risk at the head office as it is better equipped with risk management expertise and scale economies. Second, Japanese firms that export highly differentiated products or that have a dominant share in global markets tend to choose yen invoicing even for exports to advanced countries. Third, although Japanese firms have shifted their production bases to Asian countries, exports from these Asian bases tend to be invoiced in US dollars as long as the final destination market is the US, which results in US dollar invoicing even for exports from the Japanese head office to production subsidiaries in Asia. Thus, a smaller share of yen invoicing in Japanese exports even in the 2000s is due to the growing intra-firm trade promoted by the active overseas operations of Japanese electronics firms combined with products having a final destination of US markets.

While Japan's production networks in Asia reinforce the country's unique pattern of invoicing currency, country-specific foreign exchange regulations in Asia also lead to US dollar invoicing for Japanese exports to Asia. Since the Asian currency crisis in 1997, foreign exchange regulations and controls in Asian countries have been strengthened, thus reinforcing the use of US dollars in Asia.

Chapter 4 examines a data set collected from the questionnaire survey asking the same questions, the choice of invoice currency and currency risk management practices. A key benefit of sending the questionnaire as opposed to face-to-face interviews is the ability to reach an expanded number of samples, making it possible to generalize findings. However, one limitation of this approach is the inability to elaborate on questions when a respondent provides an unexpected answer.

In the previous chapter, we derived interesting findings on the determinants of invoicing-currency behaviour of Japanese major exporters using a unique data set obtained through the interview surveys. However, it should be noted that the results were obtained from a limited sample of firms with whom we conducted interviews. In this sense, we should re-examine the robustness of the derived determinants of invoicing-currency behaviour using a data set comprising a large number of sample firms. Accordingly, we conducted questionnaire surveys in both 2009 and 2013 to collect detailed information on firm-level invoicing choices of Japanese exporters. In both survey rounds, questionnaires were sent to all Japanese manufacturing firms listed on Japan's stock exchanges and that reported foreign sales in their consolidated financial statements as of fiscal years 2008 and 2012, respectively.

By conducting a large-scale questionnaire survey covering all Japanese manufacturing firms listed in Japan's stock exchanges, detailed information can be presented on firm-level invoicing choices by destination and by type of trading partner, with a particular emphasis on the difference between arm's length and intra-firm trades. We also show a summary of results from a cross-section regression analysis investigating the factors that determine Japanese export firms' choice of invoice currency. We have found that invoicing currency choice is strongly influenced by whether the trade is intra-firm or arm's-length trade. While yen invoicing tends to be chosen for arm's-length trade, there is a strong tendency for the importer's currency to be used in invoicing intra-firm trade. In exports to Asian subsidiaries, US dollars are widely used as an invoicing currency. We also reveal that firm size does affect the choice of invoice currency because the larger (smaller) the size of a firm, the more likely Japanese firms are to conduct intra-firm (arm's-length) trade. Moreover, growing and deepening regional production networks in Asia are likely to discourage yen-invoiced transactions, even by Japanese firms. Japanese production subsidiaries that export finished goods to the rest of the world tend to choose US dollar-invoiced transactions for their imports of semi-finished goods from their Japanese parent firm.

Several policy implications emerge from results obtained in the study. First, if Japanese exporters would like to increase the share of yen-invoiced trades to avoid currency risk, then developing and concentrating in globally competitive goods with high market shares is important. Second, it may be rational to expect that a large parent firm in Japan with diversified export destinations will manage currency risk on a global level, rather than leaving production or sales subsidiaries abroad to manage their own currency risk individually. Hence, dollar-invoiced trade between parent and subsidiaries seems rational. Given the fact of globalized trades with cross-border supply chains, it may not be rational to expect an increasing share of yen-invoiced trades for this type of trade. Third, whether American or European global exporters behave like Japanese exporters is an interesting question. They may have power to impose the US dollar or euro on the rest of the world as these are global key currencies, unlike the yen; or they may behave like Japanese globally active firms as they have the capacity to allow importers to choose the invoicing-currency denomination and manage multicurrency risks at the level of the parent firm. Fourth, it is also our future task to analyse Japanese importers' behaviour regarding whether they are in a position to impose yen-invoiced trades on their trade counterpart.

Chapter 5 presents new findings on Japanese firms' exchange rate risk management approaches based on the questionnaire surveys presented in Chapter 4. There are two parts to this chapter. First, we provide an overview of the varieties of Japanese firms' exchange rate risk management and summarize the results of the 2009 survey. Second, we conduct an empirical analysis using the questionnaire survey data to investigate the determinants of financial and operational hedging.

This is the first detailed and firm-specific investigation of Japanese firms' exchange rate risk management approaches. We find their characteristics as follows. First, firms with higher sales and greater dependency on foreign markets more actively engage in currency hedging activities, including financial and operational hedging. Second, Japanese firms use both financial and operational hedging complementarily. Third, US dollar invoicing is supported by both financial and operational hedging. Fourth, yen invoicing substitutes operational and financial hedging. Fifth, pass-through also substitutes financial hedging; however, most Japanese exporters cannot change their export price easily even if there was a large fluctuation in the foreign exchange rate. In addition, larger sized firms are more likely to pass it through compared with smaller firms.

To sum up our results, Japanese firms use operational hedging, financial hedging and pricing policies depending on their own choice of invoicing currency to mitigate the impact of currency fluctuations. We also confirm that small firms have little experience in conducting exchange rate risk management. Therefore, it is important for them to learn how large multinational firms use and combine exchange rate risk management tools effectively. Further, policymakers have to recognize that the financial and operational hedges play an important role in mitigating exchange rate risks, especially for firms that choose US dollar invoicing. In this sense, promoting deregulation of foreign transactions and foreign exchange markets, particularly in Asian countries, is indispensable to supporting their effective exchange rate risk management.

Chapter 6 investigates the invoice currency choices of Japanese overseas subsidiaries with a focus on production subsidiaries in Asia. We obtained firm-level information on the export (sales) and import (procurement) patterns of Japanese subsidiaries through questionnaire surveys conducted in 2010 and 2014. Specifically, Japanese manufacturing subsidiaries operating in Asia, for instance, import or procure intermediate inputs from various source countries or the domestic market and export or sell production goods in various destination countries or in local markets. For each transaction, we collected information about the currency which was used for trade invoicing.

Chapter 6 reveals the following patterns of invoice-currency choice. First, Japanese production subsidiaries in North America tend to use the US dollar in both exports and imports. Second, Japanese production subsidiaries in Europe tend to choose euros in trade with Japan, while their subsidiaries use euros or US dollars in trade with other countries. Third, Japanese production subsidiaries in Asia tend to choose yen and US dollars in both imports from and exports to Japan, while the US dollar is generally used in trade with other countries. This unique pattern of invoice-currency choice is mainly driven by intra-firm trade between Asia and Japan, where US dollar-invoiced transactions increased from the first questionnaire survey to the second survey. Asian currencies, including the renminbi (RMB), are rarely used in intra-firm trade by Japanese production subsidiaries.

Chapter 6 conducts a logit estimation to investigate the determinants of invoice currency, mainly focusing on production subsidiaries operating in Asia. First, we find that conventional determinants such as exchange rate volatility and product differentiation have little impact on the subsidiaries' choice of invoice currency. Second, we demonstrate that in the production subsidiary's exports to Japan, intra-firm trade along its production chains facilitates yen-invoiced transactions, especially in the case of intermediate-goods exports. Third, exchange risk hedging instruments such as 'marry and netting' also promote subsidiaries' yen-invoiced exports to Japan. Fourth, we find significantly negative impact of the group company's US dependence on subsidiaries' yen-invoiced exports. As long as the group company has a high dependence on the US market in terms of consolidated sales, Asia-based subsidiaries will have a lower (higher) tendency to choose the yen (US dollar) even for the subsidiaries' exports to Japan. Invoice-currency choice in intra-firm trades may be determined by the final destination at the end of the production chains.

Lastly, in Chapter 7, we look back on the history of the internationalization of the yen and discuss why measures to enhance internationalization of the yen did not result in promoting the use of the yen. The internationalization of a currency is defined as the use of a currency in six cells in the 3×2 matrix: 3 functions of money, namely 'unit of account', 'settlement', and 'store of value', and 2 sectors, 'private' and 'public'. We will argue that the shares of yen-invoicing among Japanese exports and imports may be both a cause and a result of slow progress of yen internationalization. In the latter half of the chapter, we discuss the progress, or lack thereof, in China's recent efforts toward internationalization of the RMB.

Based on the latest questionnaire survey presented in Chapter 6, we organize the results on the use of the RMB by Japanese overseas subsidiaries. Our results indicate that RMB cross-border transactions are not increasing among Japanese multinational firms at the moment. As the first step of the RMB internationalization, the Chinese government focused on promoting the use of the RMB for trade settlement without full convertibility of RMB. In addition, the Chinese government promoted the utilization of the offshore RMB (CNH) for cross-border transactions including trade settlements, deposit and direct investment. However, our survey results suggest, at least among the Japanese overseas subsidiaries, that there is a limit for the usage of the RMB as trade settlements without full liberalization in capital accounts.

As long as capital controls exist, Japanese firms do not recognize that the RMB is a convenient international currency. The above survey results suggest that there is a dilemma for the Chinese monetary authorities: unless capital controls are lifted, firms are reluctant to use the RMB due to the restrictions; but as capital controls are being lifted, the exchange rate volatility rises, which makes the firms avoid the use of that currency.

2. Choice of invoice currency in Japanese trade: industry- and commodity-level analysis

2.1 INTRODUCTION

Exporters' price-setting and invoicing currency practices have important implications for the transmission of macroeconomic shocks among countries. Indeed, a large number of studies have examined firms' pricing and invoicing behaviour in response to, or in anticipation of, exchange rate changes. However, there have only been a small number of empirical studies on invoice currency choice because detailed data on the selection of an invoice currency are not easily available. Specifically, while aggregate data on the choice of invoice currency are available in some countries, they are not sufficient for a rigorous empirical examination. In particular, detailed data and information on the choice of invoice currency by industry/commodity and by destination/source country have not been published or disclosed, with a few exceptions.

There are three strands of empirical studies on the choice of invoice currency. The first strand of research entails conducting a cross-country analysis of the invoice currency choice by collecting as much information as possible on the share of invoice currency at a country level (Goldberg and Tille, 2008; Ito and Kawai, 2016; Kamps, 2006). This approach has an advantage in enabling cross-country comparisons of invoice currency choices. However, it is usually hard to conduct empirical analyses because a relatively small number of observations are available about invoice currency decisions.

Second, a growing number of studies have used unpublished micro data for invoice currency on a customs basis. Goldberg and Tille (2016), for instance, utilized the highly detailed Canadian import data at a customs level for the period February 2002 to February 2009; these data contain rich information on source country, invoice currency, transaction value and so on. The determinants of invoicing currency choice for Canadian imports are empirically tested using a large number of observations. Chung (2016) theoretically and empirically examined how invoice currency choice is affected by an exporter's dependence on imported intermediate inputs using the highly disaggregated UK trade data recorded by Her Majesty's Revenue and Customs (HMRC). Recent studies have also investigated the effect of invoice currency choice on exchange rate pass-through (ERPT) and pricing-to-market (PTM). Gopinath et al. (2010) use US import data collected by the Bureau of Labor Statistics. Fitzgerald and Haller (2014) presented clear evidence on how an invoice currency choice affects the extent of PTM between Irish and UK markets using the highly disaggregated producer price indices of Ireland. Cao et al. (2015) empirically examined the effect of invoice currency choice on ERPT and PTM using unpublished product-level price data from Statistics Canada's Price Report Survey. This line of research is undoubtedly useful, but it is difficult to access and utilize such unpublished and highly disaggregated data.[1]

Third, Friberg and Wilander (2008) conducted a questionnaire survey analysis on Swedish exporting firms and empirically tested determinants of invoice currency choice. While this approach is innovative in terms of obtaining detailed data at a firm level, Friberg and Wilander (2008) did not provide information on the choice of invoice currency by industry/commodity. In addition, because it is based on a one-off questionnaire survey, they cannot analyse changing patterns in invoice currency decisions.

The main contribution of our research is to provide in greater detail rich information on the invoice currency choices made by Japanese manufacturing firms. Firm-level data obtained through the two rounds of interviews and four rounds of questionnaire surveys will be presented and discussed in the subsequent chapters.

The purpose of this chapter is threefold. First, we review recent developments in theoretical and empirical studies on invoice currency choices. Second, a changing pattern of invoice currency choice in Japanese exports and imports over the longer sample period is observed using publicly available data from the Ministry of Finance and the Bank of Japan (BOJ). We show that the choice of invoice currency in Japanese exports and imports differs markedly from the stylized facts and, hence, is puzzling. Third, we develop an estimation method for invoice currency choices at a detailed commodity level by using export and import price indices published by the BOJ. New evidence on the changing pattern of invoice currency choice from 2000 to 2015 is presented at a disaggregated commodity level.

The remainder of this chapter is organized as follows. Section 2.2 presents a concise review of the theory of invoice currency choice and overviews invoice currency decisions in Japanese exports and imports

---

[1] Donnenfeld and Haug (2003, 2008) also used highly detailed customs-level data on invoice currency in Canadian and US imports, respectively.

using aggregate data. Section 2.3 discusses the changing pattern of invoice currency choice in Japanese exports and imports by observing the published data, which reveals that Japanese invoicing currency patterns conflict with the stylized facts. Section 2.4 shows the new proposed method for estimation of invoice currency choices at a commodity level by using the BOJ export and import price indices. Section 2.5 presents empirical evidence on the changing pattern of invoice currency choice. Finally, Section 2.6 summarizes the empirical findings regarding commodity-level invoice currency choices.

2.2 KEY CONCEPT: INVOICE CURRENCY, EXCHANGE RATE PASS-THROUGH AND PRICING-TO-MARKET

Before observing the data on invoice currencies in Japanese trade, we overview a recent development in theoretical studies on the choice of invoice currency. We also discuss the relation among invoice currency choice, ERPT and PTM. The following discussion mainly focuses on a partial equilibrium approach where exchange rates are exogenous and the only source of uncertainty.[2]

Let us consider a trade relation between two countries, such as Japan and the US, where a Japanese firm exports its products to a US firm. The literature typically assumes (1) a simple monopoly model where an exporter is a monopolistic firm that faces a downward sloping demand curve; or (2) an oligopoly model where more than one monopolistic firm competes in the destination market. US demand for Japanese products is typically conditional on the competitor firm's pricing behaviour and variations in US customers' incomes. Moreover, as will be discussed below, the degree of competition in the US market may depend on whether the competitors are Japanese firms, US firms or third-country firms.

It usually takes several months for exporting firms to receive payment from importers after signing a contract for exports, and the exchange rate tends to fluctuate during the waiting period. Exporting firms have to set a

---

[2]   This section mainly relies on Bacchetta and van Wincoop (2005), Friberg (1998) and Giovannini (1988). See also Engle (2006). Against the background of the recent development of New Open Economy Macroeconomics, the choice of invoice currency is often analysed under a general equilibrium model. For instance, Bacchetta and van Wincoop (2005) examined the choice of invoice currency by assuming that money supply fluctuations in both domestic and foreign countries are the source of macroeconomic shocks under the two-country general equilibrium model. This chapter does not review such work and does assume that exchange rates are exogenously determined.

price before the exchange rate for receiving funds is known and, therefore, cannot avoid an exchange rate risk if the importer's currency is chosen as an invoicing currency. On the contrary, if the exporter's currency is chosen as an invoice currency, importers are exposed to currency risk. Thus, the choice of invoice (contract) currency is particularly important in determining which party – exporters or importers – will shoulder the exchange rate risk.

Exporting firms typically determine the volume of production by anticipating a certain future exchange rate level, $\bar{S}$, at the settlement date. Suppose S represents a realized exchange rate at the settlement date, and $S = \bar{S} + \varepsilon$ holds where ε is a prediction error term. Let us consider a short-run case, typically within a 3–6-month time horizon, when the distribution of exchange rate expectations, product model, production costs and the shape of demand function do not change. When we say 'a short-run change in exchange rates', the mean value of the expected future exchange rate $(\bar{S})$ does not change, and fluctuations of the realized exchange rate (S) are governed by the prediction error (ε). In the medium or long run, the mean value or distribution of expected future exchange rate $(\bar{S})$ can change, which induces a change in export and import prices, retail prices in the importer's country and the quantity of exports. Thus, in the medium and long run, the choice of invoice currency becomes less important in terms of considering the effect of exchange rate changes on export and import prices. We hereafter focus on the short run in discussing the invoice currency choice and its relation with ERPT and PTM.

2.2.1 Choice of Invoice Currency

An exporting firm in Japan sets a price for its products in a currency under conditions of exchange rate uncertainty. Suppose P_x^E denotes an export price denominated in the exporter's currency (yen), and S stands for the nominal exchange rate of the exporter's currency (yen) vis-à-vis the importer's currency (US dollars). The export price of the product denominated in the importer's currency is $P_x^I = P_x^E / S$. Invoicing in exporter's currency, which is typically called 'producer's currency pricing' (PCP) in the literature, serves to fix the export price in terms of the exporter's currency $(\bar{P}_x^E)$, irrespective of exchange rate fluctuations (that is, any realized value of ε). Invoicing in importer's currency, which is called 'local currency pricing' (LCP), serves to fix the export price in terms of the importer's currency $(\bar{P}_x^I)$. In practice, the choice of invoice currency is determined as a result of negotiation or bargaining between exporters and importers. In the standard approach to a firm's invoicing choice under the partial equilibrium model, however, the exporting firm is assumed to determine the choice of invoice currency because the exporting firm is typically considered as a monopolistic firm.

Existing studies have shown that the choice of invoice currency by monopolistic firms is conditional on the shape of the profit function, which is, in turn, affected by the demand and cost functions. Let $D(P)$ be a demand function where importers face the price P, and $C(Q)$ is a cost function of output where Q is the volume of production. Exporting firms set the price before the exchange rate is known by choosing either P_x^E in the exporter's currency (PCP) or P_x^I in the importer's currency (LCP). Profits under PCP and LCP are, respectively, given by:

$$\Pi^E = P_x^E D(P_x^E/S) - C(D(P_x^E/S)),\tag{2.1}$$

$$\Pi^I = SP_x^I D(P_x^I) - C(D(P_x^I)).\tag{2.2}$$

Clearly, the choice of invoice currency depends on the comparison of expected utility of profits between two choices:[3]

$$EU(\Pi^E) - EU(\Pi^I) = 0.5U' \frac{\partial^2 \Pi^E}{\partial S^2} \sigma^2.\tag{2.3}$$

As proved by the seminal work of Giovannini (1988), the exporter's (importer's) currency is chosen as an invoice currency when $EU(\Pi^E)$ is globally convex (concave) with respect to the exchange rate, S.

Concavity of the profit function is conditional on the curvature of the demand function. Giovannini (1988) and Bacchetta and van Wincoop (2005) showed that the more (less) differentiated the firm's export product is, the lower (higher) is the elasticity of demand for them, which leads to the choice of exporter's (importer's) currency for invoicing.[4] Thus, the degree of product differentiation and competitiveness is one of the major determinants of invoicing choice.

2.2.2 Invoice Currency, Exchange Rate Pass-through and Pricing-to-market

Based on a mark-up rule, an export price is typically set as follows:

$$P_x = (1+m^x)MC,\tag{2.4}$$

where MC stands for a marginal cost. By invoicing its exports in its own currency ($P_x = P_x^E$), an exporter (Japanese firm) can be sure to receive

---

[3] As long as firms set the export price optimally, the partial derivative of profits with respect to the exchange rate is the same ($\partial\Pi^E/\partial S = \partial\Pi^I/\partial S$), which is used to obtain equation (2.3).
[4] See, for example, Giovannini (1988), Fukuda and Ji (1994) and Friberg (1998).

$\overline{P}_x^E$ irrespective of exchange rate fluctuations. In this case, unless P_x^E itself changes, the importer's payment to the exporter in terms of the importer's currency ($P_x^I = \overline{P}_x^E / S$) will change when the exchange rate (S) fluctuates. Thus, when choosing to invoice in the exporter's currency, exchange rate changes are fully passed through from exporters to importers, which is called a 'complete' ERPT.

In contrast, when invoicing in the importer's currency ($P_x = P_x^I$), importing firms will not face any exchange rate risk; the export price in terms of the exporter's currency ($P_x^E = P_x^I \cdot S$) will change in response to exchange rate fluctuations. In this case, the export price in terms of the importer's currency is stabilized and exporters take any exchange rate risk, which is called PTM. Assuming a constant marginal cost, a mark-up factor (m_x) will be adjusted as S changes.[5]

The degree of ERPT or PTM in terms of the importer's currency can be measured by the following elasticity:

$$\rho_x^I(\varepsilon) = -(\Delta P_x^I / P_x^I)/(\Delta S / S). \tag{2.5}$$

In the short run, when the distribution of exchange rate expectation, product model, production cost and the shape of the demand function do not change, the choice of invoice currency is closely related to both ERPT and PTM. Specifically, invoicing in the exporter's currency (or PCP) has a one-to-one relation with 'complete' ERPT or 'no' PTM, where $\rho_x^I(\varepsilon) = 1$ holds. In contrast, the invoicing in the importer's currency (or LCP) is equivalent to 'no' ERPT or 'complete' PTM, where $\rho_x^I(\varepsilon) = 0$ holds.

2.2.3 Pass-through to Retail Price and Distribution Margin

The choice of invoice currency does not fully affect the retail price that consumers encounter. In the ERPT literature, it is widely known that the degree of ERPT tends to be high in import prices but low in consumer prices. Choudhri et al. (2005), for instance, presented evidence for differences in the extent of ERPT across domestic prices in the case of non-US G-7 countries, and Ito and Sato (2008) showed the different degree of ERPT along the pricing chain – from the wholesale level to the retail level – in Asian countries.

Different from a typical illustration in standard textbooks, exporting firms do not ship their products directly to local customers or consumers.

---

[5] As shown in Goldberg and Knetter (1997), PTM incorporates price discrimination in multiple markets into the ERPT research, but PTM is often used in bilateral international transactions in the literature on new open-economy macroeconomics.

Exporting firms typically ship products to local importing firms who serve as local distributors in the destination market. Burstein et al. (2003) and Campa and Goldberg (2006, 2008) investigated the role of distribution margins in lowering the degree of ERPT in consumption prices. Allowing for such local distribution channels, the above mark-up rule can be reformulated into:

$$P_R = (1 + m^m) P_x^I + d_m, \qquad (2.6)$$

where the retail price in the local market (P_R) is a sum of the import price (that is, a wholesale cost: P_x^I) multiplied by a profit margin (that is, a mark-up: $(1 + m^m)$) and distribution cost (d_m). Thus, even though exporters choose to invoice in the importer's currency or LCP ($P_x = \bar{P}_x^I$), the retail price in the local market can change, conditional upon the distribution margin (m^m) as well as distribution cost (d_m), which results in a different degree of ERPT or PTM between import and retail prices.

Which plays a more important role in explaining incomplete ERPT, wholesale costs (wholesale-level PTM) or distribution margins (retail-level mark-up)? Nakamura and Zerom (2010) and Leibtag et al. (2007) examined this question by focusing on the coffee industry. Gopinath et al. (2011) employed new and unique data on retail prices and wholesale costs at the barcode level for a single grocery chain operating in the United States and Canada,[6] and found that the variation in retail prices between two countries is explained by the variation in relative wholesale costs, which implies a widespread nature of PTM at the wholesale level.

2.2.4 Invoicing in Third-country Currency

While the above discussion assumes an invoicing choice of either exporter's or importer's currency, the choice of a third country's currency for trade invoicing is not explicitly considered. Johnson and Pick (1997) and Friberg (1998) extended the theoretical model of invoicing choice by analysing the conditions in which invoicing in a third country's currency is selected. They showed that not only the shape of the profit function but also the exchange rate volatility (variance) of both exporter's and third country's currencies against the importer's currency determine the choice of invoice currency.[7]

---

[6] Although focusing only on the US markets, Nakamura (2008) also used unique, barcode-level price data for about 7000 grocery stores in the United States and empirically investigated whether the retail price variation is explained by retail margins or wholesale costs.

[7] The following discussion is mainly based on Oi et al. (2004), who showed the conditions of third-currency invoicing using the framework of Bacchetta and van Wincoop (2005).

Suppose S^T denotes the exchange rate of the third country's currency vis-à-vis the importer's currency. Then, P_x^T is assumed to be the export price in terms of the third country's currency. When exporting firms choose third-country currency for invoicing, the profit is given by:

$$\Pi^T = (S/S^T) \cdot P_x^T \cdot D(P_x^T/S^T) - C(D(P_x^T/S^T)). \qquad (2.7)$$

The choice of invoice currency depends on the comparison of expected utility of profits not only between the third country's and importer's currencies but also between the third country's and exporter's currencies:[8]

$$EU(\Pi^T) - EU(\Pi^I) = 0.5U' \frac{\partial^2 \Pi^T}{\partial (S^T)^2} (\sigma^T)^2, \qquad (2.8)$$

$$EU(\Pi^T) - EU(\Pi^E) = -0.5U' \frac{\partial^2 \Pi^E}{\partial S^2} \sigma^2 + 0.5U' \frac{\partial^2 \Pi^T}{\partial (S^T)^2} (\sigma^T)^2, \qquad (2.9)$$

where σ and σ^T denote the variance of exchange rate of the exporter's currency, S, and the third country's currency, S^T, respectively.

First, consider the case where profit functions are concave in the exchange rates ($\partial^2 \Pi^E/\partial S^2 < 0$ and $\partial^2 \Pi^T/\partial (S^T)^2 < 0$), where export products are less differentiated, and the price elasticity of demand for the products is high. In this case, equation (2.8) indicates that importer-currency pricing leads to the highest expected profit. Which currency offers the second highest expected profit depends on the variation of exchange rates in exporter's and third country's currency vis-à-vis the importer's currency, given the inequality $\partial^2 \Pi^E/\partial S^2 > \partial^2 \Pi^T/\partial (S^T)^2$.[9] If the degree of exchange rate fluctuations in the exporter's currency is larger than that in the importer's currency ($\sigma^2 > (\sigma^T)^2$), equation (2.9) shows that the choice of the third country's currency leads to the second highest expected profit. On the other hand, if the inequality $\sigma^2 < (\sigma^T)^2$ holds, the exporter's currency will be the second highest expected profit.

Second, suppose that profit functions are convex in the exchange rates ($\partial^2 \Pi^E/\partial S^2 > 0$ and $\partial^2 \Pi^T/\partial (S^T)^2 > 0$), where the export products are more differentiated and price elasticity of demand is low. Equation (2.8) clearly shows that the choice of the third country's currency results in higher expected profits. According to equation (2.9), if the inequality $\sigma^2 > (\sigma^T)^2$ holds, the exporter's currency is chosen as trade invoice currency. However, if $\sigma^2 < (\sigma^T)^2$ holds, the third country's currency is used for trade invoicing.

---

[8] Oi et al. (2004) derived the two conditions (2.8 and 2.9).
[9] Oi et al. (2004) derive this inequality by assuming that the price elasticity of demand is larger than unity to ensure positive production by the monopolistic firms.

Thus, the decision regarding invoice currency is conditional on (1) degree of product differentiation; and (2) size of variances between the exchange rate of exporter's currency vis-à-vis importer's currency and the corresponding exchange rate between the third currency and importer's currency. When exporting less differentiated or homogeneous goods to developing countries, the choice of a developing country's currency for trade invoicing leads to the highest expected profit. However, if any restrictions are imposed on the use of the local currency, such as strict capital controls in developing countries, the local currency will not be used and a third country's currency will instead be used for trade invoicing.

2.2.5 Invoice Currency Choice in Intra-firm Trade

We have so far assumed implicitly that an export firm has no corporate ties with an import firm, which is called 'arm's length trade'. In the case of intra-firm trade, however, both exporters and importers are in the same company or the corporate group, and exporters (often the headquarters) have little incentive to impose exchange rate risk to importers (subsidiaries) in terms of consolidated accounting. For example, when exporting goods to its sales subsidiaries in the United States, a Japanese head office is likely to avoid passing through exchange rate changes to the subsidiaries; otherwise, the subsidiaries shoulder the exchange rate risk at least in the short run and lose their price competitiveness in the US market when the yen appreciates against the US dollar. Thus, on the consolidated basis, the head office will strategically choose the invoice currency to maximize the group-wide or integrated profits: $\Pi_{Group} = [\Pi_{Subsidiary}] + [\Pi_{HeadOffice}]$.

Neiman (2007) sets up a partial equilibrium model for vertically integrated firms where the head office (manufacturer) and its subsidiary (distributor) maximize their overall or integrated profits.[10] But local subsidiaries can be production subsidiaries (manufacturers) as well, in which case we need to consider the invoice currency choice along production or value chains. It is also unclear whether local subsidiaries in practice aim to maximize their profits in terms of the local currency or the home currency. If a local subsidiary, for example, imports intermediate or finished goods in the yen from its Japanese head office, the subsidiary has to manage exchange rate risk by itself. However, the subsidiary's hedging may be costly, and the Japanese head office is likely to have more advantage in exchange rate management, including hedging and diversification. Thus, Japanese firms may concentrate all exchange rate risks in the head

---

[10] See also Neiman (2010) and Bacchetta and van Wincoop (2003).

office by choosing the importer's currency or US dollar invoicing in their exports.

A key contribution of our work is to collect firm-level information through interviews and questionnaire surveys with Japanese head offices and overseas subsidiaries, which is a novel approach to reveal invoice currency decisions and exchange risk management. Before investigating the firm-level invoicing decision, let us overview the choice of invoice currency not only in Japanese aggregated exports and imports but also by industry/commodity in the rest of this chapter.

2.3 CHOICE OF INVOICE CURRENCY IN JAPANESE TRADE: 1980–2015

It is generally hard to collect detailed data on the choice of invoice currency in exports and imports, but Japan is an exception, as a Japanese governmental agency has published data on the shares of invoice currencies in Japanese exports and imports. The purpose of this section is to show the changing pattern of invoice currency choice in Japanese exports and imports by examining these published data.

This chapter also presents an estimation method for share of invoice currency in Japanese trade using the export and import price data published by the Bank of Japan (BOJ). The BOJ publishes the industry-breakdown data on invoice currency choice for both Japanese exports and imports, but these data are not too disaggregated and only December data are available. We develop a new approach to estimating the industry/commodity-breakdown share of invoice currency by utilizing the BOJ export and import price indices. The estimated results of invoicing choice by industry/commodity are presented in the next section.

2.3.1 Shares of Invoice Currencies in Japanese Exports and Imports[11]

The Japanese Ministry of Finance publishes, on a semi-annual basis, the shares of invoice currencies in Japanese exports and imports.[12] Although industry-breakdown data are not available, we can get information on the choice of invoice currency in trade with four destination and source countries (regions): the world, the US, the European Union (EU) and Asia.

---

[11]   This section partly relies on Ito et al. (2012).
[12]   The data are available from the website of the Trade Statistics of Japan from the second half of 2000 (http://www.customs.go.jp/toukei/shinbun/trade-st/tuuka.htm).

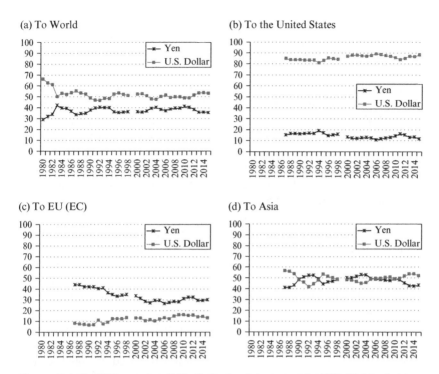

Notes: Data for 1999 are not available. September data are used for 1992–97, March data for 1998, the second half of the year data for 2000–2015.

Sources: Bank of Japan, Yushutsu Shinyojo Tokei [Export Letter of Credit Statistics]; MITI, Yushutsu Kakunin Tokei [Export Confirmation Statistics]; MITI, Yushutsu Hokukosho Tukadate Doko [Export Currency Invoicing Report]; MITI, Yushutsu Kessai Tsukadate Doko Chosa [Export Settlement Currency Invoicing]; website of Japan Customs.

Figure 2.1   Share of invoice currency in Japanese exports: 1980–2015 (%)

Invoice currency choice in Japanese exports
Figure 2.1 shows how the choice of invoice currency for Japanese exports has changed from 1980 to 2015. First, the share of yen invoicing for exports increased after changes to the foreign exchange-related laws in 1980, that is, the amendment of Foreign Exchange and Foreign Trade Control Act (FEFTCA) in 1980. Figure 2.1 shows that in Japanese exports to the world, the share of yen-invoiced transactions rose from 28.9 per cent in 1980 to 42.0 per cent in 1983. However, after 1983, the share of yen-invoiced exports declined to 33.4 per cent in 1987, even though further liberalization was put into

practice in 1984.[13] Why did such a liberalization policy fail to promote further use of the yen in Japanese exports? The fall of the yen's share of invoicing from 1983 to 1987 is generally attributed to the PTM strategy of Japanese exporters.[14] Specifically, during a period of the yen's rapid appreciation against the US dollar from 1985 to 1987, Japanese firms are said to have stabilized selling prices in the local (US) market by invoicing in US dollars to maintain their own market share. From the mid-1980s to 2015, however, the share of yen invoicing stayed within a narrow range, from 33 per cent to 41 per cent for Japan's exports to the world, even though further liberalization – the Japanese Big Bang – was put into force in April 1998.[15] The above observation suggests that the Japanese government's policy of financial liberalization for yen internationalization failed, in practice, to promote use of the yen in trade transactions.

Second, Japanese invoicing currency patterns differ across destination countries (regions). The destination-breakdown data in Figure 2.1 provide more interesting evidence, although the data are only available from 1987. The share of yen invoicing is very low in exports to the US, which may reflect the US dollar's special position as an international currency (see Tavlas and Ozeki (1992) and Tavlas (1997)). As of 2015, 88.3 per cent of Japanese exports to the US are invoiced in US dollars. In exports to the euro area, the share of yen invoicing has declined from 44.0 per cent in 1987 to 30.1 per cent in 2015. Although not reported in Figure 2.1(c), 49.6 per cent of Japanese exports to the EU were invoiced in euros as of 2015.[16] The above observation strongly suggests that Japanese firms tend to invoice in local currency when exporting to advanced countries, which is consistent with the PTM behaviour of Japanese exporting firms.[17]

Third, and more importantly, the share of yen invoicing has not increased for Japanese exports to Asia in the last 28 years. Specifically, the yen's share rose to about 50 per cent or more in the early 1990s and first half of the 1990s. However, the share of the yen declined to a large extent

---

[13] The real demand principle was abolished in April 1984 and restrictions on so-called 'yen conversion' were abolished in June 1984.

[14] See Krugman (1987), Marston (1990) and Tavlas and Ozeki (1992).

[15] The revised Foreign Exchange and Foreign Trade Law in April 1998 brought the first major step of the Japanese 'Big Bang' by deregulating domestic and foreign capital transactions and foreign exchange operations in principle, which largely affected Japanese firms' exchange rate risk management.

[16] If you include the UK pound and Swedish krona, the share of local currency invoicing in Japanese exports to the EU amounts to 56.1 per cent in the second half of 2015. See the website of the Ministry of Finance (http://www.customs.go.jp/toukei/shinbun/trade-st/tuuka.htm).

[17] For an empirical analysis of the PTM behaviour and ERPT in Japanese exports, see Knetter (1989, 1993), Marston (1990), Parsons and Sato (2008) and Takagi and Yoshida (2001).

from 49.2 per cent in 2010 to 43.2 per cent in 2015, while the US dollar's share increased from 48.7 per cent in 2010 to 52.2 per cent in 2015. At present, the share of US dollar invoicing exceeds that of yen invoicing (Figure 2.1(d)).

Such an invoicing pattern is puzzling because until around the mid-1990s, when the yen's internationalization was the subject of a lively debate, it was generally conjectured that use of the yen as an invoice currency would be growing in Asia if intra-firm trade increased between Japanese parent companies and local subsidiaries through active foreign direct investment in Asia by Japanese firms.[18] In particular, as most exports from Japan to Asia were regarded as capital goods and differentiated products, the share of yen invoicing was expected to increase steadily.

Figure 2.1(d) clearly shows, however, that the share of yen invoicing has not increased from 1990 to 2015, even though Japanese firms built a regional production network during that period. Instead, the US dollar has been used more than the yen in Japanese exports to Asia. To gain insight into this puzzling pattern of invoicing choice in Japanese exports, it is necessary to obtain detailed data on invoice currency for Japanese exports both by commodity/industry and by destination.

Invoice currency choice in Japanese imports

Let us turn to the share of invoice currencies used by Japanese importers. Figure 2.2 shows the shares of the yen and US dollar in Japanese imports from 1980 to 2015. First, in Japan's imports from the world, the share of yen invoicing increased gradually from 2.4 per cent in 1980 to 25.5 per cent in 2002 but declined to 20.8 per cent in 2014. The US dollar is the most-used currency in Japanese imports, with a share of 69.8 per cent in 2015. It is well-known that the trade of crude oil and raw materials tends to be invoiced in US dollars. Indeed, Japan has long been heavily dependent on imported oil and raw materials, but Japan's import patterns have structurally changed in recent years, with a substantial increase in procurements of manufactured products from Asian countries. As regional integration has deepened and production networks have been developed further by Japanese firms, use of the yen can be expected to increase for Japan's imports from Asia. Figure 2.2(d) shows, however, that more than 70 per cent of imports from Asia are invoiced in US dollars and the share of yen invoicing has never exceeded 30 per cent. In 2015, only 22.9 per cent of Japan's imports from Asia were invoiced in yen whilst 73.5 per

---

[18]   Kawai (1996), for instance, pointed out that international use of the yen would naturally grow as Japan's economic interdependence with Asia deepened through intra-industry trade, foreign direct investments and various types of financial flows.

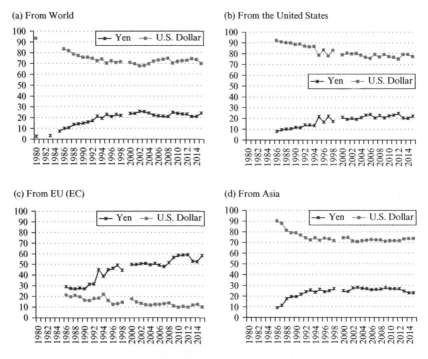

Notes: Data for 1999 is not available. For imports from the world, the data on yen
invoicing is not available for 1981, 1982 and 1984, and the data on US dollar invoicing is not
available for 1981–85. The 1986 data are the fiscal year data. September data are used for
1992–97, March data for 1998, and the second half of the year data for 2000–2015.

Sources: MITI, Yunyu Shonin Todokede Hokokusho [Import Approval Notification
Report]; MITI, Hokokushorei ni Motozuku Hokoku [Report Based on Report Guidance];
MITI, Yunyu Hokoku Tokei [Import Report Statistics]; MITI, Yunyu Hokukosho Tukadate
Doko [Import Currency Invoicing Report]; MITI, Yunyu Kessai Tsukadate Doko Chosa
[Import Settlement Currency Invoicing]; website of Japan Customs.

Figure 2.2   Share of invoice currency in Japanese imports: 1980–2015 (%)

cent are invoiced in US dollars. It is confirmed that the US dollar is still
predominantly used in trade between Japan and Asia.

2.3.2   Stylized Facts and Puzzles

When investigating the choice of invoicing currency, a main obstacle to
rigorous empirical examination is the limited data availability. Although
it is possible to collect data on the aggregated share of invoicing
currency in several countries, destination/source country-breakdown

data and industry-breakdown data are rarely published. Based on such limited information, previous studies found empirical regularities, so-called 'stylized facts',[19] which show that invoicing choices are conditional on a trading partner country and characteristics of goods traded.[20]

- Stylized fact 1: Trade in manufactured products between advanced countries tends to be invoiced in the exporter's currency, a practice known as 'Grassman's Law' (Grassman, 1973, 1976).
- Stylized fact 2: Trade of manufactured products between advanced and developing countries tends to be invoiced in the advanced country's currency or, to a lesser extent, in a major international currency such as US dollars (Grassman, 1973 and Page, 1977, 1981).
- Stylized fact 3: Differentiated products, such as machinery products, tend to be invoiced in the exporter's currency. More homogeneous products, such as crude oil and primary commodities, are typically invoiced in an international currency such as US dollars (McKinnon, 1979).

Do Japan's invoicing currency patterns conform to these stylized facts? As discussed above, Japan violates stylized facts 1 and 2. Figure 2.1 shows that in Japanese exports to the US and the EU, the share of invoicing in the importer's currency is very large. This evidence clearly conflicts with stylized fact 1, which is one of the puzzles of Japan's invoicing choice. In addition, the invoicing pattern of Japanese trade is characterized by the small share of invoicing made in the home currency (yen) and the large share of the US dollar invoicing. Table 2.1 provides an international comparison of shares in invoicing currency amongst advanced countries. The share of home currency is much lower in Japan than in European countries, while the share of the US dollar invoicing is the highest in Japan, with the exception of the US.

As discussed earlier, Figure 2.1 shows that the share of yen invoicing is lower than US dollar invoicing in Japanese exports to Asia, which contradicts stylized fact 2 – another puzzle. It is widely discussed and recognized that Japanese firms have established regional supply chains and production networks in Asia that facilitate intra-firm trade between Japan and Asia

---

[19] Ligthart and da Silva (2007) provide a good literature review and propose the following three stylized facts.

[20] See, for instance, Fukuda and Ji (1994), Ito (1993), Kawai (1996), Sato (1999) and Tavlas and Ozeki (1992) for a good summary and discussion of empirical regularities in the choice of invoice currency.

Table 2.1   International comparison of currency invoicing: advanced countries(%)

	(a) Home Currency Invoicing Ratio: Exports				(b) US Dollar Invoicing Ratio: Exports			
	1980	1988	1992–96	2002–04	1980	1988	1992–96	2002–04
United States	97.0	96.0	98.0	95.0	97.0	96.0	98.0	95.0
Germany	82.3	79.2	76.4	61.1	7.2	8.0	9.8	24.1
Japan	28.9	34.3	35.9	40.1	66.3	53.2	53.1	47.5
United Kingdom	76.0	57.0	62.0	51.0	17.0	n.a	22.0	26.0
France	62.5	58.5	51.7	52.7	13.2	n.a	18.6	33.6
Italy	36.0	38.0	40.0	59.7	30.0	n.a	23.0	n.a

	(c) Home Currency Invoicing Ratio: Imports				(d) US Dollar Invoicing Ratio: Imports			
	1980	1988	1992–96	2002–04	1980	1988	1992–96	2002–04
United States	85.0	85.0	88.8	85.0	85.0	85.0	88.8	85.0
Germany	43.0	52.6	53.3	52.8	32.3	21.3	18.1	35.9
Japan	2.4	13.3	20.5	23.8	93.1	78.5	72.2	69.5
United Kingdom	38.0	40.0	51.7	33.0	29.0	n.a	22.0	37.0
France	34.1	48.9	48.4	45.3	33.1	n.a	23.1	46.9
Italy	18.0	27.0	37.0	44.5	45.0	n.a	28.0	n.a

Notes: The 1992–1996 data denote March 1996 for the United States, 1994 for Germany, March 1996 for Japan, 1992 for the United Kingdom, 1995 for France and 1994 for Italy. The 2002–2004 data denote 2003 for the United States, 2004 for Germany, second half of 2004 for Japan, 2002 for the United Kingdom, 2003 for France, and 2004 for Italy. For Germany, France and Italy, the 2002–2004 data show the share of euro invoicing.

Source: Deutsche Bundesbank (1991); Tavlas and Ozeki (1992); Tavlas (1997); Goldberg and Tille (2008); Kamps (2006); Bank of Japan, Yushutsu Shinyojo Tokei [Export Letter of Credit Statistics]; MITI, Yunyu Shomin Todokede Hokokusho [Import Approval Notification Report]; MITI, Yushutsu Kakunin Tokei [Export Confirmation Statistics]; MITI, Yunyu Hokoku Tokei [Import Report Statistics]; MITI, Yushutsu Kessai Tsukadate Doko Chosa [Export Settlement Currency Invoicing]; MITI, Yunyu Kessai Tsukadate Doko Chosa [Import Settlement Currency Invoicing].

as a part of their global production and sales strategy. In trade within group companies, Japanese exporters may well have an incentive to choose yen invoicing trade.[21] In addition, as long as Japan exports differentiated products to Asia, the share of yen invoicing is expected to be high, as suggested by stylized fact 3. However, the actual share of yen invoicing is contrary to the conventional prediction. Thus, we have two puzzles to be tackled in this book:

- 1st puzzle: Japanese exports to advanced countries tend to be invoiced in the importer's currency, which contradicts Grassman's Law.
- 2nd puzzle: The share of US dollar invoicing is higher than that of yen invoicing in Japanese trade with Asia, even though Japanese firms have built a regional production and sales network where goods are traded between group companies or in intra-firm trade.

To begin to understand these puzzles of Japan's invoicing currency patterns, this chapter investigates the detailed data on the invoicing choices of Japanese exports and imports by commodity/industry.

2.4 INVOICE CURRENCY CHOICE BY INDUSTRY

The BOJ publishes industry-breakdown data on the shares of invoice currencies in Japanese exports and imports. Specifically, the BOJ collects export price data when a cargo is loaded in Japan at the customs clearance stage, and the free on board (FOB) prices at Japanese port of exports are surveyed. As long as goods are traded in foreign currencies, sample prices are recorded on an original contract currency basis and finally compiled as the 'export price index on the *contract currency* basis'. To compile the 'export price index on the *yen* basis', sample prices in the contract currency are converted into yen equivalents by using the yen's monthly average exchange rate vis-à-vis the contract currency. The import price index is similarly constructed using port-level information.[22]

---

[21]   Kawai (1996), for instance, pointed out that the international use of the yen would naturally grow as Japan's economic interdependence with Asia deepened through intra-firm trade, foreign direct investment and various types of financial flows.

[22]   See the BOJ website (https://www.boj.or.jp/en/statistics/pi/cgpi_2010/index.htm/) for further details.

Table 2.2   Invoice currency choice in Japanese exports and imports: BOJ data (per cent)

	Export					Import				
	Yen	USD	Euro	D.Mark	Others	Yen	USD	Euro	D.Mark	Others
1990	25.1	64.3	–	4.9	5.7	3.9	92.9	–	1.1	2.1
1991	25.2	62.3	–	8.6	3.8	4.0	92.9	–	1.1	2.1
1992	24.0	64.2	–	9.2	2.7	9.7	82.2	–	4.4	3.7
1993	22.9	65.1	–	9.4	2.5	9.4	82.5	–	4.4	3.7
1994	23.7	64.1	–	9.5	2.7	9.9	82.2	–	4.4	3.5
1995	23.8	63.3	–	9.5	3.4	10.0	82.5	–	3.7	3.7
1996	23.7	64.7	–	8.1	3.5	10.6	82.0	–	3.7	3.7
1997	27.2	64.4	–	5.7	2.6	16.6	76.6	–	2.0	4.9
1998	27.5	63.7	–	5.7	3.1	17.0	76.8	–	2.0	4.3
1999	26.7	62.4	5.8	3.0	2.1	17.0	76.9	0.8	1.2	4.1
2000	29.7	59.6	6.2	2.8	1.7	18.3	75.6	1.0	1.4	3.7
2001	24.3	62.8	8.0	2.5	2.4	18.7	74.9	2.1	0.9	3.3
2002	28.5	59.0	10.1	–	2.4	23.1	71.3	3.4	–	2.2
2003	31.8	55.5	9.8	–	2.9	23.9	70.5	3.5	–	2.1
2004	32.3	53.8	10.8	–	3.1	23.6	71.1	3.6	–	1.7
2005	33.3	53.0	11.1	–	2.6	23.4	71.1	3.5	–	2.0
2006	34.0	53.4	10.1	–	2.5	23.8	70.7	3.5	–	2.0
2007	32.1	54.4	11.0	–	2.5	23.3	71.8	3.1	–	1.8
2008	30.3	54.7	12.5	–	2.5	24.6	70.4	3.0	–	2.0
2009	30.0	55.7	11.9	–	2.4	24.0	70.6	3.2	–	2.2
2010	39.2	51.0	6.3	–	3.4	27.2	69.1	2.6	–	1.2
2011	39.1	50.7	6.7	–	3.5	27.4	68.9	2.4	–	1.3
2012	38.6	51.4	6.7	–	3.3	27.5	68.9	2.3	–	1.3
2013	38.1	51.2	7.0	–	3.6	27.2	69.1	2.3	–	1.4
2014	36.7	53.1	6.9	–	3.2	27.2	69.0	2.4	–	1.5
2015	35.9	53.3	7.1	–	3.6	25.0	71.3	2.4	–	1.3

Note: The data on the share of invoice currency in exports to and imports from the world are presented. All data are December data. 'D.Mark' denotes the Deutschmark.

Source: BOJ website.

2.4.1   Comparison of Time-series Data

Before observing the industry-breakdown data for invoicing choices, let us check differences in invoice currency shares between Figures 2.1, 2.2 and Table 2.2. Table 2.2 presents the BOJ data of invoice currency shares for both Japanese exports to and imports from the world from December 1990 to December 2015. The BOJ data show that the share of yen invoicing for Japanese exports is 25.1 per cent as of December 1990 (Table 2.2). In contrast, Figure 2.1 indicates that 37.5 per cent of Japanese exports to the world are invoiced in yen as of 1990. A similar difference is observed for Japanese imports. Figure 2.2 shows that 14.6 per cent of Japanese imports are invoiced in yen, while the BOJ data indicate that only 3.9 per cent of imports are invoiced in yen.

The difference in shares of invoice currency choices between two data sets may be due to the smaller coverage of the BOJ data. As demonstrated in Figures 2.1 and 2.2, the Ministry of Finance (MOF) collects all information on invoice currency choices at the port level, while the BOJ data set (Table 2.2) is based on a survey conducted amongst a limited number of sample firms. The difference between the BOJ data and the MOF data shrinks in the 2000s, and the two data sets become quite similar after 2010. The BOJ publishes industry-breakdown data from December 1999 and the data become more accurate, especially after 2010.

2.4.2 Industry-level Data on Invoice Currencies

Table 2.3 presents industry-breakdown data of invoice currency choice for Japanese exports and imports as of December 2015, while shares of invoice currency by destination and/or source countries are not available.[23]

First, in both exports and imports, the share of invoice currency differs across industries. Stylized fact 3 tells us that the differentiated products tend to be invoiced in the exporter's currency, and Japanese machinery products can be considered differentiated products. In the case of General Machinery, 59.4 per cent of exports are invoiced in yen (Table 2.3). In contrast, only 36.0 per cent and 29.8 per cent of exports are invoiced in yen in the Electrical Machinery and Transport Equipment segments, respectively, while approximately 50 per cent or more of exports are invoiced in US dollars as of December 2015. Thus, LCP or third currency (US dollar) invoicing accounts for the largest share of Japanese exports of the Electrical Machinery and Transport Equipment industries, indicating the strong tendency to conduct PTM behaviour. Tables 2.4 and 2.5 present invoice currency shares as of December 2005 and December 1999, respectively, which also support the above observation that the share of yen invoicing is the largest for General Machinery, while LCP or US dollar invoicing tends to predominate in the Electrical Machinery and Transport Equipment industries.

Second, imports of petroleum, coal and natural gas tend to be invoiced

---

[23] The BOJ publishes data on the invoice currency patterns by industry for every year from 1999 but only December data are available.

Table 2.3 *Share of invoice currency in Japanese exports and imports (December 2015)*

Industry	Export Price Index				Industry	Import Price Index			
	JPY	USD	EUR	Others		JPY	USD	EUR	Others
					Foodstuffs & feedstuffs (75.8)	32.1	60.9	4.2	2.8
Textiles (12.5)	9.5	79.8	10.7	0.0	Textiles (53.5)	56.4	40.1	0.5	2.9
Chemicals & related products (95.4)	26.4	70.5	1.3	1.8	Chemicals & related products (83.3)	51.3	36.4	9.8	2.5
Metals & related products (118.2)	21.9	77.4	0.6	0.0	Metals & related products (117.1)	11.9	86.1	0.0	2.0
					Wood, lumber & related products (16.5)	4.1	79.7	16.1	0.0
					Petroleum, coal & natural gas (305.4)	8.7	91.3	0.0	0.0
General Machinery (192.0)	59.4	27.7	9.6	3.3	General Machinery (53.9)	35.0	59.5	2.7	2.7
Electric & electronic products (232.9)	36.0	55.6	7.8	0.5	Electric & electronic products (184.3)	33.7	64.9	0.6	0.9
Transportation equipment (240.6)	29.8	48.3	11.4	10.5	Transportation equipment (34.1)	37.1	47.4	15.5	0.0
Other Products (108.4)	34.0	60.7	3.7	1.5	Other Products (76.1)	23.3	71.7	2.0	3.0
All Industries (1000.0)	35.9	53.3	7.1	3.6	All Industries (1000.0)	25.0	71.3	2.4	1.3

Notes: Monthly data (as of December 2015). The share (percentage) of invoice (contract) currency is presented. Figures in parentheses after the name of each industry are weights for all industries (= 1000.0). 'General Machinery' denotes 'General purpose, production & business-oriented machinery'. 'Other Products' denotes 'Other primary products & manufactured goods'.

Source: Bank of Japan, Export and Import Price Indices (2010 base).

Table 2.4 Share of invoice currency in Japanese exports and imports (December 2005)

Industry	Export Price Index			
	JPY	USD	EUR	Others
Textiles (18.5)	27.0	72.7	0.0	0.0
Chemicals & related products (76.8)	21.1	74.7	2.9	1.2
Metals & related products (64.5)	15.4	83.4	1.1	0.0
General machinery & equipment (192.4)	51.0	32.1	13.9	2.9
Electrical machinery & equipment (358.3)	36.8	53.8	9.4	0.0
Transportation equipment (203.6)	21.0	49.6	21.9	7.5
Precision instruments (25.4)	30.5	62.7	6.3	0.2
Other manufacturing industry products (60.3)	34.9	55.9	3.2	5.8
All Industries (1000.0)	33.3	53.0	11.1	2.6

Industry	Import Price Index			
	JPY	USD	EUR	Others
Foodstuffs & feed stuffs (93.1)	18.8	69.7	7.0	4.4
Textiles (74.1)	46.1	49.3	2.4	2.1
Chemicals & related products (66.7)	42.5	52.4	3.6	1.4
Metals & related products (80.9)	14.2	83.2	0.0	2.6
Wood, lumber & related products (32.3)	5.4	80.1	11.4	2.8
Petroleum, coal & natural gas (221.0)	0.3	99.7	0.0	0.0
Machinery & equipment (348.8)	36.6	57.1	4.1	2.2
Other primary products & manufactured goods (83.1)	15.2	74.3	7.4	3.0
All Industries (1000.0)	23.4	71.1	3.5	2.0

Notes: Monthly data (as of December 2005). The share (percentage) of invoice (contract) currency is presented. Figures in parentheses after the name of each industry are weights for all industries (= 1000.0).

Source: Bank of Japan, Export and Import Price Indices (2000 base).

Table 2.5 *Share of invoice currency in Japanese exports and imports (December 1999)*

Export Price Index

Industry	JPY	USD	EUR	D.Mark	Others
Textiles (21.3)	9.1	88.2	0.0	2.4	0.4
Chemicals & related products (76.8)	9.2	90.2	0.0	0.3	0.2
Metals & related products (73.0)	14.8	82.8	0.0	0.0	2.3
General machinery & equipment (212.2)	64.1	26.8	4.9	2.1	2.0
Electrical machinery & equipment (354.8)	19.7	74.8	3.4	0.5	1.6
Transportation equipment (178.0)	12.8	52.1	18.5	11.3	5.2
Precision instruments (26.9)	34.6	56.4	8.7	0.0	0.0
Other manufacturing industry products (57.0)	16.2	78.2	0.0	4.3	1.2
All Industries (1000.0)	26.7	62.4	5.8	3.0	2.1

Import Price Index

Industry	JPY	USD	EUR	D.Mark	Others
Foodstuffs & feed stuffs (119.4)	20.4	72.4	0.0	0.3	6.9
Textiles (87.5)	22.3	70.6	0.0	0.9	6.1
Chemicals & related products (75.3)	35.2	63.8	0.0	0.0	0.8
Metals & related products (112.6)	14.7	83.6	0.0	0.0	1.6
Wood, lumber & related products (51.7)	0.0	100.0	0.0	0.0	0.0
Petroleum, coal & natural gas (178.2)	0.0	100.0	0.0	0.0	0.0
Machinery & equipment (282.6)	24.9	65.4	2.7	2.1	5.0
Other primary products & manufactured goods (92.7)	13.8	68.2	0.0	5.2	12.8
All Industries (1000.0)	17.0	76.9	0.8	1.2	4.1

Notes: Monthly data (as of December 1999). The share (percentage) of invoice (contract) currency is presented. Figures in parentheses after the name of each industry are weights for all industries (= 1000.0).

Source: Bank of Japan, Export and Import Price Indices (1995 base).

in US dollars. A full 100 per cent of the above imports were invoiced in US dollars as of December 1999 (Table 2.5) and 91.3 per cent were invoiced in US dollars as of December 2015 (Table 2.3). This evidence is consistent with the stylized fact 3. Table 2.3 shows that 77.4 per cent of metal exports and 86.1 per cent of metal imports are invoiced in US dollars.

Third, for Japanese imports of three major machinery industries (General Machinery, Electrical Machinery and Transport Equipment), 33–37 per cent are invoiced in yen. The share of US dollar invoicing is much higher in these three machinery industries. More interestingly, the share of yen invoicing is higher in Japanese imports of Transport Equipment than in the corresponding exports. The relative shares of yen invoicing between exports and imports are not very different even in the Electrical Machinery industry. This result is quite interesting because the stylized fact 1 says that the machinery export trade between advanced countries tends to be invoiced in the exporter's currency.

2.5 NEW APPROACH TO ESTIMATING THE INVOICE CURRENCY SHARE

We have so far observed choices of invoice currency for Japanese exports and imports by using data published by a Japanese governmental agency and the BOJ. While the MOF publishes semi-annual data on the shares of invoice currencies in Japanese exports and imports for three destination/source countries (regions), neither industry- nor commodity-breakdown data are published. The BOJ publishes the industry-breakdown data on the choice of invoice currency from 1999 but only December data are available. In addition, more detailed data such as commodity-breakdown data are not available.

In this section we propose a new estimation method regarding choice of invoice currency in Japanese exports and imports by using price data published by the BOJ (Ito et al., 2016a). The novelty of this approach lies in its estimation of the commodity- and industry-breakdown share of invoicing currency by using monthly series of the BOJ export and import price indices. As discussed earlier, the Japanese invoicing currency pattern is puzzling in that its share of invoicing in own currency is much lower than in other advanced countries.[24] Contrary to the stylized facts of trade invoicing choice, Japanese firms tend to choose the importer's currency for invoicing when exporting to advanced countries and also conduct US dollar invoicing transactions in exports to Asian countries. By estimating the share of

---

[24] See Ito et al. (2012) for the puzzles of the Japanese-currency invoicing pattern.

invoice currency by industry/commodity, we reveal the actual invoicing currency pattern, which has not yet been analysed empirically in the literature.

2.5.1 Estimation Method of the Share of Invoice Currency

Constant parameter estimation
The BOJ publishes two types of price indices for Japanese exports and imports: (1) a *yen*-based export/import price index; and (2) *contract currency*-based export/import price index. As explained in the previous section, the BOJ collects information on export prices based on contract (invoice) currency from sample firms and then calculates the yen-based export price by using the yen's bilateral nominal exchange rate (monthly average) vis-à-vis each contract currency. For a clear exposition, let us assume that Japanese exporters use only three currencies: yen, US dollars and euros, in their exports and also that the BOJ constructs the yen-invoiced export price (P_{yen}), US dollar invoiced export price ($P_{\$}$) and euro-invoiced export price (P_{euro}).[25] Then, we can define the yen-based export price index (P_{yen}^{EX}) as follows:

$$P_{yen}^{EX} = (P_{yen})^\alpha (P_{\$} \cdot S_{yen/\$})^\beta (P_{euro} \cdot S_{yen/euro})^\gamma, \tag{2.10}$$

where α, β and γ represent the share of yen invoicing, US dollar invoicing and euro invoicing exports, respectively, and $\alpha + \beta + \gamma = 1$; $S_{yen/\$}$ and $S_{yen/euro}$ denote the yen's bilateral nominal exchange rate vis-à-vis the US dollar and euro, respectively. The export price based on contract currencies (P_c^{EX}) can be defined as $P_c^{EX} = (P_{yen})^\alpha (P_{\$})^\beta (P_{euro})^\gamma$. Thus, the yen-based export price index (P_{yen}^{EX}) can be reformulated into:

$$P_{yen}^{EX} = (P_{yen})^\alpha (P_{\$})^\beta (P_{euro})^\gamma \cdot (S_{yen/\$})^\beta \cdot (S_{yen/euro})^\gamma$$
$$= P_c^{EX} \cdot (S_{yen/\$})^\beta \cdot (S_{yen/euro})^\gamma \tag{2.11}$$

By dividing both sides of the equation by P_c^{EX} and taking the natural logarithm, we obtain:

$$\ln(P_{yen}^{EX}/P_c^{EX})_t = \beta \cdot \ln S_{yen/\$,t} + \gamma \cdot \ln S_{yen/euro,t}. \tag{2.12}$$

By definition, the share of US dollar invoicing (β) and euro invoicing (γ) can be estimated by equation (2.12). The share of yen invoicing can be

---

[25] This is not an extreme assumption. In the second half of 2015, for instance, these three currencies account for 96.3 per cent of invoice currencies of Japanese total exports (see Table 2.2).

obtained by subtracting the shares of both US dollar and euro invoicing from unity: $\alpha = 1 - \beta - \gamma$. To ensure the stationarity of variables, we use the first-difference model for OLS estimation:

$$\Delta \ln(P^{EX}_{yen}/P^{EX}_c)_t = \beta \cdot \Delta \ln S_{yen/\$,t} + \gamma \cdot \Delta \ln S_{yen/euro,t} + \varepsilon_t, \quad (2.13)$$

where Δ is the first-difference operator, and ε is an independently and normally distributed error term with zero mean and a constant variance.

Time-varying parameter estimation
Our major interest is the question as to whether shares of different invoice currencies have changed over time. To examine rigorously possible changes in the share of invoice currency, we employ the Kalman filter technique to estimate the time-varying parameter of the above empirical model. Equation (2.13) can be reformulated into the observation equation (2.14) and the state equations (2.15) and (2.16) as follows:

$$\Delta \ln(P^{EX}_{yen}/P^{EX}_c)_t = \beta_t \cdot \Delta \ln S_{yen/\$,t} + \gamma_t \cdot \Delta \ln S_{yen/euro,t} + \varepsilon_t \quad (2.14)$$

$$\beta_t = \beta_{t-1} + v_t \quad (2.15)$$

$$\gamma_t = \gamma_{t-1} + \mu_t \quad (2.16)$$

where β_t and γ_t represent the time-varying coefficient, and v_t and μ_t indicate the Gaussian disturbances with zero mean.

2.5.2 Data Description

Our analysis is based on the BOJ export and import price indices, where both yen-based and contract currency-based export and import price indices are published.[26] The export price index is classified into four levels: Group, Subgroup, Commodity Class and Commodity, as shown in Figure 2.3.

The monthly series of both yen-based and contract currency-based

---

[26] The data are downloadable from the BOJ website (http://www.boj.or.jp/en/theme/research/stat/pi/cgpi/index.htm). In the case of export price index, for example, the BOJ surveys export prices at the stage of shipment from Japan. At the beginning of every month, firms are requested to report the representative price for the previous month. The surveyed prices are chosen as a representation that is sensitive to supply and demand conditions of the commodities concerned. If commodities are exported by invoicing in a foreign currency, the surveyed prices are recorded on the original contract (invoice) currency basis. Then, the contract-currency-based prices are converted into the yen-based prices by using the monthly average spot exchange rate.

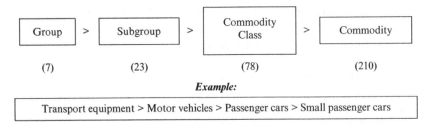

Example:

Transport equipment > Motor vehicles > Passenger cars > Small passenger cars

Note: Figures in parentheses denote the numbers compiled in each classification. Indexes for upper classification levels (Group, Subgroup, and Commodity Class) are compiled from Commodity indexes.

Figure 2.3   Classification of BOJ export price index

export price indices are available from January 1975 to the present at the Group level, while the indices at the lower classification (Subgroup, Commodity Class and Commodity) levels are available from January 1980 to the present for a limited number of commodities. We estimate the share of invoicing currencies at the Group level from January 1975 and at a more disaggregated level from January 1980 to December 2015.

All monthly series of the nominal exchange rate are taken from IMF's *International Financial Statistics*. The yen's exchange rate vis-à-vis the deutschmark (DM) is used as a substitute for the yen–Euro exchange rate from January 1975 to December 1998. To connect the yen–DM rate to the yen–euro rate, we use the euro conversion rate published on the European Central Bank's website.

2.5.3   Choice of Invoice Currency by Industry/Product

Aggregated level of time-varying invoice currency choice
Figure 2.4 shows the time-varying estimates of invoice currency choice in Japanese exports obtained from the Kalman filter estimation of equation (2.14). The time-varying invoicing share by industry (that is, at the Group level) from January 1995 to December 2015 is presented. By generating ± two-standard error confidence bands, we confirmed that time-varying estimates of US dollar invoicing share are statistically significant, while time-varying estimates of euro invoicing are not necessarily significant. To obtain the time-varying share of yen invoicing, we just subtract both shares of US dollar and euro invoicing from unity, that is, $\alpha = 1 - \beta - \gamma$, even though the share of euro invoicing is not necessarily significant. In Figure 2.4, both the estimated time-varying share of US dollar invoicing and the calculated share of yen invoicing are presented.

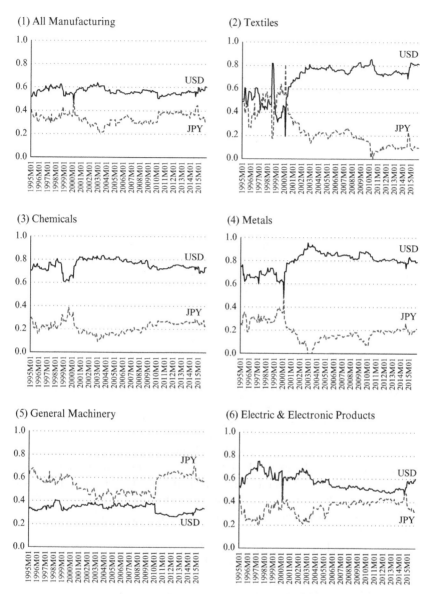

Note: Bold (black) and dotted (grey) lines show the time-varying estimates of US dollar invoicing and yen invoicing, respectively. In the vertical axis, 1.0 denotes 100 per cent, while 0.0 denotes 0 per cent.

Figure 2.4   Time-varying estimates of invoice currency share in Japanese exports

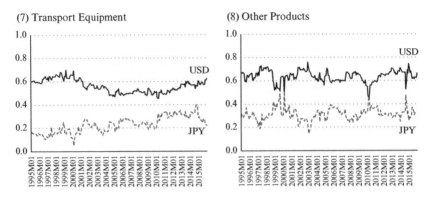

Figure 2.4   (continued)

Figure 2.4(1) indicates that the yen-invoiced share in 1995 fluctuates between 30 and 40 per cent, which is higher than the yen-invoiced share reported in Table 2.2. As discussed in section 2.4.1, the estimated share of invoice currency for Japanese trade is somewhat unusual up to around 2000, probably due to the relatively small coverage of the sample firms in the BOJ survey. Such an unusual result is more evident in the industry-level results. For instance, Japanese Textile exports in Figure 2.4(2) exhibit large fluctuations in invoice currency shares until around 2000 and estimated invoice currency shares become relatively stable in subsequent years. Thus, we hereafter assume that the time-varying invoice currency shares seem more reliable from around 2000.

Figure 2.4 clearly shows that Japanese non-machinery exports largely tend to be invoiced in US dollars. At least 70 or 80 per cent of exports are invoiced in US dollars in Textiles, Chemicals and Metals. In addition, at least from the early 2000s, the US dollar invoicing share is quite stable, though Chemicals and Metals exhibit a slight decline in US dollar invoicing share from the late 2000s. The share of yen invoicing in the above three industries is very low, fluctuating between 10 and 30 per cent from the early 2000s.

Japanese machinery exports tend to be invoiced more in yen compared with non-machinery exports, but the share of yen-invoiced exports differs between the machinery industries. Figure 2.4(6) shows that 60 per cent or more of Electric Machinery exports were invoiced in US dollars in the early 2000s, but the US dollar-invoiced share kept declining to 50 per cent or less up to the end of 2012. During that period, the yen-invoiced share increased to around 40 per cent. From the end of 2012, when the Japanese Prime Minister Abe's economic stimulus package (the so-called *Abenomics*) was initiated, the US dollar-invoiced share increased from 48 per cent to reach

60 per cent by the end of 2015, while the share of yen-invoiced transactions declined to 32 per cent during the same period.

Japanese firms typically conduct PTM behaviour in Transport Equipment exports. The share of US dollar and euro invoicing is very high, with 70–80 per cent of exports invoiced in these currencies (Figure 2.4(7)). Although not presented in Figure 2.4, the share of euro invoicing was between 20 and 30 per cent up to the late 2000s, and the share invoiced in euros started to fall rapidly from 2010, when the yen's appreciation accelerated in response to the global financial crisis and subsequent euro area fiscal crisis. During the same period, the yen-invoiced share started to rise from around 20–30 per cent or more. Thus, the share invoiced in yen exhibits a considerable increase during the recent period of yen appreciation.

It is interesting to observe the yen-invoiced share of the General Machinery industry. As shown in Figure 2.4(5), the US dollar-invoiced share is less than 40 per cent in the General Machinery industry, while the yen-invoiced share is always higher than the US dollar-invoiced share. More noteworthy is that the share of yen invoicing increased sharply from 42 per cent at the end of 2009 to 60 per cent or higher by June 2010.

The above observation indicates that Japanese machinery exporters strategically changed the share of invoice currency in response to large exchange rate fluctuations. The nominal yen–US dollar exchange rate appreciated from 106.7 in September 2008 to 76.8 in November 2011.[27] In response to such a sharp appreciation, Japanese General Machinery exporters and, to a lesser extent, Transport Equipment exporters raised their yen-invoiced share to increase the degree of ERPT. It is often pointed out that Japanese production equipment and capital goods tend to have strong market power, probably due to product differentiation and, hence, exporters can pass through the exchange rate risk to importers by invoicing in yen.

Turning to the result of the time-varying estimation in Japanese imports, it is found that the share of US dollar invoicing is 70 per cent or more from around 2000 for imports in all industries, while the yen-invoiced share is 20 per cent or more (Figure 2.5). When looking at the industry-level share of invoice currency, US dollar invoicing accounts for the largest share (70 per cent or more) in imports of Foodstuffs, Metals, Wood and Petroleum. This finding is consistent with the stylized fact that homogeneous goods tend to be invoiced in US dollars. In the case of Japanese machinery imports, more than 50 per cent of trades are invoiced in US dollars in the General Machinery, Electric Machinery and Transport Equipment. The share of

---

[27]   The monthly average nominal exchange rate is taken from the IMF's *International Financial Statistics*. On 31 October 2011, the yen–US dollar exchange rate hit 75.32, a post-war record high.

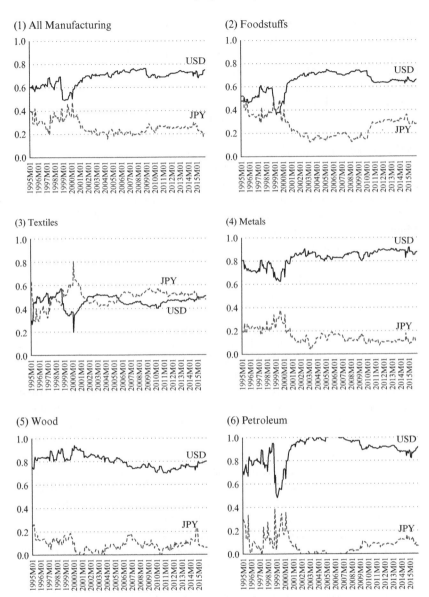

Note: Bold (black) and dotted (grey) lines show the time-varying estimates of US dollar invoicing and yen invoicing, respectively. In the vertical axis, 1.0 denotes 100 per cent, while 0.0 denotes 0 per cent.

Figure 2.5   Time-varying estimates of invoice currency share in Japanese imports

(7) Chemicals

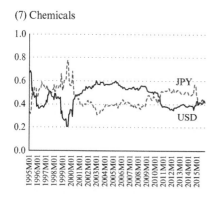

(8) General Machinery

(9) Electric & Electronic Products

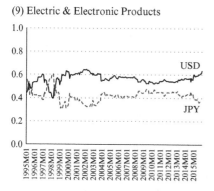

(10) Transport Equipment

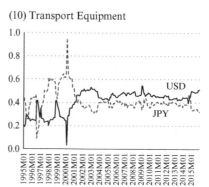

(11) Other Products

Figure 2.5   (continued)

yen invoicing is the second largest, accounting for approximately 40 per cent of imports in the three machinery industries. The share of euro invoicing, which is not presented in Figure 2.5, is 20 per cent or less in imports of these machinery industries.

Commodity-level invoice currency choices in Japanese exports

To investigate changing patterns of the invoice currency choices, we perform an OLS estimation of Equation (2.13) for each commodity and present the estimated results in Tables 2.6 and 2.7.[28]

Let us discuss the results of the estimation of invoice currency choice in Japanese exports. First, Table 2.6 shows that 70–80 per cent of Japanese exports of Textiles (Table 2.6(A)), Chemicals (Table 2.6(B)) and Metals (Table 2.6(C)) are invoiced in US dollars. It is also found that a large difference exists in the share of invoice currency across commodities. Some commodities are mostly invoiced in yen, but on average, the share of yen invoicing is more than 20 per cent in Chemicals (Table 2.6(B)) and Metals (Table 2.6(C)), while only 9 per cent of exports of Textiles (Table 2.6(A)) are invoiced in the yen during the 2012–15 period.

Second, Table 2.6(D) shows that 61 per cent of Japanese General Machinery exports are invoiced in yen during the 2012–15 period, which may reflect the strong competitiveness of General Machinery products.[29] For instance, exports of semiconductor and flat-panel/display manufacturing equipment are totally invoiced in yen, reflecting these products' strong export competitiveness and large share in the world market.

Third, in contrast, more than 50 per cent of Electric Machinery exports are invoiced in US dollars during the 2012–15 period (Table 2.6(E)); 60 per cent of electronic components and devices are invoiced in US dollars. In addition, 72 per cent of passenger cars are invoiced in US dollars (Table 2.6(F)), reflecting a strong tendency towards PTM behaviour. Interestingly, 49 per cent of internal combustion engines and motor vehicle parts are invoiced in yen in 2012–15. Engines are typically considered as differentiated products, and the larger share of yen-invoiced exports is consistent with stylized fact 3.

Commodity-level invoice currency choices in Japanese imports

Table 2.7 shows the estimated share of invoice currency in Japanese imports. Approximately 70 per cent or more of Japanese imports of

---

[28] We present the estimated invoice currency share at a level of 'Commodity Class' (Figure 2.3). Estimated invoice currency shares at a more detailed level (i.e. 'Commodity' level) are presented in Ito et al. (2016a).

[29] This finding is consistent with Ito et al. (2012).

Table 2.6 Estimated invoice currency share in Japanese exports

	Weight	US Dollar Invoicing Share				Yen Invoicing Share			
		00–03	04–07	08–11	12–15	00–03	04–07	08–11	12–15
(A) Textiles	**(12.5)**	0.74	0.76	0.75	0.80	0.29	0.23	0.16	0.09
Raw & semi-processed fibres for spun yarn	**(3.0)**	1.01	1.00	1.00	1.01	0.00	0.00	0.01	0.00
Woven fabrics	**(7.4)**	0.96	1.01	0.76	0.78	0.07	0.01	0.05	0.07
Natural fibre fabrics	(2.1)	0.96	1.01	0.77	0.75	0.07	0.01	0.10	0.30
Synthetic fibre fabrics	(5.3)	0.67	0.69	0.80	0.79	0.33	0.30	0.02	0.00
Other textile products	**(2.1)**	0.59	0.62	0.60	0.59	0.42	0.39	0.38	0.30

	Weight	US Dollar Invoicing Share				Yen Invoicing Share			
		00–03	04–07	08–11	12–15	00–03	04–07	08–11	12–15
(B) Chemicals & related products	**(95.4)**	0.82	0.79	0.74	0.71	0.16	0.18	0.24	0.26
Industrial inorganic chemicals	**(8.7)**	0.81	0.79	0.79	0.87	0.19	0.21	0.21	0.13
Industrial organic chemicals	**(61.8)**			0.89	0.85			0.10	0.14
Basic petrochemicals	(3.9)			1.00	1.00			−0.01	0.01
Aliphatic intermediates	(9.0)			1.00	1.00			−0.01	0.01
Cyclic intermediates	(21.1)	1.02	1.01	1.00	1.00	−0.01	0.00	0.00	0.00
Plastic resins & materials	(22.6)			0.73	0.71			0.26	0.27
Other industrial organic chemicals	(5.2)	0.97	0.88	0.86	0.53	0.01	0.13	0.15	0.44
Pharmaceutical products	**(6.8)**			0.25	0.22			0.75	0.72
Other chemical products	**(18.1)**			0.34	0.32			0.65	0.66

51

Table 2.6 (continued)

(C) Metals & related products	Weight	US Dollar Invoicing Share				Yen Invoicing Share			
		00–03	04–07	08–11	12–15	00–03	04–07	08–11	12–15
(C) Metals & related products	**(118.2)**	0.87	0.84	0.84	0.80	0.14	0.17	0.15	0.21
Metal materials	**(7.8)**			0.26	0.14			0.75	0.81
Iron & steel	**(60.5)**	1.01	0.98	0.99	0.95	−0.02	0.02	0.01	0.05
Ferro-alloys	(1.0)	1.01	0.98	1.01	1.01	−0.02	0.02	0.00	0.00
Hot rolled ordinary steel products	(18.5)	0.98	1.00	0.98	0.98	0.02	0.00	0.03	0.03
Cold finished & coated ordinary steel	(19.5)			0.99	1.00			0.00	0.00
Hot rolled special steel products	(9.0)			0.75	0.74			0.24	0.26
Cold finished special steel products	(4.0)			1.00	1.00			0.00	0.00
Steel pipes & tubes	(7.8)	1.02	1.00	1.00	1.00	−0.02	0.01	0.00	0.01
Cold finished bars	(0.7)	1.02	1.00	0.81	0.82	−0.02	0.01	0.19	0.19
Nonferrous metals	**(35.6)**			0.80	0.83			0.20	0.17
Unwrought metals	(20.0)		1.00	1.00	1.00		0.01	0.00	0.01
Copper and copper alloy rolled	(6.1)	0.69	0.46	0.44	0.41	0.29	0.53	0.56	0.57
Aluminium and aluminium alloy rolled	(4.1)	0.77	0.65	0.67	0.41	0.21	0.35	0.33	0.57
Other nonferrous metal rolled	(5.4)			0.61	0.98			0.40	0.05
Metal products	**(14.3)**	0.72	0.67	0.65	0.37	0.24	0.26	0.25	0.58
Wire products	(9.0)	0.73	0.76	0.72	0.25	0.35	0.26	0.23	0.75
Other metal products	(5.3)	0.69	0.52	0.54	0.54	0.08	0.25	0.27	0.31

(D) General purpose, production & business oriented machinery	Weight	US Dollar Invoicing Share				Yen Invoicing Share			
		00–03	04–07	08–11	12–15	00–03	04–07	08–11	12–15
(D) General purpose, production & business oriented machinery	**(192.0)**	0.35	0.36	0.35	0.31	0.49	0.47	0.51	0.61
General purpose machinery	**(55.5)**	0.33	0.36	0.40	0.34	0.48	0.40	0.43	0.55
Engines & parts	(13.0)	0.05	0.23	0.43	0.46	0.53	0.24	0.31	0.49
Pumps & compressors	(10.6)		0.31	0.26	0.22		0.70	0.73	0.76
Oil hydraulic & pneumatic machinery	(6.0)		0.62	0.49	0.25		0.38	0.49	0.76
Power transmission equipment & bearings	(15.9)	0.46	0.53	0.45	0.28	0.42	0.35	0.40	0.49
Refrigerating machines & appliances	(4.8)	0.51	0.32	0.39	0.48	0.10	0.07	0.00	0.01
Other general purpose machinery	(5.2)	0.34	0.10	0.42	0.43	0.67	0.77	0.58	0.58
Production machinery	**(112.8)**	0.31	0.28	0.29	0.24	0.54	0.59	0.60	0.70
Agricultural machinery	(4.5)	0.40	0.19	0.29	0.51	0.51	0.80	0.72	0.51
Construction machinery	(23.5)	0.32	0.38	0.54	0.42	0.56	0.42	0.24	0.47
Textile machinery	(6.2)	0.40	0.45	0.49	0.63	0.57	0.38	0.31	0.19
Printing, plate making & bookbinding	(3.0)		0.01	0.09	0.27		0.79	0.82	0.76
Semiconductor and flat panel & display manufacturing	(42.0)		0.12	0.05	0.00		0.88	0.95	1.00
Other special industrial machinery	(7.0)	0.65	0.41	0.30	0.18	0.35	0.59	0.69	0.82
Metal cutting machine tools	(15.2)	0.42	0.43	0.40	0.24	0.49	0.32	0.37	0.67
Metal forming machinery	(5.4)	0.32	0.47	0.41	0.38	0.32	0.42	0.58	0.64
Tools for machines and pneumatic	(3.8)	0.06	0.07	0.26	0.49	0.72	0.55	0.32	0.31
Other production machinery	(2.2)	0.37	0.37	0.39	0.39	0.24	0.25	0.35	0.60
Business oriented machinery	**(23.7)**	0.49	0.45	0.46	0.55	0.46	0.45	0.39	0.35
Instruments & appliances for measuring	(9.3)	0.32	0.32	0.21	-0.01	0.68	0.69	0.78	0.97
Medical appliances	(7.1)	0.65	0.65	0.70	0.87	0.35	0.35	0.09	0.00
Optical instruments & lenses	(7.3)	0.54	0.43	0.53	0.85	0.28	0.25	0.18	0.00

Table 2.6 (continued)

(E) Electric & electronic products	Weight	US Dollar Invoicing Share				Yen Invoicing Share			
		00-03	04-07	08-11	12-15	00-03	04-07	08-11	12-15
	(232.9)	0.60	0.55	0.51	0.54	0.34	0.37	0.40	0.39
Electronic components & devices	(130.4)	0.63	0.53	0.56	0.60	0.34	0.46	0.42	0.38
Opto electronic devices	(6.3)	0.19	0.32	0.47	0.30	0.86	0.67	0.52	0.53
Discrete semiconductors	(6.1)	0.90	0.42	0.38	0.44	0.07	0.59	0.62	0.57
Integrated circuits	(56.9)	0.78	0.53	0.66	0.71	0.21	0.48	0.32	0.27
Display devices	(11.3)		0.60	0.39	0.38		0.43	0.61	0.65
Passive components	(15.6)	0.43	0.59	0.45	0.52	0.56	0.41	0.55	0.46
Connecting components	(12.8)	0.14	0.11	0.18	0.37	0.86	0.89	0.82	0.66
Other electronic components	(21.4)		0.79	0.74	0.78		0.13	0.17	0.20
Electrical machinery & equipment	(66.5)	0.42	0.42	0.42	0.44	0.50	0.52	0.48	0.47
Heavy electrical apparatus	(15.8)			0.35	0.41			0.51	0.52
Electric bulbs and lighting & wiring devices	(5.6)	0.00	0.08	0.17	0.34	1.00	0.93	0.84	0.69
Electronic equipment	(10.0)		0.40	0.38	0.41		0.50	0.48	0.40
Electrical meters & measuring instruments	(14.6)			0.25	0.31			0.74	0.69
Other electrical machinery & equipment	(20.5)			0.52	0.60			0.27	0.23
Information & communications equipment	(36.0)	0.63	0.58	0.54	0.55	0.27	0.22	0.23	0.25
Communications equipment	(9.5)	0.00	0.16	0.14	0.23	1.00	0.81	0.79	0.67
Image & audio equipment	(17.3)	0.88	0.75	0.68	0.71	0.04	0.02	0.00	0.01
Electronic computers & computer equipment	(9.2)	0.72	0.62	0.67	0.65	0.03	0.11	0.15	0.17

(F) Transportation equipment	Weight	US Dollar Invoicing Share				Yen Invoicing Share			
		00–03	04–07	08–11	12–15	00–03	04–07	08–11	12–15
	(240.6)	0.55	0.49	0.52	0.57	0.22	0.24	0.24	0.30
Motor vehicles	**(225.1)**			0.52	0.57			0.30	0.30
Passenger cars	(125.6)	0.65	0.58	0.63	0.72	0.05	0.06	0.06	0.15
Buses	(4.4)	0.13	0.09	0.15	0.15	0.74	0.55	0.50	0.77
Trucks	(15.2)	0.46	0.48	0.41	0.26	0.49	0.23	0.18	0.58
Motorcycles	(4.3)	0.49	0.48	0.52	0.51	0.03	0.26	0.20	0.13
Internal combustion engines & motor vehicle parts	(75.6)	0.37	0.30	0.34	0.43	0.53	0.58	0.57	0.49
Other transportation equipment	**(15.5)**	0.69	0.71	0.64	0.60	0.31	0.27	0.31	0.32
Marine engines	(5.6)	0.71	0.71	0.49	0.32	0.31	0.30	0.44	0.42
Aircraft parts & aircraft engines	(6.3)	0.85	0.94	1.00	1.00	0.15	0.05	0.00	0.00
Industrial trucks & parts	(2.3)	0.46	0.44	0.36	0.20	0.54	0.40	0.43	0.74
Bicycle parts	(1.3)	0.25	0.02	0.00	0.00	0.69	0.96	1.00	1.00

(G) Other primary products & manufactured goods	Weight	US Dollar Invoicing Share				Yen Invoicing Share			
		00–03	04–07	08–11	12–15	00–03	04–07	08–11	12–15
	(108.4)	0.65	0.61	0.63	0.67	0.30	0.32	0.31	0.30
Wastepaper	**(1.3)**		1.00	0.99	0.99		0.02	0.00	0.00
Paper	**(6.1)**		0.99	0.99	1.00		0.02	0.00	0.00
Ceramic, stone & clay products	**(20.3)**	0.84	0.81	0.63	0.45	0.16	0.19	0.33	0.55
Glass & related products	(15.7)	0.84	0.81	0.61	0.40	0.16	0.19	0.35	0.63
Other ceramic, stone & clay products	(4.6)	0.64	0.66	0.51	0.59	0.37	0.31	0.42	0.35

Table 2.6 (continued)

	Weight	US Dollar Invoicing Share				Yen Invoicing Share			
		00–03	04–07	08–11	12–15	00–03	04–07	08–11	12–15
(G) Other primary products & manufactured goods	**(108.4)**	0.65	0.61	0.63	0.67	0.30	0.32	0.31	0.30
Other manufactured goods	**(80.7)**			0.64	0.68			0.30	0.28
Petroleum & coal products	(28.5)			0.77	0.74			0.22	0.26
Plastic products	(28.7)		0.37	0.41	0.57		0.52	0.51	0.38
Rubber products	(15.0)		0.67	0.71	0.81		0.09	0.06	0.13
Musical instruments & sporting goods	(4.3)	0.84	0.78	0.63	0.53	0.16	0.23	0.31	0.36
Other manufactured goods	(4.2)	0.65	0.67	0.67	0.62	0.34	0.35	0.32	0.35

Notes: Estimated invoice currency share is reported. For example, 1.00 indicates that the share of invoice currency is 100 per cent. Shaded figures in grey denote an insignificant share (coefficient). Weight indicates the share of each industry or commodity in total exports (1000).

Table 2.7 *Estimated invoice currency share in Japanese imports*

(A) Foodstuffs & feedstuffs

	Weight	US Dollar Invoicing Share				Yen Invoicing Share			
		00–03	04–07	08–11	12–15	00–03	04–07	08–11	12–15
(A) Foodstuffs & feedstuffs	**(75.8)**	0.71	0.72	0.70	0.65	0.19	0.17	0.20	0.30
Edible agriculture, livestock & fishery products	**(35.6)**			0.68	0.66			0.32	0.32
Grains	(11.0)	0.98	1.00	0.69	0.68	0.02	0.01	0.31	0.31
Beans & oilseeds	(5.6)			1.00	1.00			0.00	0.00
Other agriculture products	(4.9)	0.95	0.94	0.92	0.94	0.05	0.07	0.08	0.06
Livestock products	(14.1)	0.45	0.45	0.41	0.41	0.55	0.55	0.59	0.56
Primary processed foodstuffs	**(2.2)**	0.77	0.78	0.81	0.79	0.25	0.12	0.10	0.21
Prepared & preserved foodstuffs	**(22.4)**			0.64	0.68			0.23	0.23
Processed agriculture & fishery products	(10.3)			0.78	0.77			0.17	0.19
Other prepared & preserved foodstuffs	(12.1)			0.50	0.58			0.30	0.27
Beverages	**(5.6)**		0.33	0.38	0.55		0.32	0.19	0.18
Tobacco products	**(5.5)**			0.22	0.24			0.77	0.77
Feedstuffs	**(4.5)**	0.96	1.00	0.96	0.88	0.05	0.01	0.03	0.13

(B) Textiles

	Weight	US Dollar Invoicing Share				Yen Invoicing Share			
		00–03	04–07	08–11	12–15	00–03	04–07	08–11	12–15
(B) Textiles	**(53.5)**	0.49	0.46	0.44	0.48	0.50	0.51	0.55	0.51
Raw yarn	**(2.0)**	0.92	1.00	0.99	0.89	0.13	0.00	0.00	0.09
Yarn of natural fibres	(0.8)	0.99	0.99	0.99	1.01	0.01	0.01	0.00	0.00
Synthetic yarn	(1.2)	0.87	1.00	0.99	0.82	0.21	−0.01	0.00	0.13

Table 2.7 (continued)

(B) Textiles

(B) Textiles	Weight	US Dollar Invoicing Share				Yen Invoicing Share			
		00–03	04–07	08–11	12–15	00–03	04–07	08–11	12–15
(B) Textiles	**(53.5)**	0.49	0.46	0.44	0.48	0.50	0.51	0.55	0.51
Wowen fabrics	(1.6)	0.95	1.01	0.96	0.90	0.08	0.01	0.00	0.00
Natural fibre fabrics	(1.0)	1.00	1.01	0.93	0.83	0.00	0.01	0.00	0.00
Synthetic fibre fabrics	(0.6)	0.87	1.01	1.00	1.00	0.21	0.00	0.00	0.00
Apparel	(43.8)		0.38	0.36	0.41		0.60	0.63	0.58
Underwear	(5.2)	0.43	0.32	0.30	0.30	0.61	0.62	0.65	0.71
Shirts, blouses, polo shirts, T-shirts, sweatshirts	(8.0)		0.46	0.48	0.60		0.55	0.53	0.39
Outerwear	(23.9)	0.48	0.35	0.32	0.32	0.53	0.62	0.68	0.67
Other apparel	(6.7)		0.45	0.44	0.56		0.55	0.55	0.43
Other textile products	(6.1)	0.43	0.44	0.56	0.72	0.45	0.46	0.38	0.30

(C) Metals & related products

(C) Metals & related products	Weight	US Dollar Invoicing Share				Yen Invoicing Share			
		00–03	04–07	08–11	12–15	00–03	04–07	08–11	12–15
(C) Metals & related products	**(117.1)**	0.85	0.84	0.86	0.87	0.13	0.15	0.13	0.12
Metal materials	**(54.0)**			1.01	1.01			−0.01	0.00
Iron ores	(23.8)	0.98	0.98	0.99	1.00	0.01	0.00	0.01	0.01
Nonferrous metal ores	(23.0)	1.01	0.99	1.00	1.00	0.00	0.01	0.00	0.01
Metal scrap	(7.2)			1.00	1.00			−0.01	0.01
Iron & steel	(12.5)	0.48	0.48	0.47	0.51	0.52	0.52	0.52	0.49

	Weight	US Dollar Invoicing Share				Yen Invoicing Share			
		00–03	04–07	08–11	12–15	00–03	04–07	08–11	12–15
Ferro-alloys	(6.0)	0.96	1.00	1.00	1.01	0.05	0.00	0.00	0.00
Hot rolled ordinary steel products	(3.0)	0.00	0.00	0.00	0.00	1.00	1.00	1.00	1.00
Cold finished & coated ordinary steel products	(2.2)	0.00	0.00	0.00	0.01	1.00	1.00	1.00	0.99
Special steel products	(1.3)	0.00	0.00	0.00	0.00	1.00	1.00	1.00	1.00
Nonferrous metals	**(38.9)**		0.95	0.95	0.94		0.07	0.05	0.07
Unwrought precious metals	(10.9)		0.99	0.99	1.01		0.02	0.00	0.00
Unwrought heavy metals	(9.7)		0.99	1.00	1.00		0.02	0.00	0.00
Unwrought light metals	(11.3)	1.00	0.99	0.99	0.99	0.01	0.01	0.00	0.01
Unwrought silicon	(3.5)	0.75	0.79	1.00	1.00	0.24	0.22	0.00	0.00
Electric wires & cables	(3.5)		0.63	0.48	0.40		0.39	0.52	0.67
Metal products	**(11.7)**	0.34	0.47	0.51	0.57	0.68	0.46	0.44	0.40
Wire products	(3.8)		0.40	0.45	0.86		0.61	0.57	0.13
Other metal products	(7.9)		0.49	0.54	0.43		0.39	0.38	0.53
(D) Wood, lumber & related products	**(16.5)**	0.85	0.76	0.73	0.78	0.03	0.10	0.08	0.08
Logs	**(1.9)**	1.00	1.00	1.00	1.00	0.00	0.01	0.00	0.01
Lumber	**(4.6)**		0.55	0.52	0.59		0.23	0.20	0.08
Wood chips	(4.6)	0.86	0.86	0.77	0.91	0.02	0.02	-0.12	0.06
Processed lumber products	**(5.4)**	0.76	0.71	0.70	0.77	0.08	0.08	0.16	0.12
Plywood	(3.8)	0.99	0.92	0.93	0.96	0.01	0.09	0.07	0.06
Other processed lumber products	(1.6)	0.20	0.21	0.14	0.21	0.25	0.35	0.44	0.30

Table 2.7 (continued)

(E) Petroleum, coal & natural gas	Weight	US Dollar Invoicing Share				Yen Invoicing Share			
		00–03	04–07	08–11	12–15	00–03	04–07	08–11	12–15
(E) Petroleum, coal & natural gas	**(305.4)**	0.98	0.99	0.92	0.87	0.04	0.02	0.07	0.12
Petroleum & related products	**(206.8)**			1.01	1.00			−0.01	0.01
Crude petroleum	(164.9)	1.00	0.99	1.00	0.99	0.02	0.02	−0.01	0.00
Petroleum products	(41.9)			1.00	1.00			0.00	0.00
Coal & related products	**(37.7)**		1.01	0.86	0.68		0.00	0.14	0.30
Coal	(37.1)	0.97	1.00	0.85	0.67	0.04	0.00	0.14	0.31
Coal products	(0.6)		1.02	1.00	1.00		−0.01	0.00	0.01
Natural gas	**(60.9)**	0.98	0.95	0.74	0.65	0.02	0.07	0.28	0.35

(F) Chemicals & related products	Weight	US Dollar Invoicing Share				Yen Invoicing Share			
		00–03	04–07	08–11	12–15	00–03	04–07	08–11	12–15
(F) Chemicals & related products	**(83.3)**	0.55	0.55	0.47	0.39	0.38	0.40	0.45	0.48
Industrial inorganic chemicals	**(8.6)**			0.87	0.85			0.13	0.14
Industrial organic chemicals	**(37.0)**			0.48	0.50			0.40	0.38
Basic petrochemicals	(0.4)	0.99	1.00	1.00	1.00	0.00	0.00	0.00	0.01
Aliphatic intermediates	(03)			1.00	0.99			0.00	0.01
Plastic resins & materials	(7.8)			0.69	0.70			0.30	0.28
Other industrial organic chemicals	(28.5)			0.40	0.44			0.44	0.41
Medical material & product preparations	**(29.6)**			0.04	0.06			0.82	0.79

	Weight	US Dollar Invoicing Share				Yen Invoicing Share			
		00–03	04–07	08–11	12–15	00–03	04–07	08–11	12–15
Other chemical products	(8.1)	0.48	0.47	0.45	0.52	0.41	0.41	0.42	0.30
Chemical fertilizers	(1.6)	0.82	0.80	0.79	1.00	0.19	0.21	0.22	0.01
Other chemical products	(6.5)	0.39	0.39	0.37	0.42	0.47	0.46	0.47	0.37
(G) General purpose, production & business oriented machinery	**(53.9)**	0.67	0.56	0.55	0.62	0.17	0.25	0.34	0.36
General purpose machinery	(22.1)		0.60	0.63	0.73		0.33	0.31	0.22
Pumps	(5.9)	0.74	0.75	0.78	0.78	0.00	0.01	-0.01	0.00
Power transmission equipment & bearings	(5.6)	0.34	0.22	0.33	0.58	0.66	0.74	0.67	0.43
Refrigerating machines & appliances	(5.3)		0.68	0.66	0.69		0.33	0.33	0.32
Other general purpose machinery	(5.3)	0.79	0.76	0.73	0.84	0.22	0.25	0.28	0.16
Production machinery	(1.5)		0.00	0.00	0.00		1.00	1.00	1.00
Business oriented machinery	(30.3)		0.66	0.54	0.57		0.18	0.39	0.44
Office machinery	(3.8)	1.00	0.71	0.63	0.72	0.00	0.29	0.36	0.26
Instruments & appliances for measuring, testing	(6.6)	0.76	0.86	0.34	0.30	0.01	0.01	0.66	0.72
Medical appliances	(16.9)	0.61	0.54	0.58	0.59	0.09	0.18	0.32	0.44
Optical instruments & lenses	(3.0)		0.77	0.69	0.80		0.23	0.26	0.10

	Weight	US Dollar Invoicing Share				Yen Invoicing Share			
		00–03	04–07	08–11	12–15	00–03	04–07	08–11	12–15
(H) Electric & electronic products	**(184.3)**	0.60	0.58	0.53	0.58	0.38	0.41	0.46	0.42
Electronic components & devices	**(67.1)**			0.50	0.56			0.50	0.44
Electronic devices	(47.9)		0.63	0.49	0.53		0.36	0.50	0.49

Table 2.7 (continued)

(H) Electric & electronic products	Weight	US Dollar Invoicing Share				Yen Invoicing Share			
		00–03	04–07	08–11	12–15	00–03	04–07	08–11	12–15
(H) Electric & electronic products	**(184.3)**	0.60	0.58	0.53	0.58	0.38	0.41	0.46	0.42
Electronic components	(19.2)			0.62	0.65			0.38	0.34
Electrical machinery & equipment	**(44.7)**			0.49	0.54			0.48	0.44
Heavy electrical apparatus	(1.2)			0.35	0.31			0.31	0.34
Household electric equipment	(13.7)			0.56	0.62			0.43	0.38
Electric bulbs and lighting & wiring devices	(6.9)		0.37	0.46	0.41		0.53	0.52	0.61
Electronic equipment	(6.2)	0.40	0.37	0.35	0.38	0.60	0.63	0.66	0.59
Electrical meters & measuring instruments	(5.1)	0.83	0.66	0.68	0.71	0.15	0.29	0.23	0.22
Other electrical machinery & equipment	(11.6)			0.42	0.57			0.57	0.45
Information & communications equipment	**(72.5)**			0.61	0.63			0.39	0.37
Communications equipment	(30.7)			0.68	0.64			0.32	0.35
Image & audio equipment	(10.1)	0.67	0.66	0.52	0.61	0.33	0.36	0.47	0.39
Electronic computers & computer equipment	(31.7)			0.54	0.64			0.46	0.39

(I) Transportation equipment	Weight	US Dollar Invoicing Share				Yen Invoicing Share			
		00–03	04–07	08–11	12–15	00–03	04–07	08–11	12–15
(I) Transportation equipment	**(34.1)**	0.46	0.46	0.47	0.47	0.43	0.39	0.39	0.37
Motor vehicles	(24.9)			0.29	0.28			0.50	0.50
Passenger cars	(10.5)			0.02	0.02			0.64	0.57
Motorcycles	(1.0)			0.37	0.45			0.48	0.40
Internal combustion engines & parts	(13.4)			0.49	0.46			0.38	0.45
Other transportation equipment	**(9.2)**			0.96	0.96			0.08	0.05

	Weight	US Dollar Invoicing Share				Yen Invoicing Share			
		00–03	04–07	08–11	12–15	00–03	04–07	08–11	12–15
Aircraft parts & aircraft engines	(7.7)	0.14	0.34	0.89	0.95	0.82	0.64	0.09	0.07
Bicycles	(1.5)			0.63	1.00			0.38	0.01
(J) Other primary products & manufactured goods	**(76.1)**	0.63	0.71	0.70	0.75	0.22	0.17	0.21	0.22
Inedible agriculture, livestock & fishery products	**(5.2)**			0.95	0.94			0.04	0.06
Feathers & down	(0.3)	0.99	1.00	1.00	1.00	0.01	0.00	0.00	0.00
Natural rubber	(4.4)			1.00	1.00			−0.01	0.00
Pearls	(0.5)			0.48	0.56			0.51	0.45
Nonmetallic minerals	**(2.9)**	0.66	1.00	1.00	1.00	0.37	0.00	0.00	0.00
Pulp, paper & related products	**(7.7)**		0.46	0.45	0.44		0.55	0.55	0.57
Pulp	(2.3)	0.98	1.01	0.99	1.00	0.02	0.02	0.01	0.00
Paper	(3.6)	0.36	0.33	0.33	0.35	0.65	0.67	0.67	0.68
Paper products	(1.8)		0.00	0.00	0.02		1.00	1.00	0.99
Other manufactured goods	**(60.3)**			0.70	0.76			0.19	0.19
Plastic products	(11.4)	0.57	0.89	0.76	0.80	0.39	0.12	0.25	0.21
Ceramic, stone & clay products	(8.9)		0.52	0.62	0.70		0.39	0.30	0.22
Furniture	(5.5)			0.91	0.92			0.02	0.03
Rubber products	(9.1)		0.90	0.86	0.87		0.11	0.11	0.14
Musical instruments & sporting goods	(9.1)		0.89	0.77	0.77		0.14	0.21	0.22
Other manufactured goods	(16.3)			0.42	0.62			0.27	0.26

Note: Estimated invoice currency share is reported. For example, 1.00 indicates that the share of invoice currency is 100 per cent. Shaded figures in grey denote an insignificant share (coefficient). Weight indicates the share of each industry or commodity in total imports (1000).

Foodstuffs (Table 2.7(A)), Metals (Table 2.7(C)) and Wood (Table 2.7(D)) are invoiced in US dollars. The share of US dollar invoicing is especially high in imports of Petroleum (Table 2.7(E)). In contrast, Chemical (Table 2.7(F)) imports are denominated more in yen than US dollars.

Turning to Japanese machinery imports, more than 60 per cent of General Machinery imports are invoiced in US dollars during the 2012–15 period (Table 2.7(G)). The share of US dollar invoicing is also higher than that of yen invoicing in Electric Machinery (Table 2.7(H)) and Transportation Equipment (Table 2.7(I)) imports. Other primary products and manufactured goods (Table 2.7(J)), which are characterized as low-end and less-differentiated products, are largely invoiced in US dollars.

In the Electric Machinery industry, 42 per cent of Japanese imports are invoiced in yen (Table 2.7(H)) during the 2012–15 period. Japanese imports of these products have been increasing steadily in recent years as Japanese firms have built regional production networks in Asia. Intra-firm imports from Asian subsidiaries to Japanese parent companies may facilitate yen-invoiced trade. However, it must be noted that the share of US dollar invoicing is higher than that of yen invoicing in imports of Electric Machinery products. Taking into account the large share of US dollar invoicing in imports from Asia (Figure 2.2), we may conjecture that US dollars are still widely used in Japanese imports of machinery products from Asia. This conjecture will be checked in subsequent chapters using the firm-level information on invoice currency choices.

2.6   CONCLUSION

Over the last few decades, Japanese firms have undertaken foreign direct investment and built production and sales networks, especially in Asia. Despite the active overseas operations of Japanese firms and growing intra-firm trade, the share of yen-invoiced transactions in both Japanese exports and imports has not increased remarkably. Rather, trade invoiced in US dollars is largely observed in Japanese trade. To begin to understand this unique trade invoicing pattern, we proposed a new method of estimating the share of invoice currency at an industry/commodity level by using the BOJ price data. The share of yen invoicing was found to differ not only across industries and commodities but also over time. In the subsequent chapters, we utilize firm-level information on the choice of invoice currency. In particular, the invoice currency choice in intra-firm trade along production chains will be discussed in detail.

3. Findings from interviews with globally operating Japanese firms*

In the preceding chapter we conducted a literature survey on invoicing currency behaviour and indicated how the stylized facts discussed in the existing literature failed to explain the invoicing currency pattern displayed by Japanese exporters who have expanded their production network across the world. We are keenly aware of a limit in research with aggregated macro data alone. Hence, we have conducted two rounds of interviews with major Japanese global firms, with the first round in 2007–2008 and the second round in 2013. To solve the puzzles surrounding the invoicing currency behaviour of Japanese firms, this chapter and subsequent chapters will empirically examine firm-level invoicing behaviour for Japanese exports using unique data sets obtained through an interview survey of Japanese major exporters. We will then propose new determinants of invoicing decisions and present new evidence for both traditional and newly proposed determinants.

3.1 SAMPLE FIRMS PARTICIPATING IN THE FIRST-ROUND INTERVIEW SURVEY IN 2007–2008

To solve the puzzle of Japan's invoicing currency pattern, we conducted interviews with 23 Japanese representative exporting companies over two consecutive years: 2007 (September–November 2007) and 2008 (July–December 2008).[1] The 23 sample firms were chosen from four types of industry, namely, 'automobile', 'electrical machinery', 'general machinery' and 'electrical component industries'.[2]

---

* This chapter is based on pp. 308–18 and Tables 2–7 of Ito et al. (2012). There are minor changes in wording.

[1] In most cases, we held an interview with a director from the finance department of the sample firms based on questionnaires sent before visiting.

[2] As expected, it is very difficult to make an appointment with Japanese companies for interviews. With the help of METI and RIETI, we were finally able to interview 23 machinery companies. Due to time constraints, we could not interview many candidate companies from the machinery and electrical component industries.

Our strategy of using interview analysis enables us to focus on the two largest industries, the electrical machinery and automobile industries, in terms of value of export amounts and sales abroad. Table 3.1 shows basic information on our sample firms. We finally conducted interviews with nine firms in the automobile industry and seven firms in the electrical machinery industry. In terms of foreign sales, the nine automobile firms account for 79 per cent of all transport equipment firms listed on the Tokyo Stock Exchange (TSE) in fiscal year 2007. The share of our seven electrical machinery firms also amounts to 55 per cent of all electric appliance firms listed on TSE. Thus, although the share is very small in terms of the number of firms, the results of our interviews with sample firms provide a comprehensive picture of invoicing currency practices of major Japanese exporting firms.

In addition, we conducted further interviews with four electrical component firms and three machinery firms. Some of these firms are said to be strong competitors in exports as they have a large global market share or export highly differentiated products, which allows our analysis to take into account the invoicing currency practices of these companies. Other firms, especially electrical component firms, operate actively in Asia by building a production network and facilitating intra-firm trade. These aspects will give us new insights into the puzzle of Japanese exporters' invoicing practices.

3.2 KEY QUESTIONS

Our interviews were conducted based on questions that cover the following four topics.

1. Production and sales structure: To generate a profile of each company, we asked questions on the following four aspects: (a) production structure (whether they have overseas production subsidiaries); (b) sales structure (whether they have overseas sales subsidiaries and regional headquarters; whether they trade through *Sogo Shosha* (Japanese trading companies); whether there is any difference between physical distribution and commercial distribution of goods); (c) characteristics of goods traded (such as competitiveness and market share); and (d) basic policy on exchange rate risk management.
2. Invoice currency: Our main interest is in collecting data of invoicing currencies by destination at the firm level. Our questions aim to learn which currency firms use (a) in exports from Japan to each destination country; (b) in exports from Japan to overseas sales and/or production subsidiaries; and (c) in exports from overseas production subsidiaries

Table 3.1 Basic information on sample firms: foreign sales in FY2007

TSE industry classification	Transportation Equipments	Electric Appliance	Machinery	Total 3 industries
Number of listed firms with foreign sales (> = 10%) in FY2007	83	221	168	472
Foreign sales in FY2007 (Sum total, billion yen)	61 958	48 366	11 455	121 781
Foreign sales / Consolidated sales (sample average, %)	46%	44%	43%	–

Sample firms by industry	Automobile	Electrical Machinery	Electrical Components	General Machinery	Total sample firms
Number of sample firms [Per cent to all listed firms]	9 [11%]	7 [3%]	4 [2%]	3 [2%]	23 [5%]
Foreign sales in FY2007 (Sum total, billion yen) [Per cent to all listed firms]	48 756 [79%]	26 379 [55%]	1992 [4%]	2115 [18%]	79 243 [65%]
Foreign sales / Consolidated sales (sample average, %)	67%	52%	68%	70%	–

Notes:
1. In the industry classification of the Tokyo Stock Exchange (TSE), 'Transportation Equipment (Yuso-yo kiki)' includes companies related to automobiles, motorcycles and shipbuilding, while 'Electric Appliances (Denki Kiki)' mainly includes electrical machinery and electrical components.
2. In the Japanese accounting standard, all listed firms have to report the amount of foreign sales in their financial statement as long as their ratio of 'foreign sales-to-consolidated sales' is 10% or more.

Source: Financial statements of all listed companies with 'Foreign Sales (Kaigai Uriage-daka)' in FY2007.

to final destination markets. Furthermore, we asked whether the invoicing choice is affected by (a) inter- or intra-firm trade; and (b) characteristics of products traded, such as degree of product differentiation.
3. Exchange rate risk management: We asked questions about what kind of hedging strategies firms use (forward, future and options through market, 'marry and netting', and so on).
4. Revision of price setting: We sought to determine whether interviewed firms periodically changed the export price itself irrespective of invoicing currency choice. We also asked whether they have any explicit policy regarding price revisions in the face of sharp and large exchange rate fluctuations.

3.3 NEW EVIDENCE ON INVOICE CURRENCY CHOICE

Through the interviews, we obtained detailed data on invoicing currency from most sample firms. For anonymity, however, the actual share of invoicing currency for each sample firm will not be presented in this study. Instead, we present the evidence on sample firms' invoicing choice in the following two ways.

3.3.1 Invoicing Currency Share by Industry

We first aggregate the firm-level data into per-industry shares of invoicing currency in exports to (1) the world and (2) Asia. Sample mean (and median in parentheses) of the invoicing share for each industry are reported in Table 3.2. Not all sample firms provided the share of invoicing currency for exports to the world and Asia; 14 out of 23 firms answered the invoicing share in exports to the world and 18 out of 23 firms answered for exports to Asia. For the remaining sample firms, we reasonably assess the share of invoicing currency for each firm. Suppose some firms did not reveal invoicing share for exports to the world but did provide information on invoicing share in exports to North America (United States), the euro area and Asia. In this case, we obtained regional breakdown data on their foreign sales from annual securities reports of the sample firms concerned, which enabled us to compute the firm's invoicing share for exports to the world by employing the reasonable assumption that a firm's exports are destined for the above three regions.[3] As a result, data for 21 firms are used

---

[3]   A lack of information prevented us from reasonably assessing the invoicing share for two electrical machinery firms, whose data were treated as a missing value.

Table 3.2 *Industry breakdown of invoicing currency share: interview results (%)*

Sample firms	Share of currency for exports from Japan to the world[2]			Share of currency for exports from Japan to Asia[2]		Share of foreign sales in total sales	Share of foreign sales by region[3]		
	USD	EUR	JPY	USD	JPY		North America	Europe	Asia
All sample firms[1]	51.6 (50.6)	14.0 (15.0)	29.9 (25.0)	55.6 (57.5)	41.8 (32.2)	61.8 (68.1)	27.6 (28.3)	25.5 (25.9)	39.1 (37.5)
Automobile	40.0	15.3	36.9	32.6	65.6	64.8	31.1	23.3	31.1
Electrical machinery	70.9	15.3	12.6	93.0	6.4	52.6	32.5	34.9	32.5
General machinery	28.3	10.0	61.7	20.0	80.0	69.8	22.0	22.7	48.2
Electrical components	71.1	12.5	12.2	88.8	9.4	67.8	19.1	20.8	57.0

Notes:
1. Sample average and sample median (in parentheses) are reported.
2. 'Share of currency for exports from Japan to the world' reports the sample average share of 21 firms excluding two electrical machinery firms that provided data on invoicing-currency breakdowns. 'Share of currency for exports from Japan to Asia' presents the sample average share of 22 firms excluding one electrical machinery firm.
3. 'Share of foreign sales by region' is calculated as the share of foreign sales in each region out of total foreign sales. The data are collected from the consolidated financial statement report for the latest accounting term corresponding to the interview research period (fiscal year end of 2006 or 2007).

Source: Interviews with and financial statements of 23 major Japanese exporters.

to calculate the simple average share of invoicing currency for exports to the world and the data from 22 firms are used to estimate exports to Asia.

The following notable pattern of invoicing currency is observed in Table 3.2. First, when looking at the simple average share (all sample firms) of invoicing currencies for exports to the world, US dollars account for 51.6 per cent, the euro for 14.0 per cent and the yen for 29.9 per cent. The share of US dollar invoicing in Table 3.2 is almost the same as the share presented in Figure 2.1 in the preceding chapter, while the yen's invoicing share is lower in Table 3.2 than in Figure 2.1. This is true even for the simple average share of exports to Asia. This observation suggests that our sample firms have a tendency to use foreign currencies more (and the yen less) than indicated in Figure 2.1.

Second, turning to industry-level data, a marked difference in invoicing patterns can be found across industries. In the electrical machinery and electrical component industries, more than 70 per cent of exports to the world are invoiced in US dollars, while only about 12 per cent are in yen. In contrast, the share of machinery firms' yen invoicing for exports to the world is 61.7 per cent, which may reflect these firms' relative strength in export competitiveness.

Third, turning to exports to Asia, the difference in invoicing currency choice across industries becomes far more evident. The share of US dollar invoicing is 93 per cent in the electrical machinery industry and 88.8 per cent in the electrical components industry, whereas the share of yen invoicing is 80 per cent in the machinery industry. More interestingly, the share of yen invoicing in exports to Asia becomes much higher (65.6 per cent) in the automobile industry. To understand these seeming inconsistencies in Japan's invoicing currency pattern, namely, the high share of dollar-denominated exports to Asia, such a sharp difference across industries gives us a key to solve the puzzles posed in Chapter 2. It is important to understand how industry characteristics are related to the invoicing currency choice.

Fourth, Table 3.2 does not show any clear relation between invoicing share and share of foreign sales by region. Columns 6 to 9 in Table 3.2 report the average share and regional breakdown of these shares of foreign sales.[4] Interestingly, the share of sales in Asia differs markedly across industries. The general machinery and electrical component industries show a very high share of sales in Asia: 48.2 per cent in the machinery

---

[4] 'Foreign sales by region' as reported in the consolidated financial statement of the annual securities report are not identical to the export from Japan to each region because the former includes data on sales of overseas subsidiaries in the local market and/or abroad. Nevertheless, 'foreign sales by region' can be regarded as a proxy variable for share of exports from Japan to each region. For further details, see Ito et al. (2012).

industry and 57 per cent in the electrical component industry, respectively. However, these two industries show a very different invoicing choice pattern, as discussed above.

3.3.2 Main Invoice Currency by Region

We have so far investigated major Japanese firms' invoicing currency choices by industry. To expand our analysis to destination-specific invoicing choice while assuring the sample firms' anonymity, this subsection employs the 'main invoice currency' approach. The main invoice currency is defined as the currency most frequently used in exports to the destination country. Our analysis of the interviews revealed that firms tend to use a single currency for exports to each destination. However, several firms use two or more invoice currencies in exports to a single destination country, in which case the main invoice currency does not mean that this currency is used in 100 per cent of exports.[5]

Table 3.3 shows firms' invoicing currency choice for exports from Japan to advanced countries, including Mexico and Russia. In this table, we count the number of firms that use one of four currencies as their main invoice currency for each destination. For instance, looking at the far left of the first row, the entry [20/22] indicates that 20 out of 22 sample firms use the US dollar as the main invoice currency in exports to the US. Industry breakdown data are also reported from row 2 to row 5. No entry in a cell means that the firm does not export to the region/country in question or that no clear data could be obtained regarding the main invoice currency.

Table 3.3 shows the choice of main invoice currency by destination and industry in 2007–2008. First, invoicing in the importer's currency is prevalent in Japanese exports to advanced countries. In exports to the US, 20 out of 22 firms use the US dollar as their main invoice currency. In exports to the euro area, 14 out of 21 firms choose the euro as the main invoice currency, while the yen is the main invoice currency for 5 firms. The importer's currency is evidently chosen even in exports to the UK, Australia and Canada.

Second, in contrast to the case of advanced countries, the importer's currency is rarely used in Mexico and Russia. Instead, the US dollar is the main invoice currency in both countries. Third, even in exports to the US and euro area, several Japanese firms in the general machinery and

---

[5] For example, we regard the US dollar as a firm's main invoice currency in exports to Asia if 50 per cent of its exports to Asia are invoiced in US dollars, 30 per cent in the local currency and 20 per cent in yen. Friberg and Wilander (2008) also employed this main invoice currency approach for their questionnaire survey analysis and empirical examinations.

Table 3.3 *Invoicing currency in exports from Japan to North America, Europe and Australia*

Main invoice currency for exports		Destination country or region						
		US	Canada	Mexico	Euro area	UK	Russia	Australia
USD	Automobile	[20/22] 8	[2/10] 1	[4/5] 2	[2/21]	[1/8]	[2/3] 2	[7/7]
	Electrical machinery	7	1		2	1		4
	Machinery	2		1				3
	Electrical components	3		1				
Euro	Automobile				[14/21] 6	[1/8]		
	Electrical machinery				5			
	Machinery				1	1		
	Electrical components	–			2			
Importer's currency	Automobile	–	[8/10] 4	[1/5] 1	–	[6/8] 4	[1/3]	
	Electrical machinery	–	3		–	2		
	Machinery	–	1		–		1	
	Electrical components	–			–			
JPY	Automobile	[2/22]			[5/21] 1			
	Electrical machinery							
	Machinery	1			2			
	Electrical components	1			2			

Note: This table counts the number of firms that use one of four currencies as a main invoice currency for each destination. For instance, looking at the far left of the first row in this table, [20/22] indicates that 20 out of 22 sample firms use the US dollar as the main invoice currency in exports to the US.

Source: Interviews with 23 major Japanese exporting firms.

electrical component industries use the yen as the main invoice currency. These firms answered that such use of the yen is mainly attributed to the high export competitiveness of their products in the global market. This is consistent with stylized fact 3. Fourth, electrical machinery firms do not use the yen at all as a main invoice currency. Interestingly, US dollar invoicing is chosen even for Japanese exports to some advanced countries other than the US.

The above observation indicates the strong tendency of major Japanese exporting firms to use the importer's currency as the main invoice currency when exporting to advanced countries, which is consistent with the PTM behaviour discussed earlier. From the standpoint of foreign exchange risk management, invoicing in the importer's currency means that the foreign exchange risks are taken and managed by the Japanese exporting firms' headquarters.

Let us next turn to the choice of main invoice currency for Japanese exports to Asia, as shown in Table 3.4. First, the most distinctive feature is that for exports to Asia as a whole, the importer's currency is not used as the main invoice currency. Importer's invoicing currency is observed only for exports to a particular destination country. Interestingly, the Chinese yuan is not used at all as a main invoice currency in exports to China, even though this country is the region's largest market. This is not surprising because Japan is an advanced country and most Asian countries are still developing countries. Second, sample firms predominantly use either the US dollar or the yen as the main invoice currency: 13 out of 22 firms choose the US dollar while 9 firms use the yen. The extensive use of the US dollar is somewhat surprising since it is a third-country currency. This aspect needs further analysis. Third, invoice currency choices vary across industries. Firms in both the electrical machinery and electrical component industries tend to use the US dollar, while the automobile firms tend to choose the yen. More interestingly, the yen tends to be used more in automobile and, especially, machinery exports to Asia, which contrasts markedly with the choices made by electrical machinery and electrical component firms.

3.4 EMPIRICS OF INVOICING DECISION

3.4.1 Determinants of Invoicing Currency Choice among Japanese Exporting Firms

Through a face-to-face discussion with each firm, we obtained the following possible determinants of invoicing currency.

Table 3.4 Invoicing currency in exports from Japan to Asia

Main invoice currency for exports	Destination country or region									
	Asia[1]	China	Thai	Indonesia	Singapore	Malaysia	Korea	Hong Kong	Taiwan	India
USD	[13/22]	[6/11]	[1/6]	[2/5]	[6/7]	[1/4]	[2/4]		[2/2]	[2/2]
Automobile	3		1	1						
Electrical machinery	7	3			2	1	1			
Machinery				1	1		1		1	1
Electrical components	3	3			3				1	
Importer's currency	[2/6]		[2/6]	[1/5]	[1/7]	[2/4]	[1/4]	[1/2]		
Automobile			1	1						
Electrical machinery	1		1		1	1	1	1		
Machinery	1									
Electrical components						1				
JPY	[9/22]	[5/11]	[3/6]	[2/5]		[1/4]	[1/4]	[1/2]		[2/2]
Automobile	5	3	2	2		1		1		1
Electrical machinery	3	2								
Machinery			1				1			1
Electrical components	1									

Note: 1. 'Asia' includes China, three Asian NIEs (Korea, Taiwan and Hong Kong) and ASEAN countries. It also includes India if the sample firms export their goods from Japan to India.

Source: Interviews with 23 major Japanese exporting firms.

1. To whom to sell: intra-firm, outside firm or trading companies (*Sogo Shosha*)

Almost all sample firms clearly state that the majority of their exports to advanced countries are destined for their own local subsidiaries (that is, intra-firm trade). To free their local subsidiaries from any exchange rate risks, these firms' Japanese headquarters have a strong tendency to invoice in the importer's currency and thus manage all exchange rate risks at the finance department of its head office. In contrast, a substantial portion of exports to Asia and other developing countries are directed toward independent firms or joint ventures with a low share of ownership, in which case Japanese headquarters have less incentive to bear the exchange rate risk. In these cases, there is a tendency to invoice not in the importer's currency but in yen for exports to Asia and other developing countries. The ownership relationship with importers is different between advanced countries and developing countries, which tends to affect the choice of an invoice currency. We propose the following hypothesis, which has not yet been formally stated or tested in the literature:

Hypothesis 1: The higher (lower) the ownership ratio or equity participation of the Japanese exporter to a foreign importer, the more (less) likely Japanese firms are to choose to use the importer's currency as an invoicing currency.

In addition, Japanese general trading companies, *Sogo Shosha*, play an important role in the exporter's invoicing currency choice. In exports to developing economies, Japanese firms do not necessarily build their own distribution network. An alternative is for exporters to use *Sogo Shosha*, who have developed their own global distribution channels/network, especially in developing countries. In the interviews conducted for this study, Japanese firms answered that their exports through *Sogo Shosha* were invoiced in yen. Presumably, *Sogo Shosha* can manage currency risk very well by in-house marry, netting and other ways. Thus, the share of yen invoicing will grow if Japanese firms export more through *Sogo Shosha*. This relation has not been tested in the literature.[6]

Hypothesis 2: Japanese firms tend to invoice their export products in yen when they export through Sogo Shosha.

---

[6] When the yen's internationalization was debated in the 1980s and the early 1990s, most studies pointed out that trade through *Sogo Shosha* had prevented yen-invoiced trade, since *Sogo Shosha* tend to use the US dollar in external trade, especially in importing crude oil and other natural resources (see, for instance, Kawai, 1996 and Fukuda and Ji, 1994). Our interview analysis, however, reveals counter-evidence that exports through *Sogo Shosha* tend to be invoiced in yen.

2. Cost of exchange rate hedging

Many sample firms point out that hedging costs are one of the most important factors in choosing an invoice currency. The hedging costs of Asian currencies (except the yen) and other developing countries tend to be higher than in advanced countries mainly due to various regulations and restrictions. Japanese exporting firms will not choose those importer currencies in their invoicing to the extent that the hedging cost is high.[7] Thus, the following hypothesis is typically tested in the empirical analysis of invoicing choice behaviour:

Hypothesis 3: The higher (lower) the hedging cost between the yen and the importer's currency, the lower (higher) is the use of the importer's currency as invoice currency.

Although spot markets with underlying international transactions and investments are fully permitted in most Asian countries, onshore and offshore markets are mostly divided, which leaves Asian forward markets still undeveloped. High transaction costs or inconvenient risk hedge instruments have discouraged Japanese exporting firms from using Asian local currencies as invoice or settlement currencies.

3. Degree of market competition and differentiation of export products

As discussed earlier, invoicing in the importer's currency prevails in exports to advanced countries, reflecting the PTM behaviour of Japanese firms. Specifically, many Japanese firms, especially those in the automobile and electrical machinery industries, indicated that it was too difficult to impose exchange rate risk on importers in advanced countries due to the high degree of competition in these markets. In contrast, a firm that exports differentiated products and has the largest market share in developing countries expressed that its local subsidiaries could manage the exchange rate risk, presumably by passing through the exchange rate fluctuations to retail prices, even when the headquarter chose yen-denominated invoicing in exports to the local subsidiaries. Thus, the degree of product differentiation and market competition is an important factor in determining invoice currency.

The result of our interview analysis is consistent with both stylized fact

---

[7]   Another possible determinant is the currency's transaction costs. The US dollar is generally considered as having the lowest transaction costs. It is widely recognized that the dominant use of the US dollar as a vehicle currency in foreign exchange markets facilitates use of the US dollar as an invoice currency, even in trade between countries other than the United States. See Krugman (1980, 1984) for such a discussion.

3 explained in Chapter 2 and the recent theoretical development of invoice currency choice behaviour. Previous studies, such as those by Giovannini (1988) and Donnenfeld and Zilcha (1991), model a firm's choice of invoice currency by solving the profit maximization with uncertainty of exchange rate movements. They showed that the choice of an invoice currency depends on the shape of the firm's profit function, which is, in turn, conditional on the curvature of the demand function in the destination markets. The more (less) differentiated the firm's export product is, the lower (higher) is the elasticity of demand for the product, which leads to invoicing in the exporter's (importer's) currency.[8] Thus, it is theoretically shown that a firm's invoicing choice depends on the characteristics of the goods traded, which is consistent with the classical stylized fact 3.[9] Some machinery firms and electrical component firms in our sample, which export/sell competitive and highly differentiated products in the global market, clearly have a strong position to negotiate their invoicing currency with customers.

Hypothesis 4: Exporters tend to invoice in yen if their products are highly differentiated and/or competitive.

4. Exports from an Asian production base to the US market

Most electrical machinery and electrical components firms that choose US dollar invoicing for their exports to Asian countries have a particular trade structure in that their production subsidiaries exhibit a strong tendency to export their products to the US market or to US firms. Under this production/distribution structure, these firms typically choose US dollar invoicing not only from the local subsidiaries in Asia to the US market but also from Japanese headquarters to local subsidiaries in Asia because it is advantageous to use the same currency in both transactions.[10] This is key

---

[8] See Fukuda and Ji (1994) and Sato (1999, 2003) for the empirical estimation of invoicing practices in Japanese exporters based on the firm's maximization behaviour of expected profits.

[9] Johnson and Pick (1997) and Friberg (1998) extend the theoretical model of invoicing choice by analysing in which conditions third-currency invoicing is chosen. They show that not only the shape of the firm's profit function but also exchange rate volatility (variance) against the importer's currency determines the choice of invoice currency. While the above theoretical models are analysed under a partial equilibrium framework, recent studies apply the general equilibrium model to the choice of an invoice currency, motivated by development of the New Open Economy Macroeconomics. For instance, Bacchetta and van Wincoop (2005) analyse the choice of invoice currency under a two-country general equilibrium model and show that the producer's currency pricing (PCP) is chosen if the exporting firm's market share is larger in the destination market and if the economic size of the exporting firm's country is larger.

[10] Moreover, to manage the exchange rate risk as efficiently as possible, some major electrical-machinery and electrical-component firms adopt an efficient settlement strategy, the so-called 're-invoicing'. Specifically, suppose a Japanese firm exports parts and

to solving the second puzzle of Japan's currency invoicing pattern, namely, why a third currency, the US dollar, is used in Japanese exports to Asia.

While exports to the US previously accounted for the largest share of total exports from Japan and Asian countries, it is now well-recognized that intra-regional trade in Asia has grown in importance for these countries in recent years. Most sample firms, however, answered that the final destination market was the US, as growing intra-regional trade was largely driven by processing trade. Although this Asian trade structure has often been identified in the literature, to our best knowledge it has never been empirically tested in the literature on invoicing currency choice specifically. In the next sub-section we construct a new variable and attempt an empirical examination to take this aspect into account.

Hypothesis 5: Japanese firms tend to choose US dollar invoicing when exporting their products to production subsidiaries in Asia when the production subsidiaries export a high proportion of their products to the US market.

3.4.2   Details of Explanatory Variables

The most commonly used variables for explaining firms' invoicing currency are the shares of exports by destination. Exporters tend to choose the currency of export destination. When retail prices in the destination market are chosen to maintain the market share in competition with local producers, the pass-through tends to be low. This is known to be PTM behaviour. This can be achieved by exporters choosing the currency of the destination country. (See, for instance, Friberg and Wilander, 2008; Goldberg and Tille, 2008.) Because we use firm-level data and information, however, the above export share for each firm is difficult to obtain. Alternatively, we use the 'share of foreign sales in the region (North America, Europe or Asia) in the total foreign sales'. Since most exports from our sample firms are destined for overseas subsidiaries, the variable 'share of foreign sales in the region' can be considered a good proxy for the share of exports to a particular country/region.

In addition, we establish the following explanatory variables to empiri-

---

components to its own production subsidiary in Asia, who assembles them into finished goods. Then, the finished goods are exported directly from the subsidiary to the US. The Japanese headquarters conducts accounting transactions by first purchasing the goods from the local subsidiary and then selling the goods to the US importers (possibly its own sales subsidiary in the US). As long as all stages of accounting transactions are invoiced in US dollars, the Japanese firm can concentrate all exchange rate exposures against a single currency, the US dollar, at the headquarters. This re-invoicing strategy will impede the further use of the yen in Japan's trade with Asia.

cally investigate the determinants of invoicing currency by Japanese exporting firms.[11]

The first and second explanatory variables are associated with the determinant (1) 'intra- or inter-firm trade' (Hypothesis 1) and 'exports through *Sogo Shosha*' (Hypothesis 2). We set a 'dummy for the equity share of overseas subsidiary (> 90 per cent)' that takes 1 if firm *i* has overseas subsidiaries with more than 90 per cent shares of equity in *k* region, and 0 otherwise. Furthermore, we use a 'dummy for trade through *Sogo Shosha*' because this type of trade is regarded as a factor of promoting yen-invoiced trade.

The third explanatory variable is related to determinant (2) 'cost of exchange rate hedging' (Hypothesis 3). We use a bid–ask spread of outright forward transactions between the yen and the importing country's currency as a straightforward proxy for the cost of exchange rate hedging.

The fourth explanatory variable is based on the determinant (3) 'the degree of market competition and differentiation of exporting products' (Hypothesis 4). Three general machinery firms and one electrical-component firm answered that they tend to invoice their exports in yen because their products have strong export competitiveness. These four firms cited high market shares of their products as evidence of their products' strong export competitiveness.[12] We use a 'dummy for export competitiveness' that takes 1 for these four firms and 0 otherwise.

The fifth explanatory variable is associated with the determinant (4) 'exports from Asian production subsidiaries to the US market' (Hypothesis 5). We set a 'dummy for firm's plants in Asia to export' that takes 1 if the ratio of intra-firm sales from Asia (that is, exports to subsidiaries outside Asia) to foreign sales in Asia (that is, sales to Asian customers) is 50 per cent or over, and 0 otherwise.

3.4.3 Probit Estimation of Determinants of Invoicing Currency

We empirically test the hypothesis of determinants of invoice currency by using the above-mentioned explanatory variables. We have already discussed that a large share of Japanese exporters are invoiced in the currency of the destination country in the case of exports to the advanced countries, which is the first puzzle of Japan's currency invoicing pattern as discussed in Chapter 2. A first examination is which currency is used for invoicing Japanese exports to advanced countries: the exporter's currency

---

[11] See Ito et al. (2012) for details of these explanatory variables.
[12] In the interviews, based on the data on the global market share, it was confirmed that the export products of these firms accounted for a very large share of the world market.

(the yen) or the importer's currency. We conduct a probit estimation where the dependent variable is a binary variable that takes 1 if the importer's currency is used as the main invoice currency and 0 otherwise.

First, the estimation results for Japanese exports to the US and euro area are presented in columns (1)–(5) in Table 3.5. As a key determinant of invoicing currency, we use (1) the forward spread of the importer's currency against the yen; (2) the share of foreign sales in the region; (3) the head office's ownership (equity) share of local subsidiaries; and (4) a dummy for export competitiveness. In columns (1)–(5), the forward spreads are negative and statistically significant at least at the 5 per cent level, indicating that the larger the hedging cost, the less often is the importer's currency used for trade invoicing. In columns (1)–(5), the effect of foreign sales in the region is also included to investigate whether invoicing currency choice is affected by the extent of export dependence on the destination market. These are all positive but statistically insignificant in columns (3) and (5). Furthermore, to allow for the effect of intra-firm trade, the head office's equity share of local subsidiaries or its dummy (> 90 per cent) are included in columns (2)–(5). These are all significantly positive at least at the 5 per cent level, strongly supporting our hypothesis in that intra-firm trade facilitates invoicing in the importer's currency. Furthermore, the dummy for export competitiveness is included in columns (3) and (5), indicating that the degree of export competitiveness negatively affects the extent of invoicing in the importer's currency.

Second, columns (6)–(8) show the results of probit estimation when including the advanced countries in North America and Europe (that is, US, Canada, euro area and the UK) as a destination market. The estimated result is similar to the case of the US and euro area (columns (1)–(5)) except for the estimates of the share of foreign sales that are all positive but insignificant.

Overall, the results of the probit estimation reveal that the importer's currency is used as an invoice currency if (1) the hedging cost of the importer's currency is lower; (2) the headquarters has a high ownership (equity) share of the local subsidiaries; and/or (3) export products are less differentiated or not competitive in the destination market. The second reason is particularly important when explicating the first puzzle of Japan's invoicing currency pattern. Since most Japanese exports to advanced countries are intra-firm transactions, the headquarters of Japanese exporting firms have a strong incentive to free their overseas subsidiaries from the exchange rate risk by invoicing in the local (importer's) currency. Such invoicing in importer's currency is much more likely if the destination market is highly competitive or if the sample firm's export products are less competitive or differentiated.

We next conduct a similar estimation focusing on Asian economies

Table 3.5 Determinants of local currency invoicing

Sample	1. US and Euro Area					2. Developed countries/region in North America and Europe (US, Canada, Euro Area, and UK)		
	(1)	(2)	(3)	(4)	(5)	(6)	(7)	(8)
Cost of currency hedging	-6.045** (2.844)	-7.078** (3.117)	-6.506** (3.779)	-6.074** (2.838)	-4.778** (3.675)	-4.514* (2.628)	-4.922* (2.584)	-5.754** (2.546)
Share of foreign sales in the region	1.012* (0.534)	1.384** (0.544)	0.751 (0.478)	1.013** (0.459)	0.472 (0.375)	0.521 (0.478)	0.598 (0.469)	0.198 (0.470)
Equity participation to overseas subsidiary		1.537** (0.744)	1.218** (0.806)					
Dummy for equity share of overseas subsidiary (> 90%)				0.579*** (0.216)	0.627** (0.257)		0.308* (0.178)	0.296* (0.191)
Dummy for export competitiveness			-0.526** (0.242)		-0.434** (0.260)			-0.492*** (0.179)
# of observations	43	43	43	43	43	61	61	61

Notes:
1. Method: Probit estimation. The dependent variable is a binary variable that takes 1 if the importer's currency is the main invoice currency and 0 otherwise.
2. Each regression equation includes a constant term. The results of marginal effects are reported. Standard errors are in parentheses.
3. ***, ** and * mean that the coefficient is statistically significant at the 1%, 5% and 10% level, respectively.

Source: Authors' calculation.

where Japanese firms have built a regional production network. In this estimation, the destinations include the following eight economies: Mainland China, Korea, Hong Kong, Singapore, Malaysia, Indonesia, Thailand and the Philippines. Our main interest is in solving the second puzzle of Japan's invoicing currency pattern, that is, why US dollar invoicing is more extensive than yen invoicing in Japan's exports to Asia. In conducting probit estimation, the dependent variable for columns (1)–(5) in Table 3.6 is a binary variable that takes 1 if US dollars are used as the main invoice currency and 0 otherwise. In addition, columns (6)–(10) in Table 3.6 present the case where the dependent variable is a binary variable that takes 1 if the yen is used as the main invoice currency.

Let us first analyse the estimation results reported in columns (1)–(5) of Table 3.6 for the determinants of US dollar invoicing. First, in contrast to the results of the previous estimation for advanced countries (Table 3.5), forward spreads do not have a significant effect on invoice currency choice. The dummy for head office's ownership (equity) share of local subsidiaries affects positively US dollar invoicing choice at the 1 per cent significance level in columns (1)–(5), which implies that Japanese firms with local subsidiaries in Asia in which they own more than a 90 per cent equity share tend to choose US dollar invoicing.

Second, the dummy for 'trade through *Sogo Shosha*' consistently indicates a negative impact on US dollar invoicing, though the coefficient is significantly negative at the 5 per cent level only in columns (3) and (5).

Third, whereas the share of foreign sales in Asia does not have any significant effect on the invoicing choice (columns (1), (2) and (4)), the share of foreign sales in North America positively affects US dollar invoicing at the 5 per cent significance level in columns (1)–(5). This result is somewhat puzzling because it shows that the greater the firm's sales in North America (mainly the US), the more the US dollar will be used in the firm's exports from Japan to Asia. The clue for understanding this puzzling relation is to understand the definition used in data on 'foreign sales in the region'.[13]

---

[13]   Assuming that North America is identical to the US for simplicity, let us consider the definition of 'firm *i*'s foreign sales in the United States'. This foreign sales variable covers (1) exports of the firm *i* from Japan to the US (i.e. customers in the US except for firm *i*'s subsidiaries); (2) exports of the firm *i*'s overseas (but non-US) subsidiaries to the US; and (3) local sales of firm *i*'s subsidiaries in the US. Since, as discussed earlier, major Japanese firms tend to export their products to local subsidiaries, export channel (1) does not account for a large share of total foreign sales in the US. Based on consolidated accounting, firm *i*'s exports from Japan to local subsidiaries in the US are not directly counted in 'firm *i*'s foreign sales in the US' but are indirectly allowed for by channel (3). As reported in, for instance, METI's *White Paper 2009*, Asian countries export a large amount of finished products to the US after processing and assembling intermediate goods through intra-Asian trade, including trade between Japan and Asian subsidiaries, which is covered by channel (2).

Table 3.6 Determinants of invoicing currency in Japan's exports to Asian economies

Dependent Variables	A binary variable that takes 1 if USD is the main invoice currency					A binary variable that takes 1 if JPY is the main invoice currency				
	(1)	(2)	(3)	(4)	(5)	(6)	(7)	(8)	(9)	(10)
Cost of currency hedging	0.988 (0.827)	1.165 (0.939)	1.067 (0.937)			0.408 (0.641)	0.163 (0.425)	0.275 (0.471)		
Dummy for equity share of overseas subsidiary (>90%)	0.689*** (0.155)	0.740*** (0.155)	0.727*** (0.159)	0.610*** (0.169)	0.636*** (0.167)	−0.274* (0.148)	−0.399** (0.178)	−0.347** (0.157)	−0.355** (0.142)	−0.352*** (0.162)
Dummy for trade through the *Sogo Shosha*	−0.350 (0.232)	−0.291 (0.238)	−0.521** (0.130)	−0.265 (0.299)	−0.543** (0.134)	0.506*** (0.159)	0.748*** (0.185)	0.627*** (0.166)	0.602*** (0.161)	0.608*** (0.162)
Foreign sales in Asia	1.117 (1.179)	1.626 (1.169)		1.643 (1.245)		0.058 (0.416)			−0.621 (0.485)	
Foreign sales in North America	3.940* (2.044)	4.273** (2.015)	1.958** (0.991)	4.628** (2.104)	2.293** (0.978)		−1.861* (0.920)	−1.757 (0.831)		−1.749 (0.825)
Dummy for Asian plant to export				0.508** (0.218)	0.427* (0.208)		0.368 (0.312)			
Dummy for export competitiveness		−0.343* (0.170)	−0.286 (0.174)				0.823** (0.185)	0.584** (0.185)	0.744*** (0.159)	0.569** (0.180)
# of observations	48	48	48	48	48	48	48	48	48	48

Notes:
1. Method: Probit estimation. The dependent variable is a binary variable that takes 1 if the US dollar (columns (1)–(5)) or the yen (columns (6)–(10)) is the main invoice currency and 0 otherwise.
2. Each regression equation includes a constant term. The results of marginal effects are reported. Standard errors are in parenthesis.
3. ***, ** and * mean that the coefficient is statistically significant at the 1%, 5%, and 10% levels, respectively.

Source: Authors' calculation.

This foreign sales variable covers exports by Japanese firms' subsidiaries in Asia to the US and other external countries. Given a triangular trade pattern where Japanese production subsidiaries in Asia import intermediate goods from the Japanese head office and export finished products to the US, US dollar invoicing will be chosen at each stage of trade transactions. The positive and significant coefficient on foreign sales in North America may show the invoicing choice in the above triangular trade.

To confirm the effect of the above triangular trade on US dollar invoicing, the 'dummy for plants in Asia to export' (Asian plant dummy) is also included in columns (4) and (5) as an explanatory variable that represents exports from Japanese production subsidiaries in Asia to the US market. The coefficient on this Asian plant dummy is positive and statistically significant at the 5 per cent level in column (4) and at the 10 per cent level in column (5). In columns (2) and (3), where the dummy for export competitiveness is included, coefficients on the export competitiveness dummy have negative signs though their significant levels are marginal around the 10 per cent level. These results support our hypothesized relation that exports from an Asian production base to the US market facilitate US dollar invoicing for Japanese exports to Asian countries.

Next, the determinants of yen invoicing are analysed using the same data set. The results reported in columns (6)–(10) are consistent with those presented in columns (1)–(5). The forward spread does not have a significant effect on the extent of yen invoicing. The dummy for the head office's ownership (equity) share of local subsidiaries has negative and significant influences on the invoicing currency choice. The dummy for *Sogo Shosha* exhibits positive and statistically significant coefficients in all cases. Although the role of *Sogo Shosha* has been supposedly declining in Japanese exports, our interview analysis has shown that exports through *Sogo Shosha* still play an important role when the destination is Asia and other developing countries. The results of our estimation suggest that the share of yen invoicing will increase when exporting through *Sogo Shosha*. While the coefficient on the Asian plant dummy is not statistically significant, the dummy for export competitiveness shows all positive and significant coefficients, which suggests that Japan's exports of differentiated products to Asia have the strongest case for yen-invoiced transactions.

In summary, the second puzzle of Japan's invoicing pattern can be explained by increasing intra-firm exports from Japan to Asian subsidiaries based on regional production networks combined with the fact that Japanese production subsidiaries in Asia tend to export a large proportion of their finished goods to the US market.

3.5 CONCLUSION

This chapter empirically examines firm-level pricing behaviour of Japanese exports to propose new determinants of invoicing behaviour and present new evidence on traditional and newly proposed determinants. We interviewed 23 representative Japanese exporting firms to collect information on their invoicing currency behaviour as well as their explicit policy/strategy of choosing an invoice currency. Through interviews, we found that Japanese electronics and automobile companies have a strong tendency to choose the local currency for invoicing for exports to advanced countries, while US dollar invoicing is largely used when exporting to Asian countries, especially when exporting electronics products. Such an invoicing strategy aims to stabilize the local currency (US dollar) price of their export products in local markets, which is consistent with the PTM behaviour discussed in the literature.

This chapter proposes new determinants and hypotheses for invoice currency choice behaviour and tests those hypotheses using a newly constructed firm-level data set. Our novel findings are threefold. First, invoicing in the importer's currency is prevalent in Japanese exports to advanced countries because most of their exports are destined for local subsidiaries which face severe competition in the local markets. In this case, Japanese parent firms have a strong tendency to take an exchange rate risk by invoicing in the importer's currency, which is consistent with the PTM behaviour discussed in the literature. It also makes sense to concentrate currency risk at the company's headquarters as it is better equipped with risk management expertise as well as scale economies. Second, Japanese firms that export highly differentiated products or that have a dominant share in global markets tend to choose yen invoicing even in exports to advanced countries. Third, although Japanese firms have shifted their production bases to Asian countries, exports from these Asian bases tend to be invoiced in US dollars as long as the final destination market is the US, which results in US dollar invoicing even for exports from a Japanese head office to its production subsidiaries in Asia. Thus, a smaller share of yen-denominated invoicing for Japanese exports even in the 2000s is due to the growing intra-firm trade promoted by the active overseas operations of Japanese electronics firms combined with products' final destination being the US market.

While Japanese firms' production networks in Asia reinforce Japan's unique pattern of invoicing currency, country-specific foreign exchange regulations in Asia also cause US dollar invoicing in Japanese exports to Asia. Since the Asian currency crisis in 1997, foreign exchange regulations and controls in Asian countries have been strengthened and this has reinforced the use of US dollars in Asia.

4. Analysis of questionnaire surveys on head offices

In the previous chapter we presented interesting findings on the determinants of invoicing currency by major Japanese exporters using a unique data set obtained through our interviews. However, the results were obtained from a limited number of sample firms with whom we conducted interviews. In this sense, it is worthwhile to re-examine the robustness of the derived determinants of invoicing currency behaviour using a data set comprising a large number of sample firms.

4.1 QUESTIONNAIRE SURVEYS OF 2009 AND 2013

The primary purpose of the questionnaire survey is to collect detailed information on firm-level invoicing currency choices of Japanese exporters.

In October and November 2009, the Research Institute of Economy, Trade and Industry, Japan (RIETI) conducted the Questionnaire Survey on the Choice of Invoice Currency by Japanese Firms (henceforth, the 2009 RIETI Survey), which covered all Japanese listed firms in the manufacturing sector that reported foreign sales in their consolidated financial statements in fiscal year 2008.[1] Then, questionnaires were sent out to 928 firms by postal mail in October 2009. The RIETI received responses from 227 firms by December 2009, with a response rate of 24.5 per cent. Among the 227 sample firms, 208 firms (91.6 per cent) are manufacturing firms with capital of 1 billion yen (about USD 10 million) or more, and 174 firms (76.4 per cent) have 300 employees or more. Therefore, most respondents can be considered large companies.

In September and October 2013, the RIETI conducted a second questionnaire survey (henceforth, the 2013 RIETI Survey), in which most of the questions were the same as in the 2009 RIETI Survey. Questionnaires were sent out to 962 firms that were all listed manufacturers reporting foreign sales in their consolidated financial statements in fiscal year 2012.

---

[1] All sample firms are listed on one of five stock exchanges (Tokyo, Osaka, Nagoya, Fukuoka and Sapporo) or three emerging markets (JASDAQ, Mothers and Hercules).

The RIETI received responses from 185 firms, with a response rate of 19.2 per cent. Sixty-nine companies answered both the 2009 and 2013 Surveys.

Table 4.1 presents simple arithmetic averages of both consolidated and foreign sales for an average of 227 respondents in the 2009 Survey and 185 in the 2013 Survey. By dividing the amount of foreign sales by that of corresponding consolidated sales, we obtained the ratio of foreign sales to consolidated sales (henceforth, 'foreign sales ratio'). The foreign sales ratio for all manufacturing industries is almost identical between the respondents of these two surveys. Even at an industry level, the foreign sales ratio does not show large differences between the two sets of firms, except for the pharmaceutical industry. This observation shows that the size of our sample firms in the 2013 Survey is, on average, similar to that in the 2009 Survey. It also must be noted that not all respondents answered all questions. Hence, the number of sample firms (respondents) in the following analysis is often smaller than the total number of sample firms (227 for the 2009 Survey and 185 for the 2013 Survey).

4.2   CHOICE OF INVOICING CURRENCY

4.2.1   Invoice Currency and Settlement Currency

Before examining the firm-level invoicing choices, we first present the result of our preliminary question about whether invoice currency (currency used at the contract stage) is the same as settlement currency (currency to be used at the payments stage). It is found that in the 2009 Survey, 200 out of 226 respondents, which is equivalent to 88.4 per cent of our sample firms, answered that the same currency was used for both invoicing and settlements.[2] While the role of invoicing currency is often distinguished from that of settlement currency in theoretical studies (Friberg, 1998), our findings show that the same currency is used for invoicing and settlements in most cases, which is consistent with the findings of Friberg and Wilander (2008).

Result 1: For most Japanese firms, the same currency is used for both invoicing and settlements.

---

[2]   In the 2013 Survey, 179 out of 184 respondents (97.2 per cent) answered that currencies used for invoicing and settlements are 'mostly the same' or 'highly likely to be the same but sometimes different'.

Table 4.1 Respondent firms in 2009 and 2013 Surveys

Status of manufacturers listed in the TSE and responded firms (sample average)

Type of Industry	Responding firms in 2009 Survey				Responding firms in 2013 Survey			
	Number of responding firms	Consolidated sales (average, million yen)	Foreign sales (average, million yen)	Foreign sales / Consolidated sales (average, million yen)	Number of responding firms	Consolidated sales (average, million yen)	Foreign sales (average, million yen)	Foreign sales / Consolidated sales (average, million yen)
All manufacturers	**227**	**380951**	**190145**	**37.0**	**185**	**393235**	**191978**	**37.6**
Foods	3	483825	227374	32.3	1	34208	5396	15.8
Textiles & Apparel	9	102142	17585	23.2	8	145217	44793	30.1
Pulp & papers	0	–	–	–	2	628715	105136	19.2
Chemicals	36	273090	105240	34.7	20	258232	107326	33.9
Pharmaceuticals	3	230864	22951	10.5	1	678	593	87.5
Rubber Products	4	98511	47124	32.2	4	274893	118010	34.2
Glass & Ceramics	6	55315	25978	30.3	4	8342	1305	23.7
Steel Products	6	882765	298665	23.4	8	865763	310434	26.4
Nonferrous Metals	5	203383	30943	17.6	8	427199	144434	26.9
Metal Products	9	172879	73012	37.8	9	230205	51954	30.2
Machinery	40	158355	89751	35.7	30	190862	97307	45.1
Electrical Machinery	55	529526	231003	43.7	52	302658	136401	42.0
Transport Equipment	27	888213	631035	41.3	17	1617926	1038919	39.7
Precision Instruments	15	110474	85505	48.2	12	21368	8479	43.0
Others	9	432112	73889	34.2	9	261778	48390	27.5

Notes: Questionnaires were sent to 928 and 962 Japanese firms listed on stock exchanges in Japan in 2009 and 2013, respectively. The RIETI selected the firms that reported foreign sales in their consolidated financial statements as of fiscal year 2008 (2013), and 928 (962) firms were finally chosen. Others in the type of industry includes Oil & Coal Products and Other Products.

Source: Authors' calculation based on the 2009 and 2013 RIETI Survey.

4.2.2   Invoicing Currency in Japanese Exports to the World

Table 4.2 presents the invoicing share of Japanese exports to the world based on the 2009 and 2013 Surveys. We present two types of invoice currency shares: a simple arithmetic average share and a weighted average share. While the simple arithmetic average is a useful measure to see which currency is most frequently used for trade invoicing, it does not necessarily show the actual invoicing pattern of Japanese total exports, because the arithmetic average share does not take into account differences in export volume across sample firms. Thus, we compute the weighted average share as well, to allow for the size effect for each firm by using the amount of foreign sales as a proxy for firm's exports to the world, which is likely to show the real picture of Japanese firms' invoice-currency choice. It must be noted that destination-breakdown data on firm-level exports are not available and that we collect data on firms' foreign sales from each sample firm's annual financial statement. Since even data on destination-specific foreign sales are not available from the firms' annual financial statements, we can present the weighted average share of invoicing currency only for exports to the world.

In Table 4.2, when looking at the arithmetic average share of all manufacturing industries in the 2009 Survey, where 217 firms responded, the share of yen invoicing firms is larger (48.2 per cent) than that of US dollar invoicing firms (42.1 per cent). The share of euro invoicing firms is only 7.1 per cent, and other currencies are seldom used for invoicing (2.7 per cent). Next, turning to the weighted average share – calculated using the amount of foreign sales by respective sample firms – the share of US dollar invoicing becomes the highest, amounting to 54.1 per cent. The share of yen invoicing declines to only 28.7 per cent, which is far lower than the corresponding arithmetic average share of US dollar.

In the 2013 Survey, the arithmetic and weighted average shares of Japanese yen invoicing declines to 41.8 per cent and 21.9 per cent, respectively, while the US dollar invoicing shares increase to 49.1 per cent and 62.1 per cent, respectively (Table 4.2). The arithmetic and weighted average shares of euro invoicing also decline to 5.1 per cent and 6.8 per cent, respectively, whereas the shares of other currencies including Asian currencies increase to 4.0 per cent and 9.2 per cent, respectively. Even when we focus on the 68 sample firms that answered in both 2009 and 2013 Surveys, the arithmetic average share of yen invoicing declines from 47.6 per cent in 2009 to 42.9 per cent in 2013, while the average share of US dollar invoicing increases from 43.9 per cent to 47.6 per cent.

The above observation reveals the notable feature of Japanese firms' invoicing currency choice. Specifically, the arithmetic average share suggests that approximately a half of Japanese firms invoice their exports in yen.

Table 4.2   Share of invoicing currency for Japanese exports to the world (by firm category, sample average)

	2009 Survey						2013 Survey					
	All firms		Firms answering both surveys	Total consolidated sales			All firms		Firms answering both surveys	Total consolidated sales		
	Arithmetic average	Weighted average[1]		Large (upper 1/3)	Medium (middle 1/3)	Small (lower 1/3)	Arithmetic average	Weighted average[1]		Large (upper 1/3)	Medium (middle 1/3)	Small (lower 1/3)
# of sample firms	217	217	68	80	70	67	185	185	68	62	61	62
JPY												
All manufacturers	**48.2**	**28.7**	**47.6**	**38.1**	**50.0**	**58.3**	**41.8**	**21.9**	**42.9**	**26.2**	**45.1**	**54.9**
Chemicals	50.4	–	–	33.1	54.2	66.8	39.4	–	–	24.8	55.9	34.8
Machinery	56.2	–	–	36.8	73.8	56.5	51.0	–	–	28.6	56.9	67.7
Electrical Machinery	38.8	–	–	25.7	36.5	54.3	36.5	–	–	24.1	26.2	64.4
Transport Equipment	56.3	–	–	49.0	71.9	56.6	59.1	–	–	44.9	84.5	40.0
Precision Instruments	44.4	–	–	29.8	40.4	55.0	39.5	–	–	–	44.9	57.7
USD												
All manufacturers	**42.1**	**54.1**	**43.9**	**47.8**	**41.7**	**35.8**	**49.1**	**62.1**	**47.6**	**63.2**	**42.9**	**40.8**
Chemicals	41.0	–	–	55.9	38.7	25.9	54.7	–	–	68.7	36.7	61.8
Machinery	29.7	–	–	41.0	18.0	31.1	40.5	–	–	59.2	33.0	28.2
Electrical Machinery	50.7	–	–	59.2	51.4	41.5	51.2	–	–	65.3	51.8	34.2

Transport Equipment	33.3	–	–	35.3	23.4	41.2	30.4	–	–	44.4	12.2	29.0
Precision Instruments	44.3	–	–	42.6	51.6	39.2	52.6	–	–	–	44.4	33.3
Euro												
All manufacturers	**7.1**	**11.3**	**5.7**	**10.5**	**5.1**	**5.2**	**5.1**	**6.8**	**4.8**	**6.8**	**6.0**	**2.4**
Chemicals	7.7	–	–	10.5	5.1	7.3	5.1	–	–	5.8	6.0	3.3
Machinery	11.0	–	–	17.5	5.8	10.1	6.5	–	–	9.7	8.0	2.7
Electrical Machinery	8.2	–	–	12.8	7.8	3.8	5.5	–	–	6.6	8.2	0.5
Transport Equipment	4.5	–	–	6.1	2.7	2.1	3.1	–	–	5.8	0.2	1.0
Precision Instruments	9.0	–	–	25.4	3.0	5.8	7.5	–	–	–	5.8	9.0
Other currencies												
All manufacturers	**2.7**	**5.9**	**2.8**	**3.7**	**3.3**	**0.7**	**4.0**	**9.2**	**4.7**	**3.9**	**6.0**	**1.9**
Chemicals	0.9	–	–	0.6	2.1	0.0	0.7	–	–	0.7	1.4	0.0
Machinery	3.2	–	–	4.7	2.4	2.5	2.0	–	–	2.5	2.1	1.4
Electrical Machinery	2.5	–	–	2.3	4.9	0.3	6.8	–	–	4.0	13.8	0.8
Transport Equipment	5.9	–	–	9.6	2.0	0.1	7.4	–	–	5.0	3.2	30.0
Precision Instruments	2.3	–	–	2.2	5.0	0.0	0.5	–	–	–	5.0	0.0

Note: 1. Weighted average is calculated as average of invoicing currency share of all responded firms weighted by amount of foreign sales in FY2008 or FY2012 of each firm.

Source: Authors' calculation based on the 2009 and 2013 RIETI Survey.

Taking into consideration the firm size in terms of foreign sales, however, more than a half of Japanese exports are invoiced in US dollars. Thus, the larger the firm size in terms of foreign sales, the more frequently are foreign currencies, especially the US dollar, chosen in Japanese exports. This distinctive pattern of invoice currency choice became more prominent in 2013.

Result 2: In terms of the number of firms, Japanese firms tend to use the yen more than the US dollar for export invoicing. In terms of export amount, however, the US dollar is used more than the yen in Japanese exports to the world. The share of US dollars increases from 2009 to 2013.

Table 4.2 divides the sample firms into three categories: large (upper third), medium (middle third) and small (lower third) by firm size, which is measured by total consolidated sales.[3] In both the 2009 and 2013 Surveys, the larger (smaller) the firm size, the smaller (larger) is the share of yen invoicing. On the other hand, the larger the firm size, the larger is the share of US dollar invoicing.[4]

Result 3: Firm size does matter in the choice of invoicing currency for exports. The smaller (larger) the firm size, the larger is the share of yen (US dollar) invoicing.

4.2.3 Share of Invoicing Currency by Destination

Table 4.3 shows invoicing currency choices for Japanese exports to major advanced countries/region (US, euro area and the UK), where the simple arithmetic average shares of all manufacturers and major industries are reported.

First, the US dollar is the most used currency in Japanese exports to the US: 79.8 per cent of exports to the US are invoiced in US dollars in 2013, which increases slightly from the US dollar share (77.9 per cent) in 2009. Only 18.9 per cent of Japanese exports to the US are invoiced in the yen in 2013. Second, in exports to the euro area, the share of euro invoicing is 48.6 per cent in 2013, while 30.0 per cent of exports are invoiced in yen. The share of both euro and yen declines from 2009 to 2013, while the share of the US dollar increases from 13.6 per cent to 21.0 per cent

---

[3]   Sales data are taken from a firm's annual statement as of the reporting date immediately before the 2009 and 2013 Survey (mostly the end of March 2009 and March 2013).

[4]   Ito et al. (2012) conducted the interview analysis and revealed that Japanese export firms with active global operations and large foreign sales tend to choose the US dollar (or destination currency) as invoicing-currency.

Table 4.3 Share of invoice currency for Japanese exports to advanced economies by industry

	2009 Survey			2013 Survey		
	Destination			Destination		
	US	Euro Area	UK	US	Euro Area	UK
# of answers	168	133	65	127	102	53
A. JPY						
All manufacturers	**21.8**	**35.3**	**35.0**	**18.9**	**30.0**	**36.6**
Chemicals	16.1	28.6	22.7	20.4	30.9	46.2
Machinery	23.9	38.4	36.4	19.8	30.9	31.0
Electrical Machinery	17.0	33.5	33.7	21.8	34.6	47.4
Transport Equipment	18.5	36.6	46.8	34.2	17.3	33.5
Precision Instruments	28.5	61.7	50.0	18.3	9.0	84.0
B. USD						
All manufacturers	**77.9**	**13.6**	**18.5**	**79.8**	**21.0**	**14.2**
Chemicals	83.9	8.6	21.4	68.4	25.4	24.4
Machinery	74.8	2.1	0.0	77.2	8.8	10.3
Electrical Machinery	83.4	22.2	25.3	78.3	24.4	2.6
Transport Equipment	81.5	13.9	9.1	65.8	18.1	0.0
Precision Instruments	71.5	8.3	0.0	81.7	36.8	16.0
C. Euro						
All manufacturers	**0.3**	**51.0**	**15.7**	**0.8**	**48.6**	**18.1**
Chemicals	0.0	62.1	19.5	11.1	43.7	1.2
Machinery	1.3	59.0	25.6	0.0	59.4	28.4
Electrical Machinery	0.0	44.7	13.2	0.0	41.0	18.2
Transport Equipment	0.0	49.1	17.3	0.0	64.6	39.7
Precision Instruments	0.0	30.0	50.0	0.0	54.0	0.0
D. Importer's currency						
All manufacturers	–	–	**32.1**	–	–	**29.3**
Chemicals	–	–	36.4	–	–	28.2
Machinery	–	–	38.0	–	–	30.3
Electrical Machinery	–	–	31.7	–	–	25.9
Transport Equipment	–	–	26.8	–	–	26.8
Precision Instruments	–	–	0.0	–	–	0.0
E. Other currencies						
All manufacturers	**0.0**	**0.3**	**0.0**	**0.0**	**0.4**	**1.9**
Chemicals	0.0	0.3	0.0	0.0	0.0	0.0
Machinery	0.0	0.4	0.0	0.0	0.9	0.0
Electrical Machinery	0.0	0.4	0.0	0.0	0.0	5.9
Transport Equipment	0.0	0.4	0.0	0.0	0.0	0.0
Precision Instruments	0.0	0.0	0.0	0.0	0.2	0.0

Note: Simple arithmetic average share is reported.

Source: Authors' calculation based on the 2009 and 2013 RIETI Survey.

during that period. Third, in exports to the UK, the share of the UK
pound invoicing (importer's currency) is 29.3 per cent in 2013, while the
yen accounts for the highest share (36.6 per cent). However, if we consider
both the euro and the UK pound, European currencies account for 47.4
per cent in Japanese exports to the UK in 2013. Thus, we have found that
the importer's currency is the most used currency in Japanese exports to
advanced countries, which is consistent with the pricing-to-market (PTM)
behaviour discussed in the literature.

Table 4.4 divides the sample firms into three groups by firm size, which

Table 4.4   *Share of invoice currency for Japanese exports to advanced*
            economies by firm size

	2009 Survey			2013 Survey		
	Destination			Destination		
	US	Euro Area	UK	US	Euro Area	UK
# of answers	168	133	65	127	102	53
A. JPY						
Large	16.0	29.7	30.5	11.3	21.0	29.8
Medium	23.9	30.1	17.7	26.6	32.9	42.0
Small	26.5	49.2	65.0	20.0	43.8	54.9
B. USD						
Large	83.5	11.4	12.7	88.7	19.0	19.5
Medium	76.1	16.4	30.0	73.4	22.3	8.0
Small	72.9	13.9	21.4	77.1	23.1	4.0
C. Euro						
Large	0.7	58.8	23.6	0.0	59.5	25.1
Medium	0.0	53.2	10.7	0.0	44.2	12.0
Small	0.0	36.9	0.7	2.9	33.0	0.0
D. Importer's currency						
Large	–	–	35.7	–	–	25.6
Medium	–	–	41.7	–	–	31.3
Small	–	–	12.9	–	–	41.1
E. Other currencies						
Large	0.0	0.6	0.0	0.0	0.5	0.0
Medium	0.0	0.1	0.0	0.0	0.5	6.7
Small	0.0	0.0	0.0	0.0	0.0	0.0

Note: Simple arithmetic average share is reported

Source: Authors' calculation based on the 2009 and 2013 RIETI Survey.

shows that the larger the firm size, the higher is the share of importer's currency in Japanese exports to the US and euro area in both 2009 and 2013. In exports to the UK, the share of European currencies that consist of both the euro and the UK pound increases monotonically as the firm size becomes larger. Accordingly, the firm size is an important determinant of invoice currency choice in exports to advanced countries.

The invoice currency choice in Japanese exports to Asian countries is different from that in exports to advanced countries. First, although Figure 2.1 in Chapter 2 shows that about 54 per cent of Japanese exports to Asia are invoiced in US dollars in 2013–2014, Table 4.5 indicates that the share of yen-invoiced exports is higher than that of US dollar-invoiced exports. In the 2009 Survey, 55 per cent or more of Japanese exports to four Asian countries are invoiced in the yen. Although the share of yen-invoiced exports declined somewhat in the 2013 Survey, about 50 per cent or more of exports to Korea, Taiwan and Thailand are still invoiced in the yen. Only in exports to China is the share of US dollar invoicing (47.1 per cent) higher than that of yen invoicing (44.6 per cent) in the 2013 Survey. It must be noted, however, that Table 4.5 presents the simple arithmetic average share that tends to overestimate the share of yen-invoiced exports. If considering the size effect, the share of US dollar-invoiced exports would be much larger.

Second, Asian currencies play only a minor role in Japanese exports to Asian countries. In Japanese exports to China, the share of importer's currency (renminbi: RMB) rises from 1.3 per cent in the 2009 Survey to 8.2 per cent in the 2013 Survey. This increase in RMB-invoiced exports suggests a progress in RMB internationalization. However, the share of the RMB is still far smaller than the share of the yen and the US dollar. In exports to Korea, Taiwan and Thailand, the share of importer's currency invoicing is less than 8 per cent in the 2013 Survey. Thus, we may state that Asian currencies are not often used in Japanese exports to Asian countries.

Third, similar to exports to advanced economies, the choice of invoicing currency is strongly affected by the firm size even in exports to Asian countries. Table 4.6 clearly shows that in Japanese exports to Asian countries, the share of yen invoicing declines monotonically as the firm size increases, while the share of US dollar invoicing increases monotonically as the firm size increases.

Result 4: In terms of the number of firms, invoicing in importer's currency is chosen for exports to the US, euro area and the UK.

Result 5: The yen and US dollar are generally chosen for Japanese exports to Asia, and the yen is used more as invoice currency than the US dollar. Asian currencies are not often chosen in Japanese exports to Asian countries.

Table 4.5 *Share of invoice currency for Japanese exports to Asian countries by industry*

	2009 Survey Destination				2013 Survey Destination			
	China	Korea	Taiwan	Thailand	China	Korea	Taiwan	Thailand
# of answers	174	142	150	122	138	104	105	102
A. JPY								
All manufacturers	**55.4**	**69.0**	**62.5**	**60.1**	**44.6**	**58.4**	**49.5**	**54.6**
Chemicals	52.3	53.4	51.9	64.7	55.8	53.5	57.8	68.3
Machinery	80.4	89.3	84.2	75.5	61.7	75.6	78.4	62.4
Electrical Machinery	42.3	59.8	53.4	49.0	32.6	51.5	34.5	44.8
Transport Equipment	76.5	66.7	81.5	58.6	62.4	32.7	64.9	63.2
Precision Instruments	56.2	66.6	69.9	92.6	60.6	80.0	82.9	72.0
B. USD								
All manufacturers	**43.7**	**25.5**	**35.3**	**30.4**	**47.1**	**36.1**	**45.6**	**36.3**
Chemicals	47.7	37.9	46.3	28.8	34.2	37.4	41.2	31.7
Machinery	23.7	9.1	17.2	10.8	27.9	19.8	21.6	30.7
Electrical Machinery	57.0	35.3	43.3	42.6	54.3	44.8	57.8	48.4
Transport Equipment	16.0	8.3	9.2	21.0	35.7	65.7	21.4	16.3
Precision Instruments	38.1	33.4	30.1	7.5	39.4	20.0	17.1	0.0
C. Euro								
All manufacturers	**0.5**	**1.1**	**0.3**	**0.2**	**0.0**	**0.0**	**0.0**	**1.4**
Chemicals	0.0	2.9	1.7	0.0	0.0	0.0	0.0	0.0
Machinery	0.0	0.9	0.0	0.0	0.1	0.0	0.0	2.3
Electrical Machinery	0.7	0.1	0.0	0.5	0.0	0.0	0.0	0.0
Transport Equipment	0.0	0.0	0.0	0.3	0.0	0.0	0.0	0.0
Precision Instruments	5.0	0.0	0.0	0.0	0.0	0.0	0.0	28.0

D. Importer's currency	**1.3**	**4.5**	**2.4**	**9.4**	**8.2**	**5.4**	**4.9**	**7.8**
All manufacturers								
Chemicals	0.0	5.8	0.1	6.4	10.0	9.1	1.0	0.0
Machinery	1.6	0.7	0.0	13.8	10.3	4.6	0.0	4.6
Electrical Machinery	0.0	4.8	3.4	7.8	12.9	3.8	7.7	7.0
Transport Equipment	7.6	25.0	9.2	20.2	1.9	1.7	13.7	20.6
Precision Instruments	0.0	0.0	0.0	0.0	0.0	0.0	0.0	0.0
E. Other currencies								
All manufacturers	**0.0**	**0.0**	**0.0**	**0.0**	**0.1**	**0.0**	**0.0**	**0.0**
Chemicals	0.0	0.0	0.0	0.0	0.0	0.0	0.0	0.0
Machinery	0.0	0.0	0.0	0.0	0.0	0.0	0.0	0.0
Electrical Machinery	0.0	0.0	0.0	0.0	0.2	0.0	0.0	0.0
Transport Equipment	0.0	0.0	0.0	0.1	0.0	0.0	0.0	0.0
Precision Instruments	0.0	0.0	0.0	0.0	0.0	0.0	0.0	0.0

Note: Simple arithmetic average share is reported

Source: Authors' calculation based on the 2009 and 2013 RIETI Survey.

*Table 4.6   Share of invoice currency for Japanese exports to Asian
              countries by firm size*

	2009 Survey				2013 Survey			
	Destination				Destination			
	China	Korea	Taiwan	Thailand	China	Korea	Taiwan	Thailand
# of answers	174	142	150	122	138	104	105	102
A. JPY								
Large	45.3	62.5	53.3	54.7	29.1	38.8	41.4	41.1
Medium	60.5	68.9	63.0	57.3	46.3	61.4	41.6	60.7
Small	63.4	78.9	75.2	75.5	61.1	77.7	68.6	69.1
B. USD								
Large	52.4	32.8	42.6	35.4	64.3	51.4	53.8	49.6
Medium	40.9	25.8	35.7	32.5	41.0	35.7	48.2	30.3
Small	34.2	13.8	24.0	16.7	33.0	19.5	31.4	21.9
C. Euro								
Large	0.4	0.5	0.0	0.4	0.0	0.0	0.0	1.3
Medium	0.0	1.1	0.0	0.0	0.0	0.0	0.0	0.0
Small	1.2	1.9	1.0	0.0	0.0	0.0	0.0	3.2
D. Importer's currency								
Large	3.2	4.2	4.1	9.5	6.5	9.8	4.8	8.1
Medium	0.0	4.2	2.1	10.1	12.4	2.8	10.2	9.0
Small	0.0	5.4	0.4	7.8	5.8	2.9	0.0	5.8
E. Other currencies								
Large	0.0	0.0	0.0	0.0	0.1	0.0	0.0	0.0
Medium	0.0	0.0	0.0	0.0	0.2	0.0	0.0	0.0
Small	0.0	0.0	0.0	0.0	0.0	0.0	0.0	0.0

Note: Simple arithmetic average share is reported

Source: Authors' calculation based on the 2009 and 2013 RIETI Survey.

*Result 6: For Japanese exports to Asia, the larger (smaller) the firm size, the
higher is the share of US dollar (yen) invoicing.*

4.2.4   Type of Trading Partners and Invoice Currency Decision

Intra-firm or arm's-length trade
By using the results of the 2009 round of the questionnaire survey, we
investigate whether the choice of invoice currency is related with the type
of importers/trading partners. We consider five trading partners: (1) local

production subsidiaries; (2) local sales subsidiaries; (3) local trading agencies; (4) *Sogo Shosha* (Japanese trading companies); and (5) others. Both (1) and (2) are regarded as an *intra*-firm trade and (3) to (5) as an *inter*-firm or arm's-length trade.

Let us first check whether intra-firm trade becomes more common than arm's-length trade in Japanese exports. Panels A and B in Table 4.7 present the share of intra-firm exports to each destination by trading partners in the 2009 Survey. First, in Japanese exports to the US, the euro area and the UK (Table 4.7 Panel A), more than 50 per cent are directed toward local subsidiaries. The share of intra-firm exports is the largest in exports to the US.

Second, in exports to developing countries such as Central and Latin American countries, Russia, East European countries and African countries (Table 4.7 Panel A), about 70 per cent or more are arm's-length trade. Even in exports to Australia and New Zealand, the share of arm's-length exports is about 70 per cent, which is almost the same level as the case of East European countries. In exports to Canada, Mexico and Brazil, however, the share of intra-firm exports is about 40 per cent or less, which is higher than the case of exports to other developing countries.

Third, in exports to Asian countries (Table 4.7 Panel B), the share of intra-firm exports is much higher than in exports to other developing countries. In exports to China, Hong Kong and Thailand, the share of intra-firm exports is 54–60 per cent, which is almost equivalent to the case of exports to the euro area and the UK. In exports to Taiwan, Singapore, Malaysia and Indonesia, 40–46 per cent of exports are destined for local subsidiaries.

Fourth, the larger the firm size, the larger is the share of intra-firm trade. With only a few exceptions, the share of intra-firm trade increases monotonically as the firm size increases.

Fifth, in arm's-length trade to Asian countries as well as advanced countries, the major trading partner is 'local agencies', not *Sogo Shosha*. For example, in Japanese exports to the euro area, 25.3 per cent are destined for local agencies, while only 7.7 per cent are for *Sogo Shosha*. While the shares of local agencies and *Sogo Shosha* are almost the same in exports to China, the share of local agencies (23.2 per cent) is much higher than that of *Sogo Shosha* (8.6 per cent) in exports to Thailand. The share of *Sogo Shosha* is 22 per cent or higher only in exports to developing countries such as Central and Latin American countries, African countries, Russia and Middle East countries. A possible reason is that it is often hard to set up local subsidiaries in developing countries and, hence, Japanese firms utilize the *Sogo Shosha*'s sales network in developing countries.

Table 4.7 Japanese exports by destination, trading partner and firm size

Panel A: Japanese Exports by Trading Partner: Americas, Europe, Africa, and Pacific (all sample firms)

Sample arithmetic average (Unit: %)

	Number of answers		US	Canada	Mexico	Brazil	Central & Latin Americas	Euro Area	UK	Russia	East European countries	Australia	New Zealand	African countries
All firms	Number of answers		150	44	32	45	35	117	61	31	34	63	34	33
Export channel														
All overseas subsidiaries (a)+(b)			**70.8**	**38.7**	**38.1**	**40.5**	**22.3**	**52.1**	**55.6**	**16.1**	**30.9**	**31.5**	**26.5**	**12.2**
(a) Production Subsidiaries (plants)			20.8	10.0	11.0	28.6	6.0	12.2	15.5	1.0	20.6	6.7	8.8	3.1
(b) Sales Subsidiaries			50.0	28.7	27.1	11.8	16.3	39.8	40.1	15.1	10.3	24.7	17.6	9.1
Local agencies (no capital ties)			10.4	35.6	20.3	33.3	41.3	25.3	23.3	36.7	31.7	37.3	55.9	44.3
Via Japanese trading companies			7.6	11.6	18.7	16.4	24.9	7.7	1.3	30.7	22.7	16.4	5.6	29.6
Others			11.0	14.2	22.9	9.8	11.4	15.2	19.8	17.5	15.9	15.8	12.1	13.9
By firm size														
1. Large-size firms	Number of answers		57	28	22	28	24	52	37	16	18	35	23	21
All overseas subsidiaries (a)+(b)			**77.1**	**45.4**	**46.4**	**58.4**	**28.6**	**69.5**	**66.0**	**25.7**	**46.9**	**42.5**	**39.3**	**19.3**
(a) Production Subsidiaries (plants)			26.5	12.2	16.1	39.3	8.9	18.9	20.3	2.0	27.9	9.3	13.1	4.9
(b) Sales Subsidiaries			50.5	33.1	30.4	19.1	19.7	50.6	45.7	23.7	19.1	33.2	26.2	14.4

Local agencies (no capital ties)	4.2	27.2	20.6	17.9	32.4	12.0	16.3	26.8	15.5	30.1	47.9	45.9
Via Japanese trading companies	7.4	11.8	13.0	11.8	22.7	4.9	1.6	28.5	26.4	15.8	4.4	25.2
Others	8.9	12.4	16.0	8.6	12.6	12.0	13.7	14.8	7.9	10.8	4.4	5.3
2. Medium-size firms Number of answers	49	6	5	8	7	33	12	6	9	17	5	8
All overseas subsidiaries (a)+(b)	**75.2**	**39.2**	**20.0**	**12.5**	**0.0**	**55.3**	**72.9**	**16.7**	**22.2**	**17.6**	**0.0**	**0.0**
(a) Production Subsidiaries (plants)	26.8	0.0	0.0	12.5	0.0	8.5	16.7	0.0	22.2	0.0	0.0	0.0
(b) Sales Subsidiaries	48.4	39.2	20.0	0.0	0.0	46.8	56.3	16.7	0.0	17.6	0.0	0.0
Local agencies (no capital ties)	8.7	34.2	0.0	50.0	52.9	21.7	8.3	16.7	33.3	47.1	80.0	25.0
Via Japanese trading companies	9.6	10.0	40.0	37.5	32.9	6.6	2.1	50.0	22.2	10.6	0.0	43.8
Others	6.5	16.7	40.0	0.0	14.3	16.4	16.7	16.7	22.2	24.7	20.0	31.3
3. Small-size firms Number of answers	45	11	6	10	5	33	13	10	8	12	7	5
All overseas subsidiaries (a)+(b)	**56.6**	**18.2**	**16.7**	**9.0**	**20.0**	**20.0**	**6.2**	**0.0**	**0.0**	**16.7**	**0.0**	**0.0**
(a) Production Subsidiaries (plants)	6.7	9.1	0.0	9.0	0.0	5.2	0.0	0.0	0.0	8.3	0.0	0.0
(b) Sales Subsidiaries	49.9	9.1	16.7	0.0	20.0	14.8	6.2	0.0	0.0	8.3	0.0	0.0
Local agencies (no capital ties)	19.9	54.5	33.3	60.0	60.0	48.8	55.4	60.0	62.5	41.7	57.1	60.0
Via Japanese trading companies	5.4	10.9	19.2	11.0	20.0	12.9	0.0	19.5	12.5	25.0	12.9	20.0
Others	18.1	16.4	30.8	20.0	0.0	18.3	38.5	20.5	25.0	16.7	30.0	20.0

Table 4.7 (continued)

Panel B: Japanese Exports by Trading Partner: Asian Countries   Sample arithmetic average (Unit: %)

		Destination											
		China	Korea	Taiwan	Hong Kong	Singapore	Thailand	Malaysia	Indonesia	Philippines	Vietnam	India	Mid-East countries
All firms	Number of answers	155	131	135	96	93	110	82	77	65	56	65	57
Export channel													
All overseas subsidiaries (a)+(b)		**59.8**	**27.2**	**39.6**	**54.1**	**46.2**	**54.7**	**44.8**	**42.2**	**30.9**	**32.8**	**28.4**	**12.2**
(a) Production Subsidiaries (plants)		35.0	9.7	16.7	6.6	6.1	40.4	33.8	32.7	22.5	24.9	18.4	2.6
(b) Sales Subsidiaries		24.8	17.5	22.8	47.6	40.2	14.3	11.0	9.4	8.4	7.9	10.1	9.6
Local agencies (no capital ties)		14.2	38.3	34.6	25.6	30.5	23.2	29.9	25.1	37.9	30.9	29.7	40.6
Via Japanese trading companies		13.5	12.2	9.7	6.7	9.9	8.6	7.0	16.0	13.5	18.3	17.9	27.2
Others		13.5	22.2	16.1	13.5	13.4	13.6	19.2	16.7	17.7	20.2	24.0	20.0
By firm size													
1. Large-size firms	Number of answers	64	56	55	45	43	49	44	40	34	28	36	31
All overseas subsidiaries (a)+(b)		**63.5**	**34.8**	**52.2**	**63.6**	**60.3**	**62.7**	**54.3**	**52.1**	**45.3**	**41.7**	**44.5**	**16.2**
(a) Production Subsidiaries (plants)		32.2	10.7	21.4	4.7	8.3	48.6	44.0	36.8	30.9	29.8	27.7	1.7
Local agencies (no capital ties)		7.8	24.1	23.9	16.4	19.3	14.4	22.8	17.4	20.5	21.9	24.3	32.4

102

Via Japanese trading companies	12.6	14.4	8.6	9.7	8.4	8.5	5.4	13.1	13.8	23.4	15.9	32.3
Others	14.8	25.2	13.6	8.3	9.9	12.5	15.4	15.2	17.7	13.9	12.8	16.2
2. Medium-size firms — Number of answers	51	40	43	27	27	39	23	22	16	13	17	12
All overseas subsidiaries (a)+(b)	**67.0**	**32.7**	**36.7**	**54.3**	**41.1**	**60.2**	**47.4**	**44.1**	**10.9**	**27.9**	**11.8**	**8.3**
(a) Production Subsidiaries (plants)	44.1	17.0	20.1	11.9	4.1	50.3	27.7	43.2	7.2	27.9	11.8	8.3
(b) Sales Subsidiaries	22.9	15.7	16.6	42.4	37.0	9.9	19.7	0.9	3.8	0.0	0.0	0.0
Local agencies (no capital ties)	8.1	43.7	35.7	23.9	23.3	16.4	20.9	20.0	47.8	19.2	23.8	34.2
Via Japanese trading companies	16.5	6.0	11.6	0.0	17.0	10.8	10.4	26.4	16.3	19.2	23.2	24.2
Others	8.9	17.7	16.0	21.8	18.5	12.5	21.3	9.5	25.0	33.6	41.2	33.3
3. Small-size firms — Number of answers	41	36	38	25	24	23	16	16	16	16	13	15
All overseas subsidiaries (a)+(b)	**43.3**	**8.7**	**23.6**	**35.5**	**25.0**	**25.9**	**12.5**	**12.5**	**18.8**	**18.8**	**3.8**	**6.7**
(a) Production Subsidiaries (plants)	27.0	0.1	5.7	4.0	4.2	4.3	12.5	6.3	18.8	12.5	0.0	0.0
(b) Sales Subsidiaries	16.3	8.6	17.9	31.5	20.8	21.5	0.0	6.3	0.0	6.3	3.8	6.7
Local agencies (no capital ties)	32.1	53.6	48.0	43.2	57.5	52.2	58.8	50.0	62.5	55.0	50.0	60.0
Via Japanese trading companies	10.9	15.6	9.0	8.4	4.2	4.6	5.9	8.1	9.4	7.2	15.3	17.3
Others	16.7	22.2	19.5	13.6	13.3	17.4	25.3	29.4	9.4	19.1	30.8	16.0

Note: Simple arithmetic average share is reported.

Source: 2009 RIETI Survey.

Result 7: In exports to advanced countries and most Asian countries, intra-firm trade (exports to local subsidiaries) accounts for the largest share. In exports to developing countries, arm's-length trade (especially exports to local agencies) accounts for the largest share. The larger the firm size, the higher is the share of intra-firm trade.

4.2.5   Choice of Invoicing Currency in Intra-firm and Arm's-length Trade

Let us examine the invoicing currency pattern of Japanese exports by relationship with trading partner. Our questionnaire survey collected information not on the share of invoicing currency but on the currency that is most frequently used in exports to various trading partners in each destination. Following Friberg and Wilander (2008), we name the most frequently used currency the 'main invoice currency'.[5] Tables 4.8 and 4.9 present the simple arithmetic average share of the main invoice currency across sample firms.

Table 4.8 presents invoicing currency choices by trading partner for Japanese exports to advanced countries and non-Asian emerging/developing countries, which indicates a clear pattern of invoicing currency choice in intra-firm exports to advanced countries.

First, in exports to the US, other North American countries and Central/Latin American countries, the US dollar is the most frequently used currency in intra-firm trade. When the export destination is the US, the share of the US dollar in exports to sales subsidiaries (92.7 per cent) is higher than the share of the US dollar in exports to production subsidiaries (plants) (78.4 per cent). However, when the export destination is Canada, the share of the US dollar in exports to production subsidiaries (66.7 per cent) is larger than the share of the US dollar in exports to sales subsidiaries (58.8 per cent). Thus, it is hard to say for which type of subsidiaries Japanese firms tend to choose the US dollar in their exports.

Second, in intra-firm exports to the euro area and the UK, the importer's currency accounts for the largest share as invoice currency. When the export destination is the euro area, 69.0 per cent of exports to production subsidiaries and 64.5 per cent of exports to sales subsidiaries are invoiced in euros. When the export destination is the UK, 41.7 per cent of exports to production subsidiaries and 48.1 per cent of exports to sales subsidiaries

---

[5]   For example, we regard the US dollar as the main invoice currency used in exports to Asia: 50 per cent of Japan's exports to Asia are invoiced in US dollars, 30 per cent in the local currency and 20 per cent in the yen. Friberg and Wilander (2008) also employed this main invoice currency approach for their questionnaire survey analysis and in conducting their empirical examination.

Table 4.8 Choice of invoice currency by trading partner: Japanese exports to advanced and emerging countries

Percentage of number of 'main currency', most frequently used currency in exports from Japan to each destination, over total number of answers

						Destination						
	US	Canada	Mexico	Brazil	Central & Latin Americas	Euro Area	UK	Russia	East European countries	Australia	New Zealand	African countries
Number of answers	150	44	32	45	35	117	61	31	34	63	34	33
Production Subsidiaries (plants)												
# of answers	51	6	5	17	4	29	12	1	7	5	3	2
1. JPY	21.6	16.7	0.0	23.5	0.0	24.1	16.7	100.0	28.6	40.0	33.3	50.0
2. USD	78.4	66.7	100.0	64.7	100.0	6.9	16.7	0.0	0.0	20.0	66.7	50.0
3. Euro	0.0	0.0	0.0	11.8	0.0	69.0	25.0	0.0	71.4	0.0	0.0	0.0
4. Importer's currency	–	16.7	0.0	0.0	0.0	–	41.7	0.0	0.0	40.0	0.0	0.0
5. Others	0.0	0.0	0.0	0.0	0.0	0.0	0.0	0.0	0.0	0.0	0.0	0.0
Sales Subsidiaries												
# of answers	109	17	11	7	8	62	27	6	6	20	7	4
1. JPY	7.3	0.0	18.2	14.3	25.0	24.2	22.2	50.0	50.0	25.0	42.9	50.0
2. USD	92.7	58.8	72.7	85.7	50.0	11.3	11.1	33.3	0.0	25.0	14.3	50.0
3. Euro	0.0	0.0	0.0	0.0	25.0	64.5	18.5	16.7	50.0	5.0	0.0	0.0
4. Importer's currency	–	41.2	9.1	0.0	0.0	–	48.1	0.0	0.0	45.0	0.0	0.0
5. Others	0.0	0.0	0.0	0.0	0.0	0.0	0.0	0.0	0.0	0.0	42.9	0.0

Table 4.8 (continued)

Percentage of number of 'main currency', most frequently used currency in exports from Japan to each destination, over total number of answers

						Destination						
	US	Canada	Mexico	Brazil	Central & Latin Americas	Euro Area	UK	Russia	East European countries	Australia	New Zealand	African countries
Number of answers	150	44	32	45	35	117	61	31	34	63	34	33
Local agencies (no capital ties)												
# of answers	31	17	8	14	19	46	17	12	14	28	20	15
1. JPY	38.7	52.9	50.0	85.7	63.2	45.7	47.1	83.3	85.7	53.6	65.0	73.3
2. USD	61.3	29.4	50.0	14.3	36.8	6.5	23.5	16.7	7.1	35.7	25.0	26.7
3. Euro	0.0	0.0	0.0	0.0	0.0	47.8	0.0	0.0	7.1	0.0	0.0	0.0
4. Importer's currency	–	17.6	0.0	0.0	0.0	–	29.4	0.0	0.0	10.7	5.0	0.0
5. Others	0.0	0.0	0.0	0.0	0.0	0.0	0.0	0.0	0.0	0.0	0.0	0.0
Via Japanese trading companies												
# of answers	25	12	8	11	12	20	8	12	11	14	4	15
1. JPY	56.0	58.3	37.5	54.5	75.0	45.0	62.5	58.3	72.7	78.6	75.0	86.7
2. USD	44.0	16.7	62.5	45.5	25.0	0.0	0.0	41.7	9.1	21.4	25.0	13.3
3. Euro	0.0	8.3	0.0	0.0	0.0	55.0	25.0	0.0	18.2	0.0	0.0	0.0
4. Importer's currency	–	16.7	0.0	0.0	0.0	–	12.5	0.0	0.0	0.0	0.0	0.0
5. Others	0.0	0.0	0.0	0.0	0.0	0.0	0.0	0.0	0.0	0.0	0.0	0.0

Others

# of answers	30	11	14	10	8	29	15	10	9	14	6	9
1. JPY	43.3	27.3	50.0	80.0	62.5	48.3	40.0	60.0	55.6	71.4	50.0	66.7
2. USD	56.7	54.5	50.0	20.0	37.5	24.1	20.0	30.0	22.2	28.6	33.3	33.3
3. Euro	0.0	0.0	0.0	0.0	0.0	27.6	20.0	10.0	22.2	0.0	0.0	0.0
4. Importer's currency	–	18.2	0.0	0.0	0.0	–	20.0	0.0	0.0	0.0	0.0	0.0
5. Others	0.0	0.0	0.0	0.0	0.0	0.0	0.0	0.0	0.0	0.0	0.0	0.0

Note: The share of invoice currency is obtained by calculating the simple arithmetic average of the main invoice currency by trading partner and by destination country.

Source: Authors' calculation based on the 2009 RIETI Survey.

Table 4.9 Choice of invoice currency by trading partner: Japanese exports to Asian countries

Percentage of number of 'main currency', most frequently used currency in exports from Japan to each destination, over total number of answers

	Destination											
	China	Korea	Taiwan	Hong Kong	Singapore	Thailand	Malaysia	Indonesia	Philippines	Vietnam	India	Mid-East countries
Number of answers	155	131	135	96	93	110	82	77	65	56	65	57
Production Subsidiaries (plants)												
# of answers	93	23	36	10	12	62	35	30	16	17	15	2
1. JPY	51.6	56.5	63.9	20.0	58.3	58.1	51.4	46.7	37.5	29.4	73.3	50.0
2. USD	45.2	30.4	30.6	70.0	41.7	30.6	45.7	43.3	56.3	64.7	20.0	50.0
3. Euro	0.0	0.0	0.0	0.0	0.0	0.0	0.0	0.0	0.0	0.0	0.0	0.0
4. Importer's currency	3.2	13.0	5.6	10.0	0.0	11.3	2.9	10.0	6.3	0.0	6.7	0.0
5. Others	0.0	0.0	0.0	0.0	0.0	0.0	0.0	0.0	0.0	0.0	0.0	0.0
Sales Subsidiaries												
# of answers	75	37	44	53	48	28	14	14	9	9	10	9
1. JPY	42.7	64.9	52.3	32.1	37.5	57.1	57.1	35.7	44.4	77.8	60.0	33.3
2. USD	57.3	29.7	40.9	60.4	54.2	32.1	42.9	57.1	55.6	22.2	30.0	66.7
3. Euro	0.0	0.0	0.0	1.9	0.0	0.0	0.0	0.0	0.0	0.0	10.0	0.0
4. Importer's currency	0.0	5.4	6.8	5.7	8.3	10.7	0.0	7.1	0.0	0.0	0.0	0.0
5. Others	0.0	0.0	0.0	0.0	0.0	0.0	0.0	0.0	0.0	0.0	0.0	0.0

Local agencies (no capital ties)												
# of answers	41	63	65	33	34	31	32	23	26	20	21	25
1. JPY	68.3	73.0	66.2	60.6	85.3	87.1	68.8	69.6	76.9	75.0	71.4	68.0
2. USD	29.3	23.8	32.3	39.4	11.8	12.9	31.3	30.4	23.1	25.0	28.6	32.0
3. Euro	0.0	1.6	1.5	0.0	0.0	0.0	0.0	0.0	0.0	0.0	0.0	0.0
4. Importer's currency	2.4	1.6	0.0	0.0	2.9	0.0	0.0	0.0	0.0	0.0	0.0	0.0
5. Others	0.0	0.0	0.0	0.0	0.0	0.0	0.0	0.0	0.0	0.0	0.0	0.0

Via Japanese trading companies												
# of answers	47	28	29	10	16	21	14	23	16	19	20	26
1. JPY	76.6	82.1	79.3	70.0	68.8	76.2	71.4	82.6	87.5	78.9	90.0	65.4
2. USD	21.3	17.9	20.7	20.0	25.0	23.8	28.6	8.7	12.5	21.1	10.0	30.8
3. Euro	0.0	0.0	0.0	0.0	0.0	0.0	0.0	0.0	0.0	0.0	0.0	3.8
4. Importer's currency	2.1	0.0	0.0	10.0	6.3	0.0	0.0	8.7	0.0	0.0	0.0	0.0
5. Others	0.0	0.0	0.0	0.0	0.0	0.0	0.0	0.0	0.0	0.0	0.0	0.0

Others												
# of answers	39	45	33	20	18	27	24	21	19	18	22	16
1. JPY	56.4	68.9	60.6	45.0	88.9	70.4	62.5	71.4	68.4	72.2	86.4	37.5
2. USD	43.6	28.9	39.4	50.0	11.1	29.6	37.5	28.6	31.6	27.8	13.6	37.5
3. Euro	0.0	0.0	0.0	0.0	0.0	0.0	0.0	0.0	0.0	0.0	0.0	12.5
4. Importer's currency	0.0	2.2	0.0	5.0	0.0	0.0	0.0	0.0	0.0	0.0	0.0	12.5
5. Others	0.0	0.0	0.0	0.0	0.0	0.0	0.0	0.0	0.0	0.0	0.0	0.0

Note: Share of invoice currency is obtained by calculating the simple arithmetic average of the main invoice currency by trading partner and destination country.

Source: Authors' calculation based on the 2009 RIETI Survey.

are invoiced in the UK pound. In intra-firm exports, the importer's currency is chosen only if the export destination is advanced countries, except for exports to sales subsidiaries in Mexico.

Third, the yen is also used in intra-firm exports. In most cases, the yen accounts for the second or third largest share. For example, 21.6 per cent and 24.1 per cent of Japanese exports to production subsidiaries in the US and in the euro area, respectively, are invoiced in the yen. On the other hand, when the export destination is developing countries in Europe including Russia and East European countries, the yen appears to be the most frequently used currency in intra-firm trade, although the number of samples is quite small.

Fourth, the yen is most frequently used in arm's-length exports to local agencies, *Sogo Shosha* and other importers. In exports to local agencies (Table 4.8), for example, the yen accounts for the largest share in 9 out of 12 destinations. In exports to *Sogo Shosha* and other importers, the yen is most frequently chosen as the invoice currency in 10 out of 12 destinations.

Next, Table 4.9 presents the invoicing currency pattern for Japanese exports to Asian countries. First, the yen and US dollar are mainly and almost equally used in both intra-firm and arm's-length trades with Asian countries. In exports to plant subsidiaries, the share of the US dollar surpasses the share of the yen only in 3 out of 12 destinations: Hong Kong, the Philippines and Vietnam. In exports to sales subsidiaries, the share of the US dollar is larger than that of the yen in a half of 12 destinations.

Second, the yen is more frequently used than the US dollar in exports to local agencies in all destinations. Table 4.9 indicates that 61–85 per cent of arm's-length exports to local agencies in Asia are invoiced in the yen. The yen is also the most used currency in exports to *Sogo Shosha* and other importers.

Third, the importer's (Asian) currency is used in intra-firm exports to Asian countries, but at most 13 per cent of exports are invoiced in Asian currencies. In arm's-length exports to Asian countries, the importer's (Asian) currency is seldom used. When importers are local agencies, for example, the local currency is used only in exports to China (2.4 per cent), Korea (1.6 per cent) and Singapore (2.9 per cent).

Result 8: The importer's currency tends to be used in intra-firm trade from Japan to advanced countries/regions. The yen and US dollar are almost equally used in intra-firm trade from Japan to Asian countries.

Result 9: The share of yen invoicing is the largest in arm's-length trades, which are more prevalent in exports to Asia and other developing countries.

The share of US dollar invoicing is the second largest but is much lower than the corresponding share of yen invoicing.

4.2.6   Choice of Invoicing Currency by Production Subsidiaries

The questionnaire survey also provided information on where and in which currency Japanese production subsidiaries export their products. Since Japanese firms have built regional production networks in Asia, such information will reveal firms' invoicing behaviour in production chains, which is a well-known trade pattern in Asia. Table 4.10 summarizes the location of production subsidiaries (plants) of sample firms and, if the production subsidiaries export their products to other countries/regions, the destinations of their exports. In total, 330 sample firms of the 2009 survey have production subsidiaries (plants) in Asian countries, while 76 firms have production subsidiaries in the Americas, 45 in Europe, and 9 in Pacific & Africa. Among the 330 firms that have production subsidiaries in Asia, more than half (184 firms) have the production subsidiaries exporting their goods to other countries/regions and answered regarding the destination of their exports. These numbers show that Japanese production subsidiaries are mainly located in Asian countries/regions and many Asia-based production subsidiaries export their goods to other countries.

The question is how these production subsidiaries in Asia choose an invoice currency for both imports (of parts and semi-finished goods from Japan) and exports (of assembled goods).

Table 4.11 presents the main invoice currency used for Japanese exports to two types of production subsidiaries in Asia in the 2009 Survey. The first type is production subsidiaries, which mainly sell their products to the local market, and the second type is subsidiaries who export their products to other countries. Interestingly, 67 per cent (113 out of 168 firms) of Japanese firms' exports to local sales-oriented production subsidiaries (the first type) are invoiced in yen, but the corresponding share decreases to 51 per cent (88 out of 172 firms) for Japanese exports to the export-oriented production subsidiaries (the second type). On the other hand, the share of US dollar invoicing increases from 27 per cent (45 out of 168 firms) in exports to the first type to 43 per cent (47 out of 172 firms) in exports to the second type. This evidence suggests that yen invoicing is hindered and in turn the US dollar invoicing is promoted if Japanese exports are to export-oriented production subsidiaries.

To understand the difference of invoicing pattern in exports from Japan to two types of production subsidiaries, our focus moves to the invoice currency choice in exports from overseas production subsidiaries. Panels A and B in Table 4.12 report the invoicing pattern of exporting from production

Table 4.10 Export destinations of Japanese overseas production subsidiaries

Country/region where sample firms have subsidiaries (plants)	Number of firms having subsidiaries (plants)	# of firms to answer destination	Export destination							
			Japan	Americas	US	Europe	Euro Area	Asia	China	Pacific & Africa
Americas (total)	**76**	**28**	**6**	**36**	**9**	**9**	**7**	**5**	**2**	**0**
US	49	15	4	19	–	7	5	4	2	0
Canada	6	3	0	3	3	0	0	1	0	0
Mexico	4	3	0	3	2	0	0	0	0	0
Brazil	13	7	2	11	4	2	2	0	0	0
Central & Latin Americas	4	0	0	0	0	0	0	0	0	0
Europe (total)	**45**	**21**	**4**	**5**	**4**	**19**	**9**	**5**	**1**	**1**
Euro Area	25	10	3	3	3	7	–	4	1	1
UK	12	7	1	2	1	5	5	1	0	0
Russia	1	0	0	0	0	0	0	0	0	0
East European countries	7	4	0	0	0	7	4	0	0	0
Pacific & Africa (total)	**9**	**5**	**0**	**2**	**1**	**0**	**0**	**4**	**0**	**3**
Australia	4	3	0	1	0	0	0	4	0	2
New Zealand	3	2	0	1	1	0	0	0	0	1
African countries	2	0	0	0	0	0	0	0	0	0
Asia (total)	**330**	**184**	**103**	**41**	**40**	**33**	**31**	**169**	**19**	**5**
China	85	55	35	17	17	15	14	25	–	0
Korea	19	11	8	2	1	2	1	11	3	0
Taiwan	33	19	7	1	1	1	1	27	8	1
Hong Kong	9	6	4	1	1	2	2	5	3	0
Singapore	14	9	3	3	3	3	3	9	0	1
Thailand	58	33	20	9	9	5	5	29	1	2

Malaysia	33	17	9	1	1	1	1	20	0
Indonesia	30	14	7	2	2	2	1	23	0
Philippines	16	10	5	3	1	1	2	10	0
Vietnam	16	8	5	2	1	1	0	7	0
India	14	1	0	0	0	0	0	1	0
Mid-East countries	3	1	0	0	0	0	0	2	1

Note: Number of firms is reported.

Source: 2009 RIETI Survey.

subsidiaries in China and Thailand to various destinations of final goods. As Table 4.10 shows, China and Thailand are two Asian countries hosting the largest number of overseas production and export bases for Japanese firms. Panel A in Table 4.12 shows, notably, that the US dollar is used most frequently by Japanese production subsidiaries in China. Even in the production subsidiaries' exports to Japan, only one-third (14 out of 35 firms) are invoiced in yen and most of the rest (57 per cent; 20 out of 35) are invoiced in US dollars. For destinations besides Japan, the yen is seldom used. In contrast, the US dollar is the currency used most often in subsidiaries' exports to Asia (83 per cent; 20 out of 24) as well as to the euro area (57 per cent; eight out of 14). A similar pattern of invoice currency choice is also observed for Japanese production subsidiaries in Thailand. In exports from the production subsidiaries to Japan, only a quarter (5 out of 19 firms) are invoiced in yen, while 57 per cent (11 out of 19 firms) are invoiced in US dollars. In exports to Asian countries, more than three-quarters (17 out of 22 firms) are invoiced in US dollars while only one firm uses the yen.

Taking into account the results obtained from both Tables 4.11 and 4.12, we may interpret the invoice currency choice of Japanese production subsidiaries as follows. Japanese firms have a strong tendency to free their production subsidiaries exporting their products to other countries from currency risk exposure by matching the invoice currencies in imports and exports of the production subsidiaries. Japanese firms also tend to concentrate all currency risks in the head office in Japan that has an advantage in managing currency risk. Furthermore, Japanese head offices aim to mitigate all currency exposures by using the same invoice currency, typically US dollars, in both sides of trades with their production subsidiaries. These results are quite consistent with those obtained by our interview analysis in Chapter 3.

Thus, the intra-firm production chain trade by Japanese production subsidiaries is likely to facilitate US dollar invoicing rather than yen invoicing. The growth and deepening of Japanese firms' production networks ironically prevents yen-invoiced trade and supports dollar-invoiced transactions.

Result 10: Japanese production subsidiaries in Asia have a strong tendency to choose US dollar invoicing in their exports to Japan and other countries.

4.3   EMPIRICAL RESULTS

As the previous sections in this chapter show, we obtained detailed information on firm-level invoicing currency choice by destination and

Table 4.11   Main invoice currency used in Japanese exports to production subsidiaries in Asia

'Main currency' = Most frequently used currency in exports from Japan to each destination by each trade channel

'Main Currency'	Asia	Destination										
		China	Hong Kong	Taiwan	Korea	Singapore	Malaysia	Thailand	Indonesia	Philippines	Vietnam	India
Number of responded firms	340	93	8	36	23	14	36	62	30	12	14	12
Exports to Production Subsidiaries (Local Sales Oriented)												
# of answers	168	43	4	17	13	5	18	29	16	5	7	11
1. JPY	113	26	2	12	7	2	11	20	11	4	7	11
2. USD	45	15	2	4	5	3	5	6	4	1	0	0
3. Euro	0	0	0	0	0	0	0	0	0	0	0	0
4. Importer's currency	9	2	0	1	1	0	1	3	1	0	0	0
5. Others	0	0	0	0	0	0	0	0	0	0	0	0
Exports to Production Subsidiaries (Export Oriented)												
# of answers	172	50	4	19	10	9	18	33	14	7	7	1
1. JPY	88	22	4	11	6	7	7	16	3	5	6	1
2. USD	74	27	0	7	2	2	11	13	9	2	1	0
3. Euro	0	0	0	0	0	0	0	0	0	0	0	0
4. Importer's currency	10	1	0	1	2	0	0	4	2	0	0	0
5. Others	0	0	0	0	0	0	0	0	0	0	0	0

Note: Number of answers is reported.

Source: 2009 RIETI Survey.

Table 4.12   Choice of invoice currency used in exports by Japanese production subsidiaries in China and Thailand

Panel A: Invoice currency choice in exports from plants in China

of 'main currency', most frequently used currency in exports from plants in China to each destination / total number of answers

Destination	Japan	US	Canada	Mexico	Brazil	Central & Latin America	Euro Area	UK	Russia	East Europe	Australia	New Zealand	Africa
# of answers	35	17					14		1		1	1	
A. JPY	[14/35]						[1/14]						
B. USD	[20/35]	[17/17]					[8/14]		[1/1]		[1/1]		
C. Euro	[1/35]						[5/14]						
D. Chinese Yuan													
E. Importer's currency													

Destination	Asia	China	Korea	Taiwan	Hong Kong	Singapore	Thailand	Malaysia	Indonesia	Philippines	Vietnam	India	Mid-East Asia
# of answers	24	—	4	4	9	2	1	1	1	1			2
A. JPY	[2/24]	—	[1/4]		[1/9]								
B. USD	[20/24]	—	[3/4]	[3/4]	[7/9]	[2/2]	[1/1]	[1/1]	[1/1]				[2/2]
C. Euro		—											
D. Chinese Yuan	[2/24]	—		[1/4]	[1/9]								
E. Importer's currency		—											

Panel B: Invoice currency choice in exports from plants in Thailand to each destination

of 'main currency', most frequently used currency in exports from plants in Thailand to each destination / total number of answers

Destination	Japan	US	Canada	Mexico	Brazil	Central & Latin America	Euro Area	UK	Russia	East Europe	Australia	New Zealand	Africa	Mid-East Asia
# of answers	19	9					5	1	3	1	2	1		
A. JPY	[5/19]						[1/5]							
B. USD	[11/19]	[9/9]					[2/2]	[1/1]	[1/3]		[2/2]	[1/1]		
C. Euro							[2/2]							
D. Thai Baht	[3/19]								[2/3]	[1/1]				
E. Importer's currency														

Destination	Asia	China	Korea	Taiwan	Hong Kong	Singapore	Thailand	Malaysia	Indonesia	Philippines	Vietnam	India	Mid-East Asia
# of answers	22	1	2	2	4	5	—	1	3	1	2	1	
A. JPY	[1/22]		[1/2]				—						
B. USD	[17/22]	[1/1]	[1/2]	[2/2]	[4/4]	[4/5]	—	[1/1]	[1/3]		[2/2]	[1/1]	
C. Euro							—						
D. Thai Baht	[4/22]					[1/5]	—		[2/3]				
E. Importer's currency							—			[1/1]			

Note: Number of answers is reported.

Source: Authors' calculation based on the 2009 RIETI Survey.

by relation with importers based on the 2009 Survey. Specifically, the 2009 Survey results reveal which currency is used in intra-firm trade, that is, in exports from Japanese head office to sales and production subsidiaries in various destinations. Moreover, we also collect data on the production subsidiaries' invoicing choices for exports to each destination or local sales. It is often pointed out that Japanese overseas production subsidiaries in Asia tend to export finished goods to the US, while intermediate-input goods are procured from Japan and neighbouring economies.

4.3.1 Empirical Methodology

To empirically investigate whether the intra-firm production chain in Asia is considered an important determinant of invoicing currency choices in Japanese exports, Ito et al. (2013) conducted a probit estimation of the following specification to test the firm-level determinants of invoice currency:

$$\Pr(Currency_{i,j,k}) = a_0 + a_1\ Country_{i,j,k} + a_2\ Commodity_{i,j,k}$$
$$+ a_3\ Channel_{i,j,k} + a_4\ Company_{i,j,k} + \varepsilon_{i,j,k}, \qquad (4.1)$$

where the dependent variable takes the value of 1 if the firm i chooses a particular currency, for example the yen, as the 'main invoice currency', the most frequently used currency, in Japanese exports to trading partner k in destination country j, and 0 if the currency is not chosen as the main invoice currency.

The explanatory variables on the right-hand side are categorized into four groups of variables and an error term, $\varepsilon_{i,j,k}$.

Country is a vector of variables to capture the country-specific characteristics in terms of foreign-exchange transactions. First, we test the hypothesis that the higher (lower) the hedging cost between the yen and the importer's currency, the lower (higher) is the share of invoicing in importer's currency. As an explanatory variable, we use a bid–ask spread of outright three-month forward transactions between the yen and the importing country's currency as of April 2009 as a straightforward proxy for the cost of exchange rate hedging. Second, to take into account the effect of access to the multi-currency cash settlement system, we include a dummy variable related to a country's membership in the Continuous Linked Settlement (CLS) Bank.[6] By satisfying criteria such as the deregulation of capital account transactions and the sovereign rating of govern-

---

6   The CLS Bank had 17 currencies in its membership as of 2009, including the currencies

ment bonds, CLS Bank member countries can reduce the cost of foreign exchange settlements by accessing the multi-currency cash settlement system. Thus, we consider a dummy for the CLS Bank membership to be a useful measure of the cost of settlement in the importer's currency. Finally, we use a dummy variable for de facto dollar peg countries as of 2009, which includes China, Taiwan and Hong Kong.

Commodity is a vector of variables to control for commodity/product characteristics. First, to test whether Japanese firms tend to choose yen invoicing for their exports of highly differentiated and strongly competitive goods, we established a dummy variable for differentiated export goods. We identify the sample firm's export products listed in their financial statement and check whether these products conform to Rauch's (1999) index based on SITC (Standard International Trade Classification) Rev.2. Second, we construct a dummy for top-share goods, which is a proxy for the firm's competitiveness in the global market. We check whether the sample firm's export products listed in their financial statement match the global top-share goods listed in *Nihon Shoken Journal* (NSJ). Finally, we use a dummy variable for exports of intermediate goods obtained from our questionnaire survey.

Channel is a vector of variables to differentiate the trade channels by trading partner. We use dummy variables for four different trading partners: production subsidiaries, sales subsidiaries, *Sogo Shosha* (Japanese trading companies) and others, assuming exports to local trading agencies as a benchmark. Both coefficients on dummies for production and sales subsidiaries will show possible differences in currency invoicing decisions in intra-firm exports from those in exports to local trading agencies. In addition, we devise a dummy for production subsidiaries that export their products to other countries. By taking the interaction term between this dummy variable and the dummy for production subsidiaries, we show whether the choice of invoice currency is affected by Japanese exports to production subsidiaries that have a high export propensity. Finally, while both dummies for production subsidiaries and sales subsidiaries are regarded as proxies for intra-firm trade, we additionally set up a dummy for subsidiaries wholly owned by a Japanese head office. By taking the interaction term between this dummy variable and the dummy for production or sales subsidiaries, we will test whether strength of capital ties between the Japanese head office and local subsidiaries affects the currency invoicing decision for Japanese exports.

Company is a vector of variables to control for selected firm

of Japan, US, euro area, UK, Switzerland, Canada, Australia, Singapore, Demark, Sweden, Norway, Hong Kong, New Zealand, South Korea, South Africa, Israel and Mexico.

characteristics. First, the natural log of a firm's consolidated sales is used to control for firm size. We also consider two measures of the firm's capacity to manage exchange rate risk. In the questionnaire survey, we asked whether firms use financial hedging instruments through the foreign exchange market, including forward, currency option and other currency derivatives, and/or operational hedging instrument such as 'marry' and 'netting'. Measures are taken from these survey results. The dummy for financial hedging takes 1 if firms use any hedging tools in the market to manage their exchange rate risk. The dummy for operational hedging takes 1 if firms use operational hedging such as 'marry and netting', by which firms can offset the same amounts of exports and imports denominated in the same currency and minimise the exchange rate risk exposure. By using these dummies, we test whether the sample firm's capacity to manage currency risk affects the choice of invoice currency. Lastly, we include industry dummies to allow for possible differences across 16 industries.

4.3.2   Determinants of Invoicing Currency in Japanese Exports to All Countries

In Table 4.13 we present the results of estimation where exports to all destinations are included in the sample. The dependent variable is the choice of the yen as the main invoice currency in specifications (1) to (4), the US dollar in (5) to (8), and the importer's currency in (9) to (12), respectively. Estimated coefficients are reported as marginal effects. The pseudo R-squared takes values from 0.12 to 0.38.

Let us first look at the estimated coefficients of the explanatory variables included in the *Country* vector. The coefficient of the bid–ask spread is positive and strongly significant in specifications (1) to (4) in the yen invoicing regression, and negative and strongly significant in (5) to (12) in the dollar invoicing regression and the importer's currency invoicing regression. These results clearly show that an increase in hedging costs of the importer's currency tends to promote yen invoicing and to lower the US dollar invoicing and importer's currency invoicing. The coefficient of the dummy for multi-currency cash settlement is also statistically significant in all specifications. Among the CLS Bank member countries, costs of settlements by foreign currencies can be reduced by fully utilizing the multi-currency cash settlement system, which is likely to promote US dollar invoicing and importer's currency invoicing. Interestingly, the estimated coefficient (0.18) in the importer's currency regression is larger than that in the US dollar invoicing regression (0.04), which suggests that the participation in the multi-currency cash settlement system is likely to increase importer's currency invoicing rather than US dollar invoicing.

Table 4.13   Determinants of invoice currency in exports to all countries/region

Dependent variable	Prob(Yen = 1)				Prob(US dollar = 1)				Prob(importer's currency = 1)			
Number of Observations	2261				2261				2263			
Number of samples that dependent variable =1	1222				816				394			
	(1)	(2)	(3)	(4)	(5)	(6)	(7)	(8)	(9)	(10)	(11)	(12)
Country characteristics												
Bid–ask spread (vis-à-vis JPY, 3 months)	0.256*** (0.032)	0.259*** (0.032)	0.250*** (0.033)	0.264*** (0.033)	−0.122*** (0.030)	−0.124*** (0.030)	−0.120*** (0.031)	−0.126*** (0.031)	−0.191*** (0.022)	−0.191*** (0.022)	−0.191*** (0.022)	−0.191*** (0.022)
Dummy for multi-currency cash settlement	−0.199*** (0.024)	−0.201*** (0.024)	−0.191*** (0.024)	−0.201*** (0.024)	0.046** (0.037)	0.048** (0.023)	0.044* (0.023)	0.046** (0.023)	0.189*** (0.017)	0.189*** (0.017)	0.189*** (0.017)	0.189*** (0.017)
Dummy for US dollar peg countries/region	0.042 (0.028)	0.044 (0.028)	0.047 (0.028)	0.047 (0.029)	0.037 (0.027)	0.035 (0.027)	0.034 (0.027)	0.034 (0.027)	−0.108*** (0.011)	−0.108*** (0.011)	−0.109*** (0.011)	−0.108*** (0.011)
Commodity/Product characteristics												
Dummy for differentiated goods (Rauch)	0.329*** (0.038)	0.330*** (0.038)	0.329*** (0.038)	0.313*** (0.039)	−0.310*** (0.041)	−0.310*** (0.041)	−0.310*** (0.041)	−0.295*** (0.0422)	−0.016 (0.022)	−0.017 (0.022)	−0.017 (0.023)	−0.015 (0.022)

Table 4.13 (continued)

Dependent variable	Prob(Yen = 1)				Prob(US dollar = 1)				Prob(importer's currency = 1)			
	(1)	(2)	(3)	(4)	(5)	(6)	(7)	(8)	(9)	(10)	(11)	(12)
Number of Observations	2261				2261				2263			
Number of samples that dependent variable =1	1222				816				394			
Dummy for world's top share goods	0.093** (0.042)	0.098** (0.042)	0.114*** (0.042)	0.084* (0.043)	-0.051 (0.037)	-0.055 (0.037)	-0.061 (0.037)	-0.039 (0.038)	-0.032* (0.013)	-0.032* (0.013)	-0.032* (0.013)	-0.031* (0.013)
Dummy for intermediate goods	-0.112*** (0.029)	-0.108*** (0.029)	-0.104*** (0.029)	-0.101*** (0.029)	0.121*** (0.028)	0.117*** (0.028)	0.116*** (0.028)	0.112*** (0.028)	0.013 (0.014)	0.013 (0.014)	0.012 (0.014)	0.012 (0.014)
Trade channel dummies												
Export to Product subsidiaries	-0.170*** (0.039)	-0.094** (0.046)	-0.053 (0.051)	-0.096** (0.046)	0.098*** (0.038)	0.037 (0.044)	0.020 (0.048)	0.041 (0.044)	0.148*** (0.035)	0.141*** (0.038)	0.131*** (0.042)	0.139*** (0.038)
*Export to other countries		-0.162*** (0.049)	-0.149*** (0.050)	-0.158*** (0.049)		0.126*** (0.049)	0.120** (0.049)	0.116** (0.049)		0.009 (0.023)	0.007 (0.023)	0.010 (0.024)
*Export to 100% subsidiaries			-0.101** (0.051)				0.040 (0.048)				0.012 (0.025)	

122

Export to Sales subsidiaries	-0.290*** (0.031)	-0.293*** (0.172)	-0.239*** (0.045)	-0.286*** (0.031)	0.219*** (0.032)	0.220*** (0.032)	0.194*** (0.045)	0.213*** (0.032)	0.152*** (0.027)	0.152*** (0.027)	0.161*** (0.038)	0.152*** (0.027)
*Export to 100% subsidiaries		-0.086* (0.050)					0.038 (0.045)				-0.006 (0.019)	
Export via *Sogo Shosha*	0.171*** (0.037)	0.172*** (0.037)	0.173*** (0.037)	0.166*** (0.038)	-0.151*** (0.033)	-0.151*** (0.033)	-0.151*** (0.033)	-0.145*** (0.033)	-0.008 (0.018)	-0.008 (0.018)	-0.008 (0.018)	-0.009 (0.018)
Export to Other customers	-0.000 (0.036)	-0.000 (0.036)	-0.001 (0.036)	-0.002 (0.037)	0.029 (0.035)	0.029 (0.035)	0.029 (0.035)	0.034 (0.035)	-0.019 (0.016)	-0.019 (0.016)	-0.019 (0.016)	-0.019 (0.016)
Company characteristics												
Log of Consolidated Sales	-0.026*** (0.007)	-0.024*** (0.007)	-0.026*** (0.007)	-0.000 (0.008)	0.013** (0.006)	0.012* (0.006)	0.012* (0.006)	-0.010 (0.007)	-0.003 (0.003)	-0.003 (0.003)	-0.003 (0.003)	-0.003 (0.003)
Dummy for company engaging financial hedging activities				-0.067** (0.029)				0.061** (0.026)				0.006 (0.012)
Dummy for company engaging operational headging activities				-0.146*** (0.027)				0.151*** (0.025)				-0.002 (0.012)

Table 4.13 (continued)

Dependent variable	Prob(Yen = 1)				Prob(US dollar = 1)				Prob(importer's currency = 1)			
Number of Observations	2261				2261				2263			
Number of samples that dependent variable =1	1222				816				394			
	(1)	(2)	(3)	(4)	(5)	(6)	(7)	(8)	(9)	(10)	(11)	(12)
Industry Dummy												
Foods	-0.345*** (0.096)	-0.339*** (0.099)	-0.331*** (0.110)	-0.349*** (0.095)	0.447*** (0.094)	0.439*** (0.096)	0.437*** (0.096)	0.454*** (0.092)	-0.034 (0.031)	-0.034 (0.031)	-0.035 (0.030)	-0.035 (0.030)
Textiles & Apparel	-0.121 (0.076)	-0.103 (0.077)	-0.095 (0.077)	-0.121 (0.078)	0.183** (0.076)	0.168** (0.076)	0.165** (0.076)	0.186** (0.078)	-0.045* (0.016)	-0.046* (0.015)	-0.046* (0.013)	-0.047* (0.015)
Chemicals	-0.087* (0.049)	-0.068 (0.049)	-0.060 (0.049)	-0.099** (0.049)	0.118** (0.048)	0.104** (0.048)	0.101** (0.049)	0.141*** (0.049)	-0.045*** (0.013)	-0.045*** (0.013)	-0.046*** (0.013)	-0.046*** (0.013)
Pharmaceuticals	-0.309*** (0.087)	-0.295*** (0.090)	-0.277*** (0.093)	-0.255** (0.097)	0.324*** (0.099)	0.311*** (0.101)	0.303*** (0.102)	0.279*** (0.105)	0.005 (0.054)	0.003 (0.053)	0.001 (0.052)	0.001 (0.052)
Oil & Coal									-0.022 (0.095)	-0.022 (0.094)	-0.023 (0.093)	-0.024 (0.092)
Rubber Products	-0.141 (0.097)	-0.117 (0.099)	-0.114 (0.099)	-0.170* (0.097)	0.210** (0.098)	0.189* (0.099)	0.188* (0.099)	0.258*** (0.098)	-0.023 (0.032)	-0.024 (0.032)	-0.023 (0.032)	-0.026 (0.031)
Glass & Ceramics	-0.132 (0.081)	-0.107 (0.083)	-0.099 (0.083)	-0.127 (0.083)	0.173* (0.085)	0.152* (0.085)	0.149* (0.086)	0.185** (0.087)	-0.038 (0.020)	-0.039 (0.019)	-0.039 (0.019)	-0.040 (0.019)

Steel Products	-0.041 (0.147)	-0.027 (0.146)	-0.022 (0.146)	-0.136 (0.145)	0.086 (0.145)	0.077 (0.145)	0.075 (0.145)	0.195 (0.149)	-0.025 (0.047)	-0.025 (0.047)	-0.025 (0.047)	-0.025 (0.047)
Nonferrous Metals	-0.085 (0.101)	-0.069 (0.101)	-0.065 (0.101)	-0.134 (0.100)	0.145 (0.102)	0.133 (0.102)	0.131 (0.102)	0.206** (0.103)	0.007 (0.051)	0.006 (0.050)	0.005 (0.050)	0.004 (0.050)
Metal Products	0.167** (0.060)	0.184*** (0.059)	0.182*** (0.060)	0.096 (0.068)	-0.025 (0.063)	-0.039 (0.062)	-0.038 (0.062)	0.063 (0.071)	-0.064*** (0.008)	-0.064*** (0.008)	-0.064*** (0.008)	-0.064*** (0.008)
Machinery	0.038 (0.045)	0.059 (0.045)	0.067 (0.045)	0.050 (0.046)	-0.034 (0.042)	-0.050 (0.042)	-0.053 (0.042)	-0.037 (0.044)	-0.027* (0.014)	-0.028* (0.014)	-0.029* (0.014)	-0.030* (0.015)
Electrical Machinery	-0.146*** (0.042)	-0.119*** (0.043)	-0.109*** (0.044)	-0.086* (0.044)	0.213*** (0.042)	0.191*** (0.043)	0.187*** (0.043)	0.161*** (0.043)	-0.056*** (0.013)	-0.057*** (0.013)	-0.058*** (0.013)	-0.058*** (0.013)
Precision Instruments	0.017 (0.060)	0.044 (0.060)	0.045 (0.060)	0.028 (0.060)	0.104* (0.060)	0.082 (0.060)	0.082 (0.061)	0.109* (0.061)	-0.066*** (0.008)	-0.066*** (0.008)	-0.066*** (0.008)	-0.066*** (0.008)
Other Products	-0.233*** (0.072)	-0.219*** (0.073)	-0.210*** (0.074)	-0.192** (0.076)	0.259*** (0.076)	0.246*** (0.077)	0.241*** (0.077)	0.217*** (0.079)	-0.018 (0.026)	-0.019 (0.026)	-0.019 (0.026)	-0.020 (0.026)
Pseudo R-squared	0.176	0.179	0.181	0.190	0.125	0.127	0.127	0.141	0.384	0.384	0.385	0.384

Notes:
1. Dependent variable: Probability of the choice of invoice currency in Japan's exports to each destination by trade channel.
2. Destination: Advanced economies (US, Canada, Euro area, UK, and Australia) and Asian countries (China, Hong Kong, Taiwan, Korea, Philippines, Vietnam, Singapore, Thailand, Malaysia, Indonesia, and India).
3. Empirical method is the Probit estimation. The marginal effect and the standard errors (in parentheses) are reported in each column.
4. ***, **, and * denote the 1%, 5% and 10% significance level, respectively.

The dummy for US dollar peg country/region has negative and statistically significant coefficients in the importer's currency invoicing regression, while it has positive but insignificant coefficients in yen invoicing and US dollar invoicing regressions.

Second, among explanatory variables included in the *Commodity* vector, coefficients of both dummies for the differentiated goods (Rauch) and the world's top share goods are positive and strongly significant in the yen invoicing regression. This result is consistent with the existing literature that has found a positive impact of product differentiation and the world market share on the home currency invoicing. The dummy for intermediate goods has negative impacts on yen invoicing and positive impacts on dollar invoicing with a strongly significant level, which suggests that exports of intermediate goods are different from those of final goods in terms of currency invoicing decision.

Third, regarding the trading partner dummies in the *Channel* vector, in the specification without any interaction terms, (1), (5) and (9), coefficients of both dummies for export to product subsidiaries and sales subsidiaries are negative and highly significant in the yen invoicing regression, while positive and strongly significant in the dollar invoicing and importer's currency invoicing regressions. Estimated coefficients calculated as marginal effects show that exports to production subsidiaries and exports to sales subsidiaries decrease the probability of yen invoicing by 17 per cent and 29 per cent, respectively, as compared to exports to local trading agencies. In contrast, the intra-firm exports significantly promote dollar invoicing and importer's currency invoicing. Among the arm's-length trade, coefficients of exports via *Sogo Shosha* are positive and statistically significant in the yen invoicing regression and significantly negative in the dollar invoicing regression, while having no significant impact on importer's currency invoicing. Thus, exports via *Sogo Shosha* increase the probability of yen invoicing by 29 per cent and decrease that of dollar invoicing by 15 per cent, respectively, as compared to the exports to local trading agencies. These results strongly suggest that invoicing choice depends on whether it is intra-firm trade or arm's-length trade.

For a further check on significant difference in invoicing choice between intra-firm trade and arm's-length trade, we focus on two kinds of interaction terms related to intra-firm trade. First, by using the interaction term between the dummy for subsidiaries exporting to other country and the share of exports to production subsidiaries, we can make a distinction in the invoicing choice between Japanese exports to the local sales-oriented production subsidiaries and those to the export-oriented production subsidiaries. The interaction term takes negative and highly significant coefficient in the yen invoicing regression in (2) and significantly positive coefficient in the dollar invoicing regression in (6), while positive but insignificant coefficient in the importer's currency regression in (10). This result shows that the yen is less used for trade invoicing if Japanese firms export their products to overseas production subsidiaries that have a high export propensity. Second, by including the interaction term between the dummy for subsidiaries wholly owned by Japanese head office and the dummy for intra-firm exports, we can test whether close capital ties affect the choice of invoice currency. The estimated coefficients are negative and statistically significant only in the yen invoicing regression in (3). These additional results provide strong evidence that the invoicing choice depends significantly on the trade channel and distinction between intra-firm trade and arm's-length trade.

Finally, among firm characteristics variables included in the *Company* vector, the firm size measured by the natural log of total consolidated sales is negative and statistically significant at the 1 per cent level in the yen-invoicing regression in (1)–(3), and positive and significant at the 5 per cent or 10 per cent level in the dollar-invoicing regression in (5)–(7) after controlling for the industry dummies taking the transportation machinery as a benchmark. This result indicates that an increase in the firm size in terms of consolidated sales lowers yen-invoicing exports and increases dollar-invoicing exports. We also include two measures of firm's capacity to manage exchange rate risk in the specifications (4), (8) and (12). Both financial hedging and operational hedging dummies have significantly negative coefficients in the yen-invoicing regression and significantly positive coefficients in the dollar-invoicing regression. Interestingly, coefficients of the natural log of consolidated sales are insignificant if two measures of exchange rate management are included, which suggests that large-size firms with the capacity to use various hedging instruments are more likely to choose dollar invoicing rather than yen invoicing. Thus, in light of exchange rate risk management, the firm size does matter in the choice of invoice currency.

4.3.3 Determinants of Invoicing Currency in Japanese Exports to Advanced and Asian Countries

We also run the probit estimation for two sub-samples: the first sub-sample covers Japanese exports to five advanced economies that have international currencies with full convertibility, and the second one exports to all Asian countries. The estimated results using sub-samples enable us to show marked differences in invoicing decision between the above two destinations.

First, the coefficient of the world top share dummy is highly significant in exports to advanced economies (in (1)–(6)) but insignificant in exports

Table 4.14 Determinants of invoice currency in exports to advanced economies and Asian countries

Export destination	Advanced economies						Asian countries					
Dependent variable	Prob(Yen = 1)		Prob(US dollar = 1)		Prob(importer's currency = 1)		Prob(Yen = 1)		Prob (US dollar = 1)		Prob(importer's currency = 1)	
Number of Observations	648		653		650		1608		1608		1445	
Number of samples that dependent variable =1	214		269		345		1008		547		49	
	(1)	(2)	(3)	(4)	(5)	(6)	(7)	(8)	(9)	(10)	(11)	(12)
Country characteristics												
Bid–ask spread (vis-a-vis JPY, 3 months)	1.287*** (0.447)	1.324*** (0.449)	−3.305*** (0.494)	−3.343*** (0.497)	−5.579*** (0.584)	−5.611*** (0.587)	0.084** (0.040)	0.087** (0.041)	−0.092** (0.040)	−0.094** (0.040)	0.001 (0.008)	0.001 (0.007)
Dummy for multi-currency cash settlement							−0.061* (0.033)	−0.056* (0.034)	0.033 (0.032)	0.028 (0.032)	0.021** (0.010)	0.021** (0.010)
Dummy for US dollar peg countries/ region							−0.050 (0.031)	−0.049 (0.031)	0.052* (0.030)	0.051* (0.030)	−0.003 (0.006)	−0.003 (0.006)
Commodity/Product characteristics												
Dummy for differentiated goods (Rauch)	0.106 (0.064)	0.102 (0.065)	−0.160** (0.079)	−0.161** (−.079)	−0.015 (0.086)	−0.005 (0.086)	0.402*** (0.047)	0.384*** (0.048)	−0.393*** (0.049)	−0.368*** (0.051)	0.008 (0.010)	0.005 (0.011)

	(1)	(2)	(3)	(4)	(5)	(6)	(7)	(8)	(9)	(10)	(11)	(12)
Dummy for world's top share goods	0.266*** (0.086)	0.267*** (0.088)	-0.133* (0.069)	-0.132* (0.070)	-0.211** (0.079)	-0.192** (0.083)	0.037 (0.046)	0.026 (0.047)	-0.030 (0.043)	-0.014 (0.045)	-0.003 (0.009)	-0.005 (0.008)
Dummy for intermediate goods	-0.099* (0.048)	-0.100* (0.048)	0.128** (0.056)	0.130** (0.056)	0.016 (0.061)	0.012 (0.062)	-0.101*** (0.033)	-0.083** (0.033)	0.107*** (0.032)	0.091*** (0.033)	-0.001 (0.006)	-0.007 (0.006)
Trade channel dummies												
Export to Product subsidiaries	-0.142** (0.058)	-0.109 (0.071)	0.039 (0.079)	0.006 (0.088)	0.192** (0.077)	0.184** (0.088)	-0.148*** (0.045)	-0.071 (0.053)	0.091** (0.044)	0.026 (0.051)	0.083*** (0.037)	0.062*** (0.034)
*Export to other countries		-0.094 (0.092)		0.088 (0.111)		-0.011 (0.121)		-0.166*** (0.057)		0.136** (0.057)		0.017 (0.016)
Export to Sales subsidiaries	-0.311*** (0.043)	-0.308*** (0.043)	0.194*** (0.058)	0.189*** (0.059)	0.328*** (0.056)	0.319*** (0.057)	-0.239*** (0.040)	-0.237*** (0.041)	0.189*** (0.040)	0.187*** (0.041)	0.064*** (0.021)	0.067*** (0.030)
Export via *Sogo Shosha*	0.213*** (0.075)	0.209*** (0.075)	-0.167** (0.069)	-0.160** (0.070)	-0.163** (0.079)	-0.168** (0.079)	0.159*** (0.039)	0.155*** (0.040)	-0.161*** (0.036)	-0.157*** (0.036)	0.020 (0.021)	0.020 (0.021)
Export to Other customers	0.040 (0.062)	0.043 (0.063)	0.021 (0.070)	0.019 (0.070)	-0.142* (0.074)	-0.149** (0.074)	-0.025 (0.008)	-0.020 (0.042)	0.026 (0.041)	0.037 (0.041)	-0.003 (0.012)	-0.002 (0.012)
Company characteristics												
Log of Consolidated Sales	-0.036*** (0.012)	-0.028** (0.014)	0.002 (0.013)	-0.006 (0.015)	0.023 (0.014)	0.015 (0.016)	-0.025*** (0.008)	0.005 (0.009)	0.027*** (0.007)	-0.004 (0.009)	-0.001 (0.001)	-0.000 (0.002)
Dummy for company engaging financial hedging activities		-0.012 (0.049)		-0.003 (0.053)		0.073 (0.058)		-0.081** (0.032)		0.100*** (0.030)		-0.008 (0.008)

Table 4.14 (continued)

Export destination	Advanced economies						Asian countries					
Dependent variable	Prob(Yen = 1)		Prob(US dollar = 1)		Prob(importer's currency = 1)		Prob(Yen = 1)		Prob (US dollar = 1)		Prob(importer's currency = 1)	
Number of Observations	648		653		650		1608		1608		1445	
Number of samples that dependent variable =1	214		269		345		1008		547		49	
	(1)	(2)	(3)	(4)	(5)	(6)	(7)	(8)	(9)	(10)	(11)	(12)
Dummy for company engaging operational hedging activities		−0.047 (0.046)		0.080* (0.048)		0.012 (0.053)		−0.178*** (0.030)		0.184*** (0.030)		−0.004 (0.006)
Industry Dummy												
Foods	−0.078 (0.189)	−0.088 (0.186)	0.141 (0.223)	0.164 (0.220)	−0.043 (0.223)	−0.059 (0.223)	−0.410*** (0.123)	−0.405*** (0.124)	0.538*** (0.096)	0.538*** (0.097)		
Textiles & Apparel	−0.066 (0.110)	−0.058 (0.113)	0.028 (0.137)	0.027 (0.138)	0.022 (0.152)	0.001 (0.154)	−0.172 (0.093)	−0.185** (0.095)	0.300*** (0.092)	0.317*** (0.094)	−0.014 (0.005)	−0.014 (0.005)
Chemicals	−0.164** (0.064)	−0.160** (0.065)	0.014 (0.089)	0.017 (0.089)	0.148 (0.092)	0.141 (0.093)	−0.073 (0.057)	−0.102* (0.059)	0.207*** (0.061)	0.250*** (0.062)	−0.024*** (0.006)	−0.025*** (0.006)
Pharmaceuticals	0.063 (0.229)	0.090 (0.232)	−0.214 (0.176)	−0.209 (0.178)	0.029 (0.242)	0.003 (0.245)	−0.401*** (0.101)	−0.336*** (0.115)	0.484*** (0.092)	0.423*** (0.108)	−0.008 (0.011)	−0.006 (0.012)

	(1)	(2)	(3)	(4)	(5)	(6)	(7)	(8)	(9)	(10)	(11)	(12)
Oil & Coal					0.055 (0.596)	0.069 (0.594)						
Rubber Products			0.290 (0.242)	0.304 (0.243)			−0.130 (0.109)	−0.184* (0.111)	0.256** (0.110)	0.320*** (0.108)	−0.014 (0.004)	−0.014 (0.004)
Glass & Ceramics	−0.074 (0.112)	−0.067 (0.116)	−0.101 (0.144)	−0.089 (0.148)	0.157 (0.140)	0.140 (0.145)	−0.179 (0.109)	−0.183* (0.104)	0.334*** (0.098)	0.344*** (0.100)		
Steel Products	0.164 (0.389)	0.149 (0.391)	−0.028 (0.373)	−0.008 (0.383)	−0.181 (0.367)	−0.144 (0.384)	−0.041 (0.158)	−0.177 (0.166)	0.109 (0.162)	0.277* (0.164)	0.003 (0.032)	−0.002 (0.022)
Nonferrous Metals	−0.255** (0.060)	−0.256** (0.055)	−0.139 (0.220)	0.158 (0.221)	0.375* (0.120)	0.373* (0.122)	0.024 (0.105)	−0.040 (0.114)	0.090 (0.116)	0.170 (0.122)	−0.007 (0.014)	−0.018*** (0.005)
Metal Products	0.179 (0.127)	0.156 (0.131)	−0.085 (0.115)	−0.052 (0.123)	−0.252** (0.113)	−0.235* (0.120)	0.0133* (0.063)	0.045 (0.077)	0.013 (0.077)	0.139 (0.090)		
Machinery	−0.131** (0.060)	−0.125* (0.067)	−0.034 (0.077)	−0.031 (0.080)	0.169*** (0.079)	0.151* (0.083)	0.115** (0.048)	0.125** (0.049)	−0.023 (0.054)	−0.032 (0.055)	−0.018*** (0.006)	−0.019*** (0.005)
Electrical Machinery	−0.095 (0.064)	−0.076 (0.271)	0.092 (0.076)	0.073 (0.077)	−0.007 (0.081)	−0.027 (−.083)	−0.177*** (0.051)	−0.107** (0.052)	0.300*** (0.053)	0.231*** (0.055)	−0.027*** (0.007)	−0.026*** (0.007)
Precision Instruments	0.137 (0.113)	0.139 (0.115)	0.023 (0.113)	0.036 (0.115)	−0.251** (0.107)	−0.263** (0.107)	−0.034 (0.069)	−0.026 (0.069)	0.183** (0.074)	0.182** (0.076)	−0.019*** (0.004)	−0.018*** (0.004)
Other Products	−0.259*** (0.046)	−0.254*** (0.049)	0.181 (0.136)	0.160 (0.140)	0.287** (0.109)	0.269* (0.115)	−0.180* (0.096)	−0.131 (0.097)	0.346*** (0.092)	0.303*** (0.097)		
Pseudo R-squared	0.180	0.183	0.132	0.136	0.261	0.263	0.161	0.184	0.167	0.195	0.166	0.175

Notes:

1. Dependent variable: Probability of the choice of invoice currency in Japan's exports to each destination by trade channel.
2. Destination: Advanced economies (US, Canada, Euro area, UK, and Australia) and Asian countries (China, Hong Kong, Taiwan, Korea, Philippines, Vietnam, Singapore, Thailand, Malaysia, Indonesia, and India).
3. Empirical method is the Probit estimation. The marginal effect and the standard errors (in parentheses) are reported in each column.
4. ***, **, and * denote the 1%, 5% and 10% significance level, respectively.

to Asian countries (in (7)–(12)). The export competitiveness with a large market share is clearly an important determinant of invoicing choice in exports to advanced countries, but such strong competitiveness does not necessarily affect the choice of currency invoicing in exports to Asian countries.

Second, the interaction term between the dummy for export to other countries and the dummy for export to production subsidiaries does not show any significant coefficients in exports to advanced economies, but negative and significant coefficients in exports to Asian countries. Moreover, when including the above interaction term in exports to Asian countries (in (8) and (10)), the dummy for exports to production subsidiaries becomes insignificant in both the yen-invoicing regression and the dollar-invoicing regression, which indicates that Japanese exporters tend to lower (increase) yen- (dollar-) invoicing transactions only in exports to the export-oriented production subsidiaries, which is consistent with our findings from Tables 4.11 and 4.12. Thus, the Japanese production network built in Asia, characterized by the production chain trades by Japanese production subsidiaries, tends to lower the yen-invoiced transactions, given that exports of production subsidiaries in Asia are typically invoiced in US dollars as shown in Tables 4.11 and 4.12.

Finally, coefficients of both financial hedging and operational hedging dummies are insignificant in most exports to advanced economies (in (2), (4) and (6), but coefficients of two dummies are statistically significant in exports to Asian countries in both yen- and dollar-invoicing regressions (in (8) and (10)). This evidence suggests that hedging activities play a more important role in the invoicing choice of Japanese exports to Asian countries, mainly due to the relatively large currency risk in trade with Asian countries.

4.4   CONCLUSION

By conducting a large-scale questionnaire survey covering Japanese manufacturing firms listed in Japan-based stock exchanges, detailed information is presented on firm-level invoicing choices by destination and type of trading partner, with a particular emphasis on the difference between arm's-length and intra-firm trades. We have also shown the results of the cross-section regression analysis investigating the determinants of Japanese export firms' choice of invoice currency. We have found that a firm's invoicing choice is strongly influenced by whether the trade is intra-firm or arm's-length. While yen-denominated invoicing tends to be chosen in arm's-length trades, there is a strong tendency for the importer's currency to be used when invoicing intra-firm trade. In exports to Asian subsidiaries, the US dollar is widely used as an invoicing currency. We have also revealed that the firm size does affect invoice currency choice; the larger (smaller) the firm's size, the more likely it is to conduct intra-firm (arm's-length) trade. Moreover, growing and deepening regional production networks in Asia are likely to discourage yen-invoiced transactions even by Japanese firms. Japanese production subsidiaries that export finished goods to the rest of the world tend to choose US dollar-invoiced transactions for their imports of semi-finished goods from their Japanese parent.

A few policy implications emerge from results obtained in this analysis. First, if Japanese exporters wish to increase the share of yen-invoiced trades to avoid currency risk, then developing and concentrating in globally competitive goods with high market shares is important. Second, it may be rational to expect that large parent firms in Japan with diversified export destinations to manage global currency risk, rather than having production or sales subsidiaries abroad, manage their own currency risk individually. Hence, dollar-invoiced trade between the parent and subsidiaries seems rational. Given the globalized trades with a cross-border supply chain, it is unlikely that yen-invoiced trade transactions will increase in the future.

5. Exchange rate risk management in Japanese firms

5.1 INTRODUCTION

Volatile foreign exchange rate movements often exert a large influence on both the business performance of globally active firms in the short term as well as their corporate strategies, including the placement of production bases in the medium to long term. The degree of these influences may depend on individual firms' exchange rate risk management. It is said that firms use a combination of financial and operational hedges to manage their currency exposure. While firms implement financial hedges to hedge their currency exposure using foreign exchange derivatives in foreign exchange markets, operational hedges are conducted through the operational set-up within the firm and often used among a firm's international subsidiaries to reduce their foreign exchange exposure. With the development over recent decades of sophisticated financial hedge techniques in foreign exchange markets, such as forward contracts, currency swaps and currency options, firms can hedge their currency exposure effectively. However, these transactions can only ensure a certain amount of earnings in terms of the home currency in a certain period. Firms cannot fully avoid the influence of long-term appreciation of the home currency itself. For example, in response to the yen's appreciation in 1995, Japanese exporting firms increasingly chose to transfer their production bases overseas or increased the capacity of existing overseas bases and the share of imported components from overseas. They adopted such an operational hedging structure to avoid the negative effect caused by the yen's appreciation.

A strong currency can also quickly turn into an economic and political issue in countries having massive export sectors, such as Japan and other East Asian countries, because many Asian export firms invoice their exports in US dollars. A stronger home currency reduces overseas sales income of exporting firms when their foreign currency earnings are converted into the home currency. If their exports are invoiced in the home currency, their business performance will not be affected by currency appreciation, at least in the short run. As a consequence, the choice of invoicing currency itself is strongly related to the choice of exchange rate risk management tools.

Furthermore, whether firms can make their price revisions in response to foreign exchange fluctuations (exchange rate pass-through) and how frequently they can do so are also related to their exchange rate risk management. If firms have a sufficiently competitive product and can, therefore, always revise their prices in response to the yen's appreciation to maintain constant earnings, then exchange rate fluctuations will not have any severe impact on their performance, at least within a certain period while trading volumes do not change. Accordingly, the effectiveness of exchange risk management, the choice of invoicing currency and the decision regarding the exchange rate pass-through are interdependent.

This chapter presents new findings on Japanese firms' exchange rate risk management approaches based on the questionnaire survey presented in Chapter 4.[1] The questionnaire survey (hereafter, 2009 RIETI Survey) offers rich information not only on the firms' foreign exchange rate risk management but also on the firms' choice of invoicing currency and price revision (pass-through) strategy. The survey results are classified by industry and by firm size using the annual financial reports of sample firms, so that we can illustrate our new evidence for Japanese firms' exchange rate risk management, such as the use of financial and operational hedging and price revision in tandem. Our analysis shows how Japanese firms combine three different tools of exchange rate risk management, such as operational hedging, financial hedging and exchange rate pass-through, under their own choice of invoicing currency to mitigate the influence of exchange rate risk. Given Japanese firms' growing regional production networks, our findings based on the questionnaire surveys will have important implications for both government and firms to consider a more suitable exchange rate policy and effective exchange rate risk management under current volatile exchange rate markets.

There are five sections in this chapter. Section 5.2 summarizes the methodologies of exchange rate risk management and overviews the foreign exchange market condition presented by the BIS quarterly survey. Section 5.3 describes the characteristics of Japanese firms' exchange rate risk management approaches from the 2009 RIETI Survey results. Section 5.4 conducts an empirical analysis to investigate the relation between each risk management tool, including the choice of invoice currency and price revision strategy (pass-through). Section 5.5 concludes the chapter.

---

[1] This questionnaire survey was conducted by the Research Institute of Economy, Trade and Industry (RIETI) in October to November 2009.

5.2 VARIETY OF EXCHANGE RATE RISK MANAGEMENT

5.2.1 Types of Exchange Rate

Firms that use foreign currency-denominated transactions face a foreign exchange rate risk. Exchange rate risk is defined as the variability of a firm's value as a result of unpredictable exchange rate changes. To measure and manage this foreign exchange rate risk, we need to identify the types of risks to which a firm is exposed. According to many previous studies, such as Shapiro (1996), Hakala and Wystup (2002) and Döhring (2008), we can consider the following three main types of exchange rate risk:

1. Transaction risk: transaction risk is based on actual transactions. It deals with the effect of exchange rate moves on transactional account exposure related to receivables (export contracts), payables (import contracts) or repatriation of dividends. An exchange rate change in the denomination currency of the above contracts affects the receivable or payable amounts in terms of the home currency, which will result in a transaction risk to the firm directly. Firms often try to hedge their transaction risk by using financial derivatives in the foreign exchange market. In this study, we basically focus on this risk as an exchange rate risk management tool.
2. Translation risk: in contrast to transaction risk, translation risk usually involves no actual cash flow. A firm's translation exposure is the extent to which its financial reporting is affected by exchange rate movements. All firms must generally prepare financial statements for reporting purposes. Multinational firms need to translate their foreign assets and liabilities or financial statements of foreign subsidiaries from the foreign to home currency as part of their consolidation accounting process. Although a translation exposure may not affect a firm's cash flows, it could sometimes have a significant impact on a firm's reported earnings and, therefore, its stock price. The greater the proportion of asset, liability equity classes denominated in a foreign currency, the greater is the translation risk.
3. Economic risk: economic risk reflects the risk from exchange rate movements to the present value assigned to the firm's future operating cash flows. In other words, economic risk concerns the effect of exchange rate changes on revenues and operating expenses. For example, if a firm has foreign subsidiaries, its market value is influenced by unexpected exchange rate fluctuations. Such exchange rate adjustments may severely affect the firm's market share with regard to

Hedging Instruments	Financial Hedges		Operational Hedges		Choice of Invoice Currency		Pricing Policy (Pass through)
Classification in Financial Statements	Derivative Hedges	Natural Hedges		+	**Home currency (yen) or US dollar**	+	Yes/No
Examples	**Forward Options** Others	Foreign Currency Debt	Overseas Diversification Operational matching of revenues and expenditure **(marry/netting)**				

Note: The section on 'Hedging instruments' is from Döhring (2008).

Figure 5.1   Concept of exchange rate risk management

its global competitors, its future cash flows and, ultimately, its value. Economic risk is usually applied to the present value of future cash flow operations of a firm's parent company and foreign subsidiaries.

As mentioned above, multinational firms usually employ a number of foreign exchange hedging strategies. Transaction exposure is often managed either through the use of foreign exchange derivatives, such as forward contracts, swaps options, or with operational techniques such as leads and lags in receipts and payments to marry their foreign exposure and invoicing currency. A number of empirical studies have examined how firms deal with the foreign exchange rate risk. Figure 5.1 shows a conceptual diagram of corporate exchange rate risk management strategies by partly employing the framework of Döhring (2008).

Usually, firms use two different methods to hedge the exchange rate risk. One is a financial hedge through financial market instruments, such as exchange rate derivatives or foreign currency debt, the other is an operational hedge through the operational set-up of the exporting firm. To manage long-term exchange rate risks effectively, firms should build operational hedging structures in addition to widely used financial hedging strategies. So far, most empirical studies have specifically examined financial and operational hedging.[2] These studies analyse the relation between operational and financial hedging and underscore the effectiveness of both strategies by conducting empirical analyses based on firms' stock returns. For example, Pantzalis et al. (2001), using a sample of 220 US multinational firms, found that operational and financial hedges are

---

[2]   For example, Carter et al. (2001) investigated the impact of firm-wide risk management practices for US multinational corporations and reported that currency risk can be reduced effectively through transactions in the forward exchange market.

complementary risk management strategies. Hommel (2003) showed that operational hedging creates flexibility, a strategic complement to financial hedging. Allayannis et al. (2001) also investigated both financial and operational exchange rate risk management strategies of multinational firms and confirmed that operational hedging strategies benefit shareholders only when used in combination with financial hedging strategies. On the other hand, Kim et al. (2006) investigated how operational hedging is related to financial hedging. They confirm that firms' usage of operational hedging are less dependent on the usage of financial derivatives.[3]

The relation between invoicing currency and hedging has rarely been investigated so far. The exception, to the best of our knowledge, is the study by Döhring (2008), who conducted the first survey study of both choice of invoicing currency and financial/operational hedging. It is shown that invoicing choice is a substitute for derivative hedging such as exchange rate forwarding in eliminating transaction risk. This study also shows that firms would be expected to opt for either strategy depending on their relative cost. Conducting a survey of actual hedging strategies and techniques employed by large corporations from a euro area perspective, Döhring (2008) concluded that whether invoicing in a domestic currency and hedging are substitutes or complements depends crucially on the size and geographical orientation of the exporting firm and on the structure of the destination market.

Regarding the relation between pass-through and hedging, Bartram et al. (2010) showed empirically that firms pass-through some porting of currency changes to customers and use both operational and financial hedges for the remainder of their foreign exchange exposure. They assumed that corporate financial managers can use pricing (pass-through) policy, operational hedging financial hedging strategies to mitigate the impact of currency fluctuations. Using a sample of 1150 manufacturing firms in 16 countries, it is empirically shown that pass-through and operational hedging each reduce exposure by 10–15 per cent, whereas financial hedging with foreign debt lowers exposure by 40 per cent.

As for Asian country-specific studies, Chiand and Lin (2007) examined financial and operational hedge strategies of foreign exchange exposures using multiple-horizon data on Taiwanese non-financial firms from 1998–2005 and found that the use of operational hedging strategies does not help reduce Taiwanese firms' foreign exchange exposures. Pramborg (2005) compared the hedging practices between Swedish and Korean

---

[3] They used a sample of 424 firm observations from the COMPUSTAT Geographic Segment files for 1998.

Table 5.1   Global foreign exchange market turnover by currency (%)

(Percentage shares of average daily turnover in April)

Currency	2004	2007	2010	2013
US dollar	88.0	85.6	84.9	87.0
Euro	37.4	37.0	39.1	33.4
Japanese yen	20.8	17.2	19.0	23.0
Pound sterling	16.5	14.9	12.9	11.8
Australian dollar	6.0	6.6	7.6	8.6
Swiss franc	6.0	6.8	6.4	5.2
Canadian dollar	4.2	4.3	5.3	4.6
Hong Kong dollar	1.8	2.7	2.4	1.4
Korean won	1.1	1.2	1.5	1.2
Singapore dollar	0.9	1.2	1.4	1.4
Chinese renminbi	0.1	0.5	0.9	2.2
Thai baht	0.2	0.2	0.2	0.3
Others	17.0	21.8	18.4	19.9

Note: The sum of the percentage shares of individual currencies totals 200%.

Source: BIS Triennial Central Bank Survey of foreign exchange and derivatives market activity.

non-financial firms and showed that Korean firms were more dependent on foreign debt than derivatives and used much smaller financial derivatives than Swedish firms. Both studies highlight the difficulties in effective exchange rate risk management in underdeveloped foreign exchange markets such as Taiwan and Korea. Although Japanese exporting firms tend to face large volatility in the yen–US dollar exchange rate, surprisingly few studies have conducted firm-level analysis of hedging and exchange rate risk management of Japanese firms.[4]

5.2.2   Foreign Exchange and Derivatives Market Activities in Japan

Before discussing the questionnaire survey results, we overview the characteristics of foreign exchange and derivatives market activity in Japan according to the triennial central bank survey coordinated by the Bank for International Settlements (BIS). Table 5.1 summarizes developments

---

[4]   As for research using Japanese data, Jayasinghe and Tsui (2008) examined the exchange rate exposure of sectoral indexes in Japanese industries and report significant evidence of exposed returns and asymmetric conditional volatility of exchange rate exposure by employing a bivariate GJR-GARCH model.

Table 5.2 Amounts outstanding of OTC foreign exchange derivatives (in billions of US dollars)

	2009	2010	2011	2012
By instrument and maturity				
Total contracts	49181	57796	63349	67358
Forwards and swaps	39683	47704	53317	57138
with maturity one year or less	24767	31619	38089	40697
maturity between 1 and 5 years	7555	8139	10532	11485
maturity over 5 years	7311	7947	4696	4956
Options	9543	10092	10032	10220
with maturity one year or less	5847	6368	7255	7438
maturity between 1 and 5 years	2157	1996	2223	2243
maturity over 5 years	1539	1727	554	539
By currency				
US dollar	40921	48741	54035	57600
Euro	20364	21913	22497	23797
Japanese yen	11238	12574	13068	14111
Pound sterling	5929	6584	7023	7825
Swiss franc	3106	4213	4876	3832
Canadian dollar	1858	2421	2862	3099
Others	14946	19146	42337	24452

Source: BIS Quarterly Review, Table 20A, 20 B, 20C.

in foreign exchange market turnover by currency since 2004. As the US dollar's share stays at more than 80 per cent for the entire period, its role as the world's dominant vehicle currency remains unchallenged. The euro is the second most important currency worldwide; however, its global market share decreased from 39.1 per cent in 2010 to 33.4 per cent in 2013, which is the lowest value since the introduction of the common currency. While the euro's role as an international currency declined over the period, the Japanese yen is the third most used currency in the world, substantially increasing from 17.2 per cent in 2007 to 23.0 per cent in 2013. As for emerging currencies, it is striking that the Triennial Survey shows a consistent and significant rise in the global importance of the Chinese renminbi (RMB). RMB turnover soared from $34 billion in 2010 to $120 billion in 2013, which is mostly driven by a significant expansion of offshore RMB trading, which had a share of 2.2 per cent in 2013.

Table 5.2 indicates the outstanding amounts of OTC (Over-the-Counter) foreign exchange derivatives since 2008. Total contract amounts rose steadily from 49181 billion at the end of 2009 to 67358 billion at the end of

Table 5.3   Share of foreign exchange transaction by currency in Japan (%)

	April 2004	April 2007	Change	April 2010	Change
USD/JPY	60.6	58.2	Δ2.3	62.3	+4.0
Euro/USD	11.7	10.8	Δ0.9	9.5	Δ1.3
Euro/JPY	6.9	5.9	Δ1.0	8.6	+2.7
Others	20.8	25.1	+4.2	19.7	Δ5.4

Source: Bank of Japan.

2012. Among the types of contract, forward and swap transactions with maturity dates of one year or less were the most used and on the rise; on the other hand, the use of options remains unchanged. The two tables above indicate that the US dollar dominates the world foreign exchange market and such a pattern remains unchanged despite the expansion of the global foreign exchange market.

Based on country data presented by the Bank of Japan, we confirm the same results as above. Table 5.3 shows the share of foreign exchange transactions in Japan by currency. It indicates that the share of USD–JPY transactions increased from 58.2 per cent in April 2007 to 62.3 per cent in April 2010. The share of Euro–JPY transactions also increased from 6.9 per cent in April 2004 to 8.6 per cent in April 2010, while transactions against other currencies decreased from 25.1 per cent in April 2007 to 19.7 per cent in April 2010.

5.2.3   Effectiveness of Japanese Firms' Exchange Rate Risk Management

We summarized the features of Japanese firms' exchange risk management in the previous section and confirmed that financial hedges, operational hedges, choice of invoicing currency and exchange rate pass-through are viewed as four key approaches employed by Japanese exporting firms to avoid exchange rate risk. Because these methods are closely related, it is very difficult to establish an order of priority in terms of which should be utilized first. As described herein, we put these four components in the following order: (1) choice of invoicing currency (share of yen or US dollar invoicing); (2) with or without an operational hedge ('marry and netting'); (3) degree of financial hedge (hedge ratio of the forward contract); and (4) with or without an exchange rate pass-through (price revision). From these four perspectives, we consider the effectiveness of Japanese firms' exchange rate risk management in reducing their exchange rate exposure.

Choice of invoicing currency (share of yen or US dollar invoicing)
As shown by Ito et al. (2010a, 2010b), Japanese firms exporting highly differentiated products or having a dominant share in global markets tend to
choose yen invoicing. If their exports are invoiced in the yen instead of the
US dollar, their business performance will not be affected by a stronger yen,
at least in the short run. However, most firms are not usually sufficiently
competitive to decide their invoicing currency for their own sake but negotiate it with their customers or merely follow their customers' decision. For
each firm, the choice of invoice currency reflects a unique mix and balance
of factors, and depends not only on competitiveness but also on other
factors such as firm size, products, trading partners, trading countries and
financial characteristics. Although firms that invoice exclusively in yen are
robust against the yen's sudden appreciation because they have no foreign
currency exposure, firms with a high share of US dollar invoicing are vul-
nerable because of their foreign currency exposure. In this case, they must
use operational or financial hedging to manage the resultant risk. From the
standpoint of invoice currency choice only, the higher the US dollar (the
yen) invoicing share, the larger (the smaller) is the exchange rate exposure.

With or without an operational hedge ('marry and netting')
In response to the yen's severe appreciation in 1995, Japanese exporting
firms have stepped up the transfer of production bases overseas, increased
capacity of existing overseas bases and/or increased the proportion of
imported components from overseas, along with other measures to ensure
the benefits of a strong yen. In such cases, firms often use 'marry and
netting' in their intra-trade transactions.[5] However, not all firms can use
this technique. For example, firms that produce goods made using only
Japanese materials and export them abroad cannot engage in 'marry or
netting' because they have no payable foreign currency.

From the standpoint of operational hedge, applying the 'marry and
netting' technique can reduce a firm's foreign currency exposure. For firms
with a higher US dollar invoicing share, 'marry and netting' presumably
works more effectively to reduce their currency exposure.

Degree of financial hedge (hedging ratio of forward contracts)
For Japanese firms, 'forward contracts' are the most useful hedging
instrument available through the foreign exchange market. However, no
specific choice of hedging ratio for 'forward contracts' seems to exist either

---

[5]   There is another technique of operational hedging, namely using foreign currency-
denominated debt to cancel out foreign currency exposure. In this book, we regard 'marry
and netting' as a major technique of operational hedging by Japanese firms.

by industry or firm size, which suggests that deciding the hedging ratio depends on each firm's foreign exchange risk management strategy. From the standpoint of financial hedging, the higher the US dollar invoicing share, the greater is the use of financial hedges to reduce the exchange rate exposure. Firms with almost 100 per cent yen invoicing have no need to use financial hedging because they have no foreign currency exposure.

With or without an exchange rate pass-through
Whether firms can implement price revisions in response to foreign exchange fluctuations (foreign exchange pass-through) and how frequently they do so are also related to the firm's robustness against the yen's sudden appreciation. If firms are sufficiently competitive to revise their prices to maintain constant earnings in terms of the Japanese yen, then foreign exchange fluctuations impose no severe impact on their performance, at least while sales volumes do not change. From the standpoint of exchange rate pass-through, two different patterns depend on the invoicing currency share: for a larger share of yen invoicing firms, no existence of price revision in 2008 is more robust against the yen's appreciation, and for a larger share of US dollar invoicing firms, existence of price revision in 2008 is more robust against the yen's appreciation.

5.3 QUESTIONNAIRE SURVEY: CASE OF JAPANESE FIRMS' RISK MANAGEMENT

In this section we present the results of the 2009 RIETI Survey related to Japanese firms' exchange rate risk management. To elucidate these features, we classify our results by firm size, for which we set two measures: total consolidated sales and foreign sales ratio. The first category is based on total consolidated sales immediately before the survey (mostly as of March 2009) and splits all listed manufacturers into three categories, comprising large (upper third), medium (middle third) and small (lower third). The second category is also based on foreign sales ratio (total foreign sales/ total consolidated sales), splitting all listed manufacturers into high (upper third), medium (middle third) and low (lower third).

5.3.1 Share of Invoicing Currency in Japanese Exports to the World

Table 5.4 presents the results of questionnaires on the invoicing currency choice for Japanese firms' exports to the world, where a simple arithmetic average of the invoicing share is reported. First, for all manufacturing industries (217 firms responded), the share of yen invoicing is the largest

Table 5.4 Invoicing currency share in exports from Japan to the world (by industry)

Sample average (Unit: %)

Type of industry		All manufacturers	Foods	Textiles & Apparel	Chemicals	Pharmaceuticals	Steel Products	Rubber Products	Glass & Ceramics
# of firms		**217**	2	7	36	3	6	4	6
Invoicing	JPY	**48.2**	50.0	50.0	50.4	54.0	35.7	38.0	57.2
Currency	USD	**42.1**	50.0	41.3	41.0	20.3	63.5	54.3	40.8
Share	Euro	**7.1**	0.0	3.7	7.7	17.0	0.0	7.5	1.0
	Others	**2.6**	0.0	5.0	0.9	8.7	0.8	0.3	1.0

Type of industry		Nonferrous Metals	Metal Products	Machinery	Electrical Machinery	Transport Equipment	Precision Instruments	Other Products
# of firms		5	9	38	51	27	14	9
Invoicing	JPY	23.6	57.2	56.2	38.8	56.3	44.4	47.9
Currency	USD	70.4	41.7	29.7	50.7	33.3	44.3	45.1
Share	Euro	5.0	1.0	11.0	8.2	4.5	9.0	4.7
	Others	1.0	0.1	3.2	2.5	5.9	2.3	2.3

Source: The results of the 2009 RIETI Survey.

(48.2 per cent); US dollar invoicing is the next largest (42.1 per cent). The share of euro invoicing accounts for only 7.1 per cent; the share of other invoicing currency is very low (2.7 per cent). Second, when looking at industry-breakdown data, the share of yen-denominated invoicing is large in the glass and ceramics, metal products, machinery and transport equipment industries. On the other hand, the share of US dollar invoicing is largest in the rubber product, steel products, nonferrous metals and electrical machinery industries. Third, invoicing in other currencies typically accounts for a small share, although the share of euro invoicing is around 10 per cent or more in the pharmaceuticals and machinery industries.

Let us next examine the invoicing currency share across the firm size (Table 5.5). In terms of the consolidated sales, it is clearly shown that the smaller the firm, the higher is its share of yen-denominated invoicing. In contrast, the larger the firm, the higher is the share of US dollar invoicing. In terms of the foreign sales ratio, however, no clear pattern of invoicing currency choice is observed.

Result 1: The yen and US dollar are mainly used in Japanese total exports to the world. The smaller (larger) the firm, the higher is the share of yen (US dollar) invoicing.

5.3.2   Number of Foreign Currencies Handled

We asked firms to choose the foreign currencies it handles from a range of 20 foreign currencies, including the US dollar, with multiple answers allowed. Table 5.6 shows 227 firms' responses. According to the survey results, the mean of the number of foreign currencies handled in the manufacturing industry is 3.1. We conclude that approximately three different foreign currencies are used by one company on average. An electrical machinery firm answered that it handles 15 currencies at a maximum.[6] According to type of industry, the mean of the number of foreign currencies handled is 4, 3.5 and 3.3, respectively, in 'Transport Equipment', 'Electrical Machinery' and 'Machinery' industries. These results indicate that Japanese representative industries that develop production networks abroad handle various foreign currencies.[7]

Table 5.7 presents a summary of the number of foreign currencies handled in five major industries according to firm size (total consolidated

---

[6]   The number 0 denotes that no foreign currency is handled; Japanese yen are used for all trade.

[7]   Although the number of answers is only 3, the mean of the 'Pharmaceutical' industry is 3.7, which is higher than that of other industries as well.

Table 5.5 *Invoicing currency share in exports from Japan to the world (by firm category)*

	Total consolidated sales			Sample average (Unit: %) Total foreign sales / Total consolidated sales		
	Large (upper 1/3)	Medium (middle 1/3)	Small (lower 1/3)	High (upper 1/3)	Medium (middle 1/3)	Low (lower 1/3)
# of sample firms	80	70	67	64	70	83
JPY						
All manufacturers	**38.1**	**50.0**	**58.3**	**41.2**	**52.2**	**50.2**
Chemicals	33.1	54.2	66.8	52.1	50.1	49.8
Machinery	36.8	73.8	56.5	47.5	67.3	55.0
Electrical Machinery	25.7	36.5	54.3	25.1	48.9	50.7
Transport Equipment	49.0	71.9	56.6	47.5	47.0	77.9
Precision Instruments	29.8	40.4	55.0	43.8	63.5	21.3
USD						
All manufacturers	**47.8**	**41.7**	**35.8**	**45.5**	**39.0**	**42.1**
Chemicals	55.9	38.7	25.9	39.4	41.7	40.9
Machinery	41.0	18.0	31.1	31.3	19.8	35.8
Electrical Machinery	59.2	51.4	41.5	62.4	41.8	40.7
Transport Equipment	35.3	23.4	41.2	40.2	38.0	19.5
Precision Instruments	42.6	51.6	39.2	37.8	27.3	73.8
Euro						
All manufacturers	**10.5**	**5.1**	**5.2**	**11.0**	**5.7**	**5.3**
Chemicals	10.5	5.1	7.3	8.4	6.4	9.2
Machinery	17.5	5.8	10.1	18.5	9.6	5.9
Electrical Machinery	12.8	7.8	3.8	10.3	6.8	6.2
Transport Equipment	6.1	2.7	2.1	7.0	4.4	1.3
Precision Instruments	25.4	3.0	5.8	16.8	8.5	0.0

Table 5.5   (continued)

	Total consolidated sales			Sample average (Unit: %)		
				Total foreign sales / Total consolidated sales		
	Large (upper 1/3)	Medium (middle 1/3)	Small (lower 1/3)	High (upper 1/3)	Medium (middle 1/3)	Low (lower 1/3)
# of sample firms	80	70	67	64	70	83
Other currencies						
All manufacturers	**3.7**	**3.3**	**0.7**	**2.5**	**3.0**	**2.5**
Chemicals	0.6	2.1	0.0	0.1	1.8	0.1
Machinery	4.7	2.4	2.5	3.0	3.3	3.2
Electrical Machinery	2.3	4.9	0.3	2.6	2.6	2.4
Transport Equipment	9.6	2.0	0.1	5.3	10.6	1.3
Precision Instruments	2.2	5.0	0.0	1.6	0.7	5.0

Source: The results of the 2009 RIETI Survey.

sales) and foreign sales ratio (total foreign sales/total consolidated sales). The number of foreign currencies handled tends to increase monotonically as firm size increases. According to industry type, this tendency is particularly remarkable in 'Chemical', 'Machinery' and 'Electrical Machinery' (upper table) industries. In addition, the number of the foreign currencies handled tends to increase monotonically as the ratio of total foreign sales over total consolidated sales rises. This tendency is remarkable in the 'Transport Equipment' (lower table) industry.

Result 2: The average Japanese firm uses three foreign currencies for exports. Larger firms or firms with higher exposure to foreign markets use more currencies.

5.3.3   Financial Hedging

Instruments of financial hedging
Regarding financial hedging through the foreign exchange markct, we asked firms what instruments they use. Table 5.8 presents a summary of

Table 5.6 How many kinds of foreign currencies are used for international trade (by industry)?

Type of Industry	All manufacturers	Foods	Textiles & Apparel	Chemicals	Pharmaceuticals	Steel Products	Rubber Products	Glass & Ceramics
# of answers	**227**	3	9	36	3	6	4	6
Number of foreign currencies for international trade — Average	**3.1**	2.3	2.9	2.7	3.7	2.0	3.0	2.7
Max	**15**	3	6	9	5	6	5	7
Min	**0**	2	1	1	2	1	1	1

Type of Industry	Nonferrous Metals	Metal Products	Machinery	Electrical Machinery	Transport Equipment	Precision Instruments	Other Products
# of answers	5	9	40	55	27	15	9
Number of foreign currencies for international trade — Average	2.8	2.3	3.3	3.5	4.0	2.1	2.6
Max	4	8	12	15	14	4	5
Min	1	0	0	0	0	1	1

Source: The results of the 2009 RIETI Survey.

148

Table 5.7 How many kinds of foreign currencies are used for international trade (by firm category / by six major types of industry)?

		All manufacturers	All manufacturers	Chemicals	Machinery	Electrical Machinery	Transport Equipment	Precision Instruments
	Type of Industry	# of firms	**Average**	Average	Average	Average	Average	Average
	Total consolidated sales							
Number of foreign currencies for international trade	Large (upper 1/3)	86	**4.4**	3.2	5.0	5.5	5.5	3.0
	Medium (middle 1/3)	73	**2.7**	2.8	3.2	2.9	1.7	1.8
	Small (lower 1/3)	68	**1.9**	2.0	1.7	1.8	3.0	2.0

		All manufacturers	All manufacturers	Chemicals	Machinery	Electrical Machinery	Transport Equipment	Precision Instruments
	Type of Industry	# of firms	**Average**	Average	Average	Average	Average	Average
	Total foreign sales / Total consolidated sales							
Number of foreign currencies for international trade	High (upper 1/3)	69	**3.7**	2.6	3.7	3.5	6.4	2.7
	Medium (middle 1/3)	71	**3.2**	3.3	3.0	4.6	3.0	2.2
	Low (lower 1/3)	87	**2.5**	1.9	3.2	3.0	2.3	1.3

Source: The results of the 2009 RIETI Survey.

Table 5.8 Instruments of currency hedging through exchange rate markets (by industry)

Type of industry		All manufacturers	Foods	Textiles & Apparel	Chemicals	Pharmaceuticals	Steel Products	Rubber Products	Glass & Ceramics
	# of sample firms (A)	**227**	3	9	36	3	6	4	6
Firms to answer any instrument of currency hedging	# of answers (B)	**166**	3	8	24	3	4	3	4
	(B)/(A)(%)	**73.1**	100.0	88.9	66.7	100.0	66.7	75.0	66.7
Forward	# of answer "yes" (C)	**158**	2	8	24	3	4	2	4
	(C)/(B)(%)	**95.2**	66.7	100.0	100.0	100.0	100.0	66.7	100.0
Currency option	# of answer "yes" (D)	**40**	1	1	4	0	0	1	2
	(D)/(B)(%)	**24.1**	33.3	12.5	16.7	0.0	0.0	33.3	50.0
Other currency derivatives	# of answer "yes" (E)	**5**	1	0	2	0	0	0	0
	(E)/(B)(%)	**3.0**	33.3	0.0	8.3	0.0	0.0	0.0	0.0

Type of industry		Nonferrous Metals	Metal Products	Machinery	Electrical Machinery	Transport Equipment	Precision Instruments	Other Products
	# of sample firms (A)	5	9	40	55	27	15	9
Firms to answer any instrument of currency hedging	# of answers (B)	4	3	33	42	18	9	8
	(B)/(A)(%)	80.0	33.3	82.5	76.4	66.7	60.0	88.9
Forward	# of answer "yes" (C)	4	3	32	38	18	8	8
	(C)/(B)(%)	100.0	100.0	97.0	90.5	100.0	88.9	100.0
Currency option	# of answer "yes" (D)	0	1	4	13	7	4	2
	(D)/(B)(%)	0.0	33.3	12.1	31.0	38.9	44.4	25.0
Other currency derivatives	# of answer "yes" (E)	0	0	0	2	0	0	0
	(E)/(B)(%)	0.0	0.0	0.0	4.8	0.0	0.0	0.0

Source: The results of the 2009 RIETI Survey.

the results by industry type. Among the 166 respondent firms, 73.1 per cent of firms use hedging instruments of some kind through the foreign exchange market. Specifically, using 'Forward' is most common (95.2 per cent) followed by 'Currency option' (24.1 per cent) and 'Other currency derivatives' (3.0 per cent). By industry breakdown, 'Pharmaceuticals', 'Steel Products' and 'Nonferrous Metals' industries use 'Forward' only, whereas almost 40 per cent firms in the 'Electrical Machinery', 'Transport Equipment' and 'Precision Instruments' industries use 'Currency option' in combination with 'Forward'.

In Table 5.9, we present a summary of the above results by firm size (total consolidated sales) and foreign sales ratio (total foreign sales/total consolidated sales). The ratio of firms using some kind of currency hedging

Table 5.9   Instruments of currency hedging through exchange rate markets (by firm category)

	Firm category	Total consolidated sales			Total foreign sales / Total consolidated sales		
		Large (upper 1/3)	Medium (middle 1/3)	Small (lower 1/3)	High (upper 1/3)	Medium (middle 1/3)	Low (lower 1/3)
	# of sample firms (A)	86	73	68	69	71	87
Firms to answer using any instrument of currency hedging	# of answers (B)	79	51	36	58	51	57
	(B)/(A)(%)	91.9	69.9	52.9	84.1	71.8	65.5
Forward	# of answer "yes" (C)	79	47	32	55	49	54
	(C)/(B)(%)	100.0	92.2	88.9	94.8	96.1	94.7
Currency option	# of answer "yes" (D)	27	6	7	23	8	9
	(D)/(B)(%)	34.2	11.8	19.4	39.7	15.7	15.8
Other currency derivatives	# of answer "yes" (E)	2	2	1	1	2	2
	(E)/(B)(%)	2.5	3.9	2.8	1.7	3.9	3.5

Source: The results of the 2009 RIETI Survey.

instruments increases monotonically as firm size increases. In addition, the ratio of firms using 'Forward' and 'Currency option' tends to rise as firm size becomes larger. Firms with large consolidated sales or large foreign sales actively use currency hedging instruments through foreign exchange markets.

Result 3: Around three-quarters of Japanese firms use some foreign exchange hedging instruments through the foreign exchange market. Larger firms or firms with higher exposure to foreign markets use more hedging instruments to manage their foreign exchange risk.

Internal rule for the hedging ratio

The next questions we examine are (1) whether firms hedge their foreign currency exposures by an internal rule or discretionarily; and (2) how high the average hedging ratio of Japanese exporters is. We first ask if firms have any internal rules regarding a hedging ratio. Then, we ask those firms responding affirmatively about their hedging ratio on their foreign currency exposures. Table 5.10 presents a summary of these results by industry type. Among the 212 respondent firms, 54.2 per cent have an internal rule while 45.8 per cent have no internal rule. Among the firms that have some internal rule on their hedging foreign currency exposures, the ratio of 'around 50 per cent' hedging is the highest (41.7 per cent of firms) followed by 'around 100 per cent' hedging (23.5 per cent). We can confirm that almost one-quarter of foreign currency exposures are hedged 100 per cent and that more than 60 per cent of foreign currency exposure are hedged more than 50 per cent. According to industry breakdowns, no specific choice exists by industry type, which suggests that deciding choice of hedging ratio depends on each firm's foreign exchange risk management strategy.

Table 5.11 details the results presented above by firm size (total consolidated sales) and foreign market ratio (total foreign sales/total consolidated sales). The ratio of firms having an internal rule for the hedge ratio of foreign currency exposure rises monotonically as the firm size increases. That result indicates that larger firms or firms with higher exposure to foreign markets are more likely to adopt an internal rule for their hedge ratio. Firms with no internal rule for their hedging ratio indicated that they chose a hedging ratio depending on the conditions and prospects of the foreign exchange market.

Result 4: Approximately half of Japanese firms have internal rules regarding the hedge ratio of foreign exchange exposure. Larger firms or firms with higher exposure to foreign markets are more likely to adopt an internal rule for their hedge ratio.

Table 5.10 Is there an internal rule dictating the percentage of foreign exchange exposure (by industry)?

	Type of industry	All manufacturers	Foods	Textiles & Apparel	Chemicals	Pharmaceuticals	Oil & Coal Products	Rubber Products	Glass & Ceramics
Firms to answer whether they have any internal rules on FX exposure	# of firms (A)	212	3	9	34	3	1	4	6
1. Yes, we have a rule	# of answers (B)	115	2	3	21	0	1	3	3
	(B)/(A)(%)	54.2	66.7	33.3	61.8	0.0	100.0	75.0	50.0
Hedge ratio on FX exposure — around 30%	# of answers (C)	13	0	0	1	0	0	0	1
	(C)/(B)(%)	11.3	0.0	0.0	4.8		0.0	0.0	33.3
around 50%	# of answers (D)	48	0	3	7	0	0	1	2
	(D)/(B)(%)	41.7	0.0	100.0	33.3		0.0	33.3	66.7
almost 100%	# of answers (E)	27	2	0	7	0	1	2	0
	(E)/(B)(%)	23.5	100.0	0.0	33.3		100.0	66.7	0.0
others	# of answers (F)	26	0	0	6	0	0	0	0
	(F)/(B)(%)	22.6	0.0	0.0	28.6		0.0	0.0	0.0
2. No, we do not have a rule	# of answers (G)	97	1	6	13	3	0	1	3
	(G)/(A)(%)	45.8	33.3	66.7	38.2	100.0	0.0	25.0	50.0

		Steel Products	Nonferrous Metals	Metal Products	Machinery	Electrical Machinery	Transport Equipment	Precision Instruments	Other Products
	Type of industry								
Firms to answer whether they have any internal rules on FX exposure	# of firms (A)	6	4	7	39	54	24	12	6
1. Yes, we have a rule	# of answers (B)	2	1	4	22	29	12	9	3
	(B)/(A)(%)	33.3	25.0	57.1	56.4	53.7	50.0	75.0	50.0
Hedge ratio on FX exposure — around 30%	# of answers (C)	2	0	0	2	3	1	3	0
	(C)/(B)(%)	100.0	0.0	0.0	9.1	10.3	8.3	33.3	0.0
around 50%	# of answers (D)	0	0	2	13	11	6	2	1
	(D)/(B)(%)	0.0	0.0	50.0	59.1	37.9	50.0	22.2	33.3
almost 100%	# of answers (E)	0	1	0	2	7	2	2	1
	(E)/(B)(%)	0.0	100.0	0.0	9.1	24.1	16.7	22.2	33.3
others	# of answers (F)	0	0	2	5	7	3	2	1
	(F)/(B)(%)	0.0	0.0	50.0	22.7	24.1	25.0	22.2	33.3
2. No, we do not have a rule	# of answers (G)	4	3	3	17	25	12	3	3
	(G)/(A)(%)	66.7	75.0	42.9	43.6	46.3	50.0	25.0	50.0

155

Table 5.11 *Is there an internal rule dictating the percentage of foreign exchange exposure (by firm category)?*

	Firm category	Total consolidated sales			Total foreign sales / Total consolidated sales		
		Large (upper 1/3)	Medium (middle 1/3)	Small (lower 1/3)	High (upper 1/3)	Medium (middle 1/3)	Low (lower 1/3)
Firms to answer whether they have an internal rules on FX exposure	# of firms (A)	82	68	62	66	67	79
1. Yes, we have a rule	# of answers (B)	64	32	19	47	36	32
	(B)/(A)(%)	78.0	47.1	30.6	71.2	53.7	40.5
Hedge ratio on FX exposure — around 30%	# of answers (C)	5	4	4	4	5	4
	(C)/(B)(%)	7.8	12.5	21.1	8.5	13.9	12.5
around 50%	# of answers (D)	27	15	6	17	14	17
	(D)/(B)(%)	42.2	46.9	31.6	36.2	38.9	53.1
almost 100%	# of answers (E)	15	7	5	12	9	6
	(E)/(B)(%)	23.4	21.9	26.3	25.5	25.0	18.8
others	# of answers (F)	16	6	4	13	8	5
	(F)/(B)(%)	25.0	18.8	21.1	27.7	22.2	15.6
2. No, we do not have a rule	# of answers (G)	18	36	43	19	31	47
	(G)/(A)(%)	22.0	52.9	69.4	28.8	46.3	59.5

Source: The results of the 2009 RIETI Survey.

5.3.4 Operational Hedging: 'Marry and Netting'

Along with the aforementioned hedging instruments through the foreign exchange market, another solution to hedging foreign exchange exposure is operational hedging. Operational hedging is a strategy designed to manage risks through operational means, such as providing firms with flexibility in supply chains, financial positions, distribution patterns and market-facing activities by allowing dynamic adjustments in the locations used to manufacture, source and sell products. When deployed carefully, such flexibility can help to reduce the impact on costs and revenues arising from large and long-term shifts in currency values. Having faced volatile foreign exchange fluctuations for a long time, many Japanese exporting firms have built overseas production networks to enable the use of several operational hedging techniques. For example 'marry and netting' is commonly used by Japanese exporting firms. 'Marry and netting' is the practice of offsetting foreign receivables against foreign payables to avoid any foreign exchange risk entirely. In our questionnaire survey, we ask whether a firm uses 'marry and netting' as a currency risk management technique.

Table 5.12 presents answers related to use of 'marry and netting', with specific data available regarding what foreign currencies and what types of transactions by industry type. Among the 222 respondent firms, 40.1 per cent use 'marry and netting'. According to industry categories, the ratio of affirmative answers is greater than 50 per cent in 'Electrical Machinery' and 'Transport Equipment' industries. Regarding the target currency for 'marry and netting', the US dollar is the highest (97.8 per cent) followed by the euro (41.6 per cent). Furthermore, among firms using 'marry and netting', it is used mainly for trade between the head office and subsidiaries (85.4 per cent).

Table 5.13 summarizes results presented above by firm size (total consolidated sales and total foreign sales/total consolidated sales). The share of firms using 'marry and netting' increases monotonically as either total consolidated sales increase and/or degree of exposure to overseas markets rises.

Result 5: Approximately 40 per cent of Japanese firms use 'marry and netting' as a means of foreign exchange risk management. Larger firms or firms with higher exposure to foreign markets are more likely to use 'marry and netting'.

Table 5.12 Do you use marry and/or netting as a means of exchange rate risk managements (by industry)?

	Type of industry	All manufacturers	Foods	Textiles & Apparel	Chemicals	Pharmaceuticals	Steel Products	Rubber Products	Glass & Ceramics
Firms to answer whether they conduct marry and/or netting	# of firms (A)	**222**	3	9	36	3	6	4	6
1. Yes, we do	# of answers (B)	**89**	1	4	13	1	0	0	1
	(B)/(A) (%)	**40.1**	33.3	44.4	36.1	33.3	0.0	0.0	16.7
For what kind of currency?	US dollar								
	# of answers (C)	**87**	1	4	13	1	0	0	1
	(C)/(B) (%)	**97.8**	100.0	100.0	100.0	100.0			100.0
	Euro								
	# of answers (D)	**37**	1	0	3	1	0	0	0
	(D)/(B) (%)	**41.6**	100.0	0.0	23.1	100.0			0.0
	Other currencies								
	# of answers (E)	**8**	0	0	0	0	0	0	0
	(E)/(B) (%)	**9.0**	0.0	0.0	0.0	0.0			0.0

For what kind of transaction?		Total	Nonferrous Metals	Metal Products	Machinery	Electrical Machinery	Transport Equipment	Precision Instruments	Other Products
Trade between head office and subsidiaries	# of answers (F)	**76**	0	3	11	1	0	0	1
	(F)/(B) (%)	**85.4**	0.0	75.0	84.6	100.0			100.0
Others	# of answers (G)	**15**	1	1	2	0	0	0	0
	(G)/(B) (%)	**16.9**	100.0	25.0	15.4	0.0			0.0
2. No, we don't	# of answers (H)	**133**	2	5	23	2	6	4	5
	(H)/(A) (%)	**59.9**	66.7	55.6	63.9	66.7	66.7	100.0	83.3

Type of industry	Nonferrous Metals	Metal Products	Machinery	Electrical Machinery	Transport Equipment	Precision Instruments	Other Products
# of firms (A)	5	9	39	55	25	13	9
1. Yes, we do — # of answers (B)	1	1	14	32	14	3	4
(B)/(A) (%)	20.0	11.1	35.9	58.2	56.0	23.1	44.4

Table 5.12 (continued)

	Type of industry	Nonferrous Metals	Metal Products	Machinery	Electrical Machinery	Transport Equipment	Precision Instruments	Other Products
For what kind of currency?	US dollar # of answers (C)	1	1	13	32	13	3	4
	(C)/(B) (%)	100.0	100.0	92.9	100.0	92.9	100.0	100.0
	Euro # of answers (D)	0	0	10	15	5	2	0
	(D)/(B) (%)	0.0	0.0	71.4	46.9	35.7	66.7	
	Other currencies # of answers (E)	0	0	2	2	4	0	0
	(E)/(B) (%)	0.0	0.0	14.3	6.3	28.6	0.0	0.0
For what kind of transaction?	Between head office and subsidiaries # of answers (F)	1	1	14	26	11	3	4
	(F)/(B) (%)	100.0	100.0	100.0	81.3	78.6	100.0	100.0

Others	# of answers (G)	0	0	0	5	6	0	0
	(G)/(B) (%)	0.0	0.0	0.0	15.6	42.9	0.0	0.0
2. No, we don't	# of answers (H)	4	8	25	23	11	10	5
	(H)/(A) (%)	80.0	88.9	64.1	41.8	44.0	76.9	55.6

Source: The results of the 2009 RIETI Survey.

161

Table 5.13 Do you use marry and/or netting as a means of exchange rate risk managements (by firm category)?

Firm category			Total consolidated sales			Total foreign sales / Total consolidated sales		
			Large (upper 1/3)	Medium (middle 1/3)	Small (lower 1/3)	High (upper 1/3)	Medium (middle 1/3)	Low (lower 1/3)
Firms to answer whether they conduct marry and/or netting		# of firms (A)	85	71	66	67	71	84
1. Yes, we do		# of answers (B)	49	23	17	45	22	22
		(B)/(A)(%)	57.6	32.4	25.8	67.2	31.0	26.2
For what kind of currency?	US dollar	# of answers (C)	47	23	17	44	21	22
		(C)/(B)(%)	95.9	100.0	100.0	97.8	95.5	100.0
	Euro	# of answers (D)	25	8	4	22	6	9
		(D)/(B)(%)	51.0	34.8	23.5	48.9	27.3	40.9
	Other currencies	# of answers (E)	8	0	0	4	2	2
		(E)/(B)(%)	16.3	0.0	0.0	8.9	9.1	9.1
For what kind of transaction?	Trade between head office and subsidiaries	# of answers (F)	40	22	14	40	19	17
		(F)/(B)(%)	81.6	95.7	82.4	88.9	86.4	77.3
	Others	# of answers (G)	12	0	3	7	3	5
		(G)/(B)(%)	24.5	0.0	17.6	15.6	13.6	22.7
2. No, we don't		# of answers (H)	36	48	49	22	49	62
		(H)/(A)(%)	42.4	67.6	74.2	32.8	69.0	73.8

Source: The results of the 2009 RIETI Survey.

162

5.3.5 Pass-through of Exchange Rate Fluctuations to the Export Price

Exchange rate pass-through to the export price is one interesting topic related to the choice of invoicing currency. We ask whether firms pass through exchange rate fluctuations to the export price and, if so, how often. Table 5.14 summarizes the results by industry type. Among 215 respondent firms, the share of firms that chose 'it depends on the circumstances and management decision' is the highest (51.2 per cent), followed by 'no, we hardly ever pass through to the export price' (32.1 per cent). It is surprising that only 16.7 per cent of firms have an internal rule to pass through exchange rate fluctuations to the export price. These results suggest that Japanese exporters cannot easily change their export prices even when large fluctuations occur in the foreign exchange rate.

In Table 5.15, we summarize the results presented above by firm size (total consolidated sales and total foreign sales/total consolidated sales). Judging from firm size measured by total consolidated sales, the share of firms that have an internal price revision rule increases monotonically as total consolidated sales rise. Furthermore, judging from firm size as measured by the ratio of total foreign sales to total consolidated sales, the share of firms that only slightly pass through an exchange rate fluctuation to the export price increases as the ratio of total foreign sales to total consolidated sale falls.

Appreciation of the Japanese yen in 2008
We now turn to the second question of whether firms passed through to the export price the substantial appreciation of the Japanese yen that occurred in 2008 and, if so, to which currencies they passed it through. Table 5.16 presents a summary of the results by type of industry. Among the 209 respondent firms, the share that passed through exchange rate fluctuations to the export price in 2008 is 43.1 per cent, which is a smaller segment than those that did not (56.9 per cent). A surprising result is that more than half of Japanese firms did not pass through such changes even in circumstances where the Japanese yen appreciated approximately 20 per cent against the US dollar. Regarding the target currency of the price revision (multiple answers allowed), the US dollar's share is the highest (84.4 per cent) followed by the euro (47.8 per cent). According to the industry categories, no firms in 'Pharmaceuticals' and 'Steel Products' industries executed a pass-through, whereas more than half of firms in 'Textiles and Apparel', 'Chemicals', 'Machinery' and 'Precision Instruments' did execute a pass-through.

Table 5.17 summarizes the results presented above by firm size (total consolidated sales and total foreign sales/total consolidated sales). Judging from firm size, the share of firms that pass through increases monotonically as the firm size increases.

Table 5.14   Is there an internal rule to pass through the exchange rate fluctuation to the export price (by industry)?

Type of industry	All manufacturers	Foods	Textiles & Apparel	Chemicals	Pharmaceuticals	Steel Products	Rubber Products	Glass & Ceramics
# of firms (A)	215	3	7	35	3	6	4	6
1. Yes, there is a rule								
# of answers (B)	36	0	0	4	1	0	1	1
(B)/(A) (%)	16.7	0.0	0.0	11.4	33.3	0.0	25.0	16.7
2. No, we hardly ever pass through to the export price								
# of answers (C)	69	0	3	10	2	3	2	0
(C)/(A) (%)	32.1	0.0	42.9	28.6	66.7	50.0	50.0	0.0
3. It depends on the circumstances and management decisions								
# of answers (D)	110	3	4	21	0	3	1	5
(D)/(A) (%)	51.2	100.0	57.1	60.0	0.0	50.0	25.0	83.3

Type of industry		Nonferrous Metals	Metal Products	Machinery	Electrical Machinery	Transport Equipment	Precision Instruments	Other Products
	# of firms (A)	5	9	39	51	25	14	8
1. Yes, there is a rule	# of answers (B)	2	1	8	9	6	3	0
	(B)/(A) (%)	40.0	11.1	20.5	17.6	24.0	21.4	0.0
2. No, we hardly ever pass through to the export price	# of answers (C)	3	6	10	20	6	0	4
	(C)/(A) (%)	60.0	66.7	25.6	39.2	24.0	0.0	50.0
3. It depends on the circumstances and management decisions	# of answers (D)	0	2	21	22	13	11	4
	(D)/(A) (%)	0.0	22.2	53.8	43.1	52.0	78.6	50.0

Source: The results of the 2009 RIETI Survey.

Table 5.15   Is there an internal rule to pass through the exchange rate fluctuation to the export price (by firm category)?

Firm category		Total consolidated sales			Total foreign sales / Total consolidated sales		
		Large (upper 1/3)	Medium (middle 1/3)	Small (lower 1/3)	High (upper 1/3)	Medium (middle 1/3)	Low (lower 1/3)
	# of firms (A)	80	69	66	65	68	82
1. Yes, there is a rule	# of answers (B)	18	10	8	17	4	15
	(B)/(A)(%)	22.5	14.5	12.1	26.2	5.9	18.3
2. No, we hardly pass through to the export price	# of answers (C)	20	31	18	18	22	29
	(C)/(A)(%)	25.0	44.9	27.3	27.7	32.4	35.4
3. It depends on the circumstances and management decisions	# of answers (D)	42	28	40	30	42	38
	(D)/(A)(%)	52.5	40.6	60.6	46.2	61.8	46.3

Source: The results of the 2009 RIETI Survey.

Table 5.16 Did you pass through substantial appreciation of Japanese yen in 2008 to the export price (by industry)?

Type of industry		All manufacturers	Foods	Textiles & Apparel	Chemicals	Pharmaceuticals	Steel Products	Rubber Products	Glass & Ceramics
# of firms (A)		**209**	3	7	34	3	6	4	6
1. Yes, we did	# of answers (B)	**90**	1	4	19	0	0	1	1
	(B)/(A) (%)	**43.1**	33.3	57.1	55.9	0.0	0.0	25.0	16.7
For what kind of currency?	US dollar # of answers (C)	**76**	1	4	14	0	0	1	1
	(C)/(B) (%)	**84.4**	100.0	100.0	73.7			100.0	100.0
	Euro # of answers (D)	**43**	0	3	10	0	0	0	0
	(D)/(B) (%)	**47.8**	0.0	75.0	52.6			0.0	0.0
	Other currencies # of answers (E)	**14**	0	0	3	0	0	0	0
	(E)/(B) (%)	**15.6**	0.0	0.0	15.8			0.0	0.0

Table 5.16 (continued)

Type of industry		All manufacturers	Foods	Textiles & Apparel	Chemicals	Pharmaceuticals	Steel Products	Rubber Products	Glass & Ceramics
2. No, we didn't	# of answers (F)	119	2	3	15	3	6	3	5
	(F)/(A) (%)	56.9	66.7	42.9	44.1	100.0	100.0	75.0	83.3

Type of industry			Nonferrous Metals	Metal Products	Machinery	Electrical Machinery	Transport Equipment	Precision Instruments	Other Products
1. Yes, we did		# of firms (A)	5	8	36	50	25	14	8
		# of answers (B)	2	3	18	16	12	8	5
		(B)/(A) (%)	40.0	37.5	50.0	32.0	48.0	57.1	62.5
For what kind of currency?	US dollar	# of answers (C)	1	3	16	15	10	6	4
		(C)/(B) (%)	50.0	100.0	88.9	93.8	83.3	75.0	50.0

Euro	# of answers (D)	0	3	5	10	11	0	1
	(D)/(B) (%)	0.0	37.5	41.7	62.5	61.1	0.0	50.0
Other currencies	# of answers (E)	2	1	5	1	2	0	0
	(E)/(B) (%)	25.0	12.5	41.7	6.3	11.1	0.0	0.0
2. No, we didn't	# of answers (F)	3	6	13	34	18	5	3
	(F)/(A) (%)	37.5	42.9	52.0	68.0	50.0	62.5	60.0

Source: The results of the 2009 RIETI Survey.

Table 5.17 Did you pass through substantial appreciation of Japanese yen in 2008 to the export price (by firm category)?

	Firm category		Total consolidated sales			Total foreign sales / Total consolidated sales		
			Large (upper 1/3)	Medium (middle 1/3)	Small (lower 1/3)	High (upper 1/3)	Medium (middle 1/3)	Low (lower 1/3)
	# of firms (A)		77	67	65	62	67	80
1. Yes, we did	# of answers (B)		41	25	24	32	28	30
	(B)/(A)(%)		53.2	37.3	36.9	51.6	41.8	37.5
For what kind of currency?	US dollar	# of answers (C)	35	21	20	30	22	24
		(C)/(B)(%)	85.4	84.0	83.3	93.8	78.6	80.0
	Euro	# of answers (D)	27	7	9	18	14	11
		(D)/(B)(%)	65.9	28.0	37.5	56.3	50.0	36.7
	Other currencies	# of answers (E)	8	3	3	5	5	4
		(E)/(B)(%)	19.5	12.0	12.5	15.6	17.9	13.3
2. No, we didn't	# of answers (F)		36	42	41	30	39	50
	(F)/(A)(%)		46.8	62.7	63.1	48.4	58.2	62.5

Source: The results of the 2009 RIETI Survey.

Result 6: Many Japanese firms do not pass through exchange rate fluctuations to their export price. However, larger firms or firms with higher exposure to foreign markets are more likely to pass such changes through.

5.3.6   Relations Among Four Tools of Exchange Rate Risk Management

Summarizing the results presented above, we seek to determine how each tool affects the others. We first classify respondents' answers by choice of invoicing currency into those with a high share of yen invoicing and others. The reason for this division is that the choice of invoicing currency is presumed to be crucial to determining a firm's hedging policy. For example, a firm with 100 per cent yen invoicing needs not use financial hedging. Accordingly, the necessity of operational or financial hedging differs between firms with a high yen invoicing share and firms with other invoicing currency patterns.

Figure 5.2 shows the relationship between choice of invoice currency and operational hedges (in this case, 'marry and netting'). Firms with greater than 75 per cent yen invoicing share are classified as 'high share of yen invoicing' and other firms are classified as 'others'. Results show that 85.9 per cent of firms with a high share of yen invoicing do not implement 'marry and netting'. In addition, although 53.5 per cent of firms with a high share of yen invoicing implement forward transactions, 77.9 per cent of firms without a high share of yen invoicing implement forward transactions. These findings are consistent with the assertion of Döhring (2008), who found that invoicing in the domestic currency allows the elimination of transaction risk, much like hedging with an exchange rate forward.

Figure 5.3 shows the relation between operational and financial hedges. Following previous studies, our focus is whether operational and financial hedging strategies are complementary. Our results show that more than 80 per cent of firms employing 'marry and netting' use forward transactions. This share is higher than the share of firms using forward transactions that do not also use 'marry and netting' (62.4 per cent). These results indicate that Japanese firms use both operational and financial hedging as complements rather than as substitutes.

It is difficult to clarify the relation between the four tools of exchange rate risk management. However, the choice of invoicing currency is apparently a key factor in Japanese firms' decisions regarding use of operational and financial hedges. In terms of the relationship between operational and financial hedges, we confirm that Japanese firms use both operational and financial hedging as complements rather than substitutes. In addition, our results suggest that some large Japanese firms are able to use their pricing policy (pass-through) as one method of exchange rate risk management. Overall, to mitigate the impact of currency fluctuations, Japanese firms use

Choice of Invoice Currency and Operational Hedges

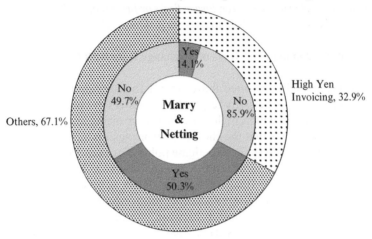

Choice of Invoice Currency and Financial Hedges

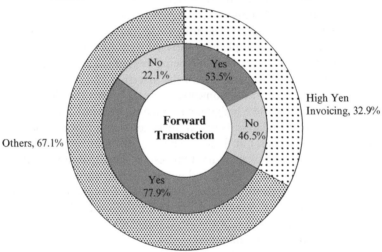

Note: Firms with more than 75% yen invoicing share are classified as having 'high yen invoicing' and other firms are classified as 'others'. The outer circle shows the choice of invoice currency. The inner circle shows the answer regarding hedges.

Source: The results of the 2009 RIETI Survey.

Figure 5.2   Relation between choice of invoice currency and hedges

Operational Hedge and Financial Hedge in 2008

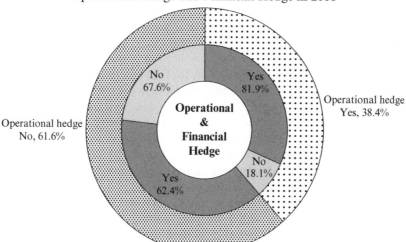

Note: Outer circle relates to marry and netting. The inner circle relates to forward transactions.

Source: The result of 2009 RIETI Survey.

Figure 5.3   Relation between operational and financial hedges

operational and financial hedging strategies and pricing policies depending on their choice of invoicing currency.

5.4 DETERMINANTS OF FINANCIAL AND OPERATIONAL HEDGING

In this section we conduct an empirical analysis to investigate the determinants of financial and operational hedging from the results of the 2009 RIETI Survey. In relation to the previous studies, we specifically examine the following questions:

1. Does yen invoicing supplement hedging?
2. Are operational and financial hedging strategies complements or substitutes?
3. Does pass-through alternate with financial hedging?

To explore these questions, we employ the following specification:

Prob $(\beta_i^{FH} = 1) = \alpha_0 + \alpha_1$ *Size*$_i$ + α_2 *Foreign Sales Ratio* + α_3 *Number of Foreign Currency*$_i$ + β_1 *Share of Japanese yen Invoicing*$_i$ + β_2 *Share of US dollar Invoicing*$_i$ + γ_1 *Dummy for Marry/Netting*$_i$ + γ_2 *Dummy for Pass-through*$_i$ + ε_i (5.1)

where β_i^{FH} is a financial hedging dummy for firm i on the left-hand side and Prob $(\beta_i^{FH} = 1)$ denotes the probability that a firm uses at least one kind of financial hedging tool. Because the basic explanatory variables are on the right-hand side, we first include a *size* of firm i measured by the log of total consolidated sales, a *foreign sales ratio*, which is a proxy for foreign market exposure and which is calculated as the total foreign sales of firms i divided by total consolidated sales and the *number of foreign currencies* used by firm i as extracted from the questionnaire survey.

After controlling for these basic variables, we examine the impacts of adoption of other hedging strategies on financial hedging. *Share of Japanese yen (US dollar) invoicing* is defined as the percentage of Japanese yen (US dollar) invoicing out of all exports to the world by firm i as extracted from the questionnaire survey. The *Dummy for marry/netting* is a dummy variable that takes 1 if firm i answered that it conducted 'marry and netting' in its trade, whereas the *Dummy for pass-through* is a dummy variable that takes 1 if firm i answered that its pricing policy had an internal rule to change export prices in the case of exchange rate fluctuations between the time of contract and time of settlement. We ran both a probit estimation and ordered probit estimation.

Table 5.18 presents the estimated results. The results of probit estimation in specifications (1)–(5) show that the log of total consolidated sales has a positive and statistically significant coefficient at the 1 per cent level across all specifications. This result means that larger firms use financial hedging more actively. The estimated coefficient on the foreign sales ratio is positive but not statistically significant. Regarding the variables on invoicing currency, the share of Japanese yen invoicing has a statistically significant negative coefficient at the 5 per cent level in specifications (1) and (4). This result is consistent with the hypothesis that the firms with larger shares of Japanese yen invoicing have a lower tendency to use financial hedging. In contrast, the share of US dollar invoicing has a statistically significant positive coefficient at the 5 per cent level in specifications (2) and (3), which suggests that firms with larger shares of foreign currency denominated invoicing engage more actively in financial hedging through the market to address exchange rate risk. The number of foreign currencies that a firm uses also has statistically significant positive impacts on use of financial hedging. The dummy for 'marry and

Table 5.18   *Impacts of invoice currency and pricing policy on the use of financial hedging*

Dependent variable: Dummy for the use of financial hedging

Model	Probit Model					Ordered Probit Model				
Dependent variable	0 = No use of financial hedging 1 = Use of financial hedging					0 = No use of currency hedging 1 = One kind of financial hedging 2 = More than two kinds of financial hedging				
	(1)	(2)	(3)	(4)	(5)	(6)	(7)	(8)	(9)	(10)
Log of total consolidated sales	0.230*** (0.080)	0.236*** (0.080)		0.253*** (0.083)	0.260*** (0.083)	0.245*** (0.062)	0.246*** (0.062)		0.237*** (0.062)	0.238*** (0.063)
Total foreign sales / total consolidated sales	0.008 (0.006)	0.008 (0.006)		0.010 (0.006)	0.010 (0.006)	0.011** (0.004)	0.011** (0.004)	0.011** (0.004)	0.011** (0.005)	0.011** (0.005)
Share of Japanese yen invoicing in total exports	-0.707** (0.309)			-0.788** (0.323)		-0.572** (0.258)			-0.598** (0.265)	
Share of USD invoicing in total exports		0.791** (0.333)	0.712** (0.301)		0.831** (0.346)		0.716*** (0.271)	0.756*** (0.274)		0.719** (0.279)
Number of foreign currencies to be used	0.139** (0.067)	0.156** (0.067)		0.154** (0.072)	0.172** (0.072)	0.085** (0.037)	0.092** (0.037)		0.100** (0.042)	0.109*** (0.042)
Dummy for marry & netting			0.390* (0.209)					0.368* (0.189)		

Table 5.18 (continued)

Dependent variable: Dummy for the use of financial hedging

Model	Probit Model					Ordered Probit Model				
Dependent variable	0 = No use of financial hedging 1 = Use of financial hedging					0 = No use of currency hedging 1 = One kind of financial hedging 2 = More than two kinds of financial hedging				
	(1)	(2)	(3)	(4)	(5)	(6)	(7)	(8)	(9)	(10)
Dummy for pass-through				-0.600*** (0.231)	-0.579** (0.229)				-0.362** (0.182)	-0.348* (0.181)
# of observations	196	196	212	185	185	196	196	194	185	185
McFadden R-squared / Pseudo R-squared	0.171	0.173	0.053	0.186	0.185	0.162	0.167	0.075	0.157	0.161

Notes:
1. Estimated coefficient and its standard error (in parentheses) are reported in each column.
2. ***, ** and * mean that the estimated coefficients are statistically significant at 1%, 5% and 10%, respectively.

Source: Authors' calculation.

netting' has a positive coefficient but is statistically significant only at the 10 per cent level. Lastly, the dummy for pass-through pricing policy has a statistically significant negative coefficient, which means that firms able to impose currency risks against their customers in negotiations have a lower tendency to use financial hedging.

We also estimated the ordered probit model using a dependent variable that takes the value of 2 if the firm uses more than two types of financial hedging tools, and 1 if only one financial hedging tool is used. Alternatively, it is zero if no financial hedging is undertaken. Estimated results are similar to those of the probit model except for the statistical significance of the estimated coefficient for 'foreign sales ratio'. The foreign sales ratio in specifications (6) to (10) has a statistically significant positive coefficient at the 5 per cent level, which means that firms that are more dependent on the overseas market more actively engage in financial hedging.

In addition, we conducted another estimation by replacing the dependent variable with the probability of using operational hedging (implementation of 'marry and netting'). Table 5.19 presents these estimated results. We again confirm that larger firms use operational hedging more actively. The estimated coefficient on the foreign sales ratio is positive and statistically significant. In addition, the share of yen invoicing has statistically significant negative coefficient at the 1 per cent level in specification (2), and the share of US dollar invoicing has a statistically significant positive coefficient at the 1 per cent level in specifications (1), (3) and (4). This result is consistent with the hypothesis that firms with larger shares of yen invoicing have a lower tendency to use operational hedging; on the other hand, a firm that uses US dollar invoicing is more likely to utilize 'marry and netting'. Furthermore, a firm that has an internal rule regarding a hedging ratio is more likely to use 'marry and netting', which means that a firm with more systematic risk management utilizes operational hedging.

$$\text{Prob}(\beta_i^{OH} = 1) = \alpha_0 + \alpha_1 \, Size_i + \alpha_2 \, Foreign \, Sales \, Ratio + \alpha_3 \, Number \, of \, Foreign \, Currency_i + \beta_1 \, Share \, of \, Japanese \, yen \, Invoicing_i + \beta_2 \, Share \, of \, US \, dollar \, Invoicing_i + \gamma_1 \, Number \, of \, Financial \, Hedging \, Tool_i + \gamma_2 \, Dummy \, of \, Internal \, Rule \, of \, Hedging \, Ratio_i + \varepsilon_i \qquad (5.2)$$

where β_i^{OH} is the operational hedging dummy for firm i.

To summarize our empirical analyses, we confirm the following findings: first, Japanese firms use both operational and financial hedging complementarily; second, yen invoicing substitutes for operational and financial hedging; third, adoption of a pricing policy consistent with the exchange

Table 5.19 *Impacts of invoice currency on use of operational hedging*

Dependent variable: Dummy for the use of operational hedging (marry & netting)

Model	Probit Model			
Dependent variable	0 = No use of operational hedging; 1 = Use of operational hedging			
	(1)	(2)	(3)	(4)
Log of total consolidated sales	0.162*** (0.063)	0.143*** (0.064)		
Total foreign sales / total consolidated sales	0.022*** (0.005)	0.022*** (0.005)	0.022*** (0.005)	
Share of Japanese yen invoicing in total exports		−1.335*** (0.306)		
Share of USD invoicing in total exports	1.293*** (0.316)		1.309*** (0.319)	0.956** (0.420)
Number of financial hedging tool			0.309* (0.164)	
Internal rule of hedge ratio (%)				0.010** (0.005)
# of observations	194	194	194	101
McFadden R-squared	0.201	0.211	0.188	0.067

Notes:
1. Estimated coefficient and its standard error (in parentheses) are reported in each column.
2. ***, ** and * mean that the estimated coefficients are statistically significant at 1%, 5% and 10%, respectively.

Source: Authors' calculation.

rate pass-through also substitutes for financial hedging; and fourth, a firm with more systematic risk management is more likely to utilize operational hedging.[8]

5.5   CONCLUSION

As described in this chapter, this is the first detailed investigation of the exchange rate risk management policies utilized by Japanese firms. From the results of the 2009 RIETI Survey and our subsequent empirical analysis using this survey's results, the features of Japanese exporting firms' exchange risk management behaviour can be summarized as follows. First, firms with higher sales and greater dependency on foreign markets more actively engage in exchange rate risk management. Second, Japanese firms use both financial and operational hedging complementarily. Third, yen denominated invoicing itself can reduce firms' exposure. Our contribution lies in demonstrating how Japanese exporting firms combine three different exchange rate risk management policies, namely, operational and financial hedging and exchange rate pass-through under their own choice of invoicing currency. Given Japanese firms' growing regional production networks, our findings based on the questionnaire study will have important implications for exporting firms seeking to expand their overseas operations in the future.

As our results indicated, small-sized firms have little experience in conducting exchange rate risk management. Therefore, it is important for them to learn how large multinational firms use and combine exchange rate risk management tools effectively. In addition, policymakers have to recognize that both financial and operational hedging play important roles in mitigating exchange rate risk, especially for the firms choosing US dollar invoicing. In this sense, promoting deregulation of foreign transactions and foreign exchange markets particularly in Asian countries is indispensable to supporting firms' effective exchange rate risk management. As a consequence, our new findings have important implications not only for Japanese firms' exchange rate risk managers seeking to build a more efficient exchange risk management system but also for policymakers

---

[8]   Ito et al. (2016b) investigated the relation between Japanese firms' exposure to exchange rate risk and their risk management instruments, which were taken from the same questionnaire survey. Our results confirm that the higher a firm's US dollar invoicing share, the greater its foreign exchange exposure, which can be reduced by both financial and operational hedging.

aiming to support both current and future expansion of Japanese firms' regional production networks.

The questionnaire method employed in this study has well-known limitations as well as benefits. Supplementary sources such as firms' financial reports were therefore used to strengthen the analysis. Some of our results are not sufficiently strong because there were insufficient items in the questionnaire survey; this should be partially reinforced by another source, such as firms' financial reports. Particularly for operational hedges, we use only 'marry and netting' as a proxy for operational hedges. However, other aspects reflect firms' operational hedging behaviour, such as foreign debt ratio, R&D investment and number of foreign subsidiaries. These remain issues to be investigated in future studies.

6. Invoice currency choice in global production and sales networks

6.1 INTRODUCTION

Invoice currency decisions in international trade are important for firms' overseas operations and global business strategies. Through active foreign direct investment, large firms in advanced countries have built global sales and procurement networks. Japanese firms, for instance, have developed regional production networks in Asia. Typically, they export parts to an Asian country to be manufactured into intermediate goods with other parts and local labour. Then the semi-finished goods are exported to yet another country to be assembled into finished goods. Then finished goods are exported to advanced countries, such as the US or Europe. How do the global firms accommodate the impact of volatility of multiple exchange rates in their pricing or invoicing decisions in terms of their global production and sales networks?

In Chapter 2 we provided two puzzles of the Japanese invoicing currency pattern, and the second puzzle is the large share of US dollar-invoiced trade between Japan and Asian countries despite growing intra-firm trade along production and supply chains. To solve the second puzzle, it is necessary to collect information on invoice currency choices made by Japanese overseas subsidiaries especially operating in Asia. However, to our knowledge, previous studies have neither collected information on subsidiaries' choice of invoice currency nor empirically examined what determines the invoice currency along their production chains.[1]

This chapter presents rich information on firm-level invoicing choices made by Japanese overseas subsidiaries, which were obtained from the large-scale questionnaire survey rounds conducted in 2010 and 2014. We particularly focus on the production subsidiaries' choice of invoice

---

[1] Recently several studies used information on the invoice currency choice obtained from unpublished customs-level data. See, for instance, Chung (2016), Devereux et al. (2017), Goldberg and Tille (2016), Gopinath and Rigobon (2008) and Gopinath et al. (2010). However, no studies have analysed the choice of invoice currency made by overseas subsidiaries.

currency along their regional and global production chains. Specifically, we obtained information on which currency is used for production subsidiaries' imports/procurements and exports/sales, identity of trading partners (intra-firm trade or arm's-length trade) and from (to) which source (destination) country the subsidiary imports (exports). Product names of import and export goods are also obtained to identify whether each product is a differentiated product in terms of Rauch (1999). By utilizing product-level information, we empirically investigate what factors determine the choice of invoice currency in overseas subsidiaries' exports along regional and global production chains.

Friberg and Wilander (2008), who carried out a questionnaire survey with Swedish exporters, have found that the customer's (importer's) currency is most often used in both intra-firm trade and arm's-length trade. In contrast, our two rounds of questionnaire surveys reveal that Japanese production subsidiaries operating in Asia tend to choose both the yen and the US dollar in their trade with Japan-based headquarters and group companies. The US dollar share increased from the first questionnaire survey to the second survey, especially in Asian exports to Japan. We also find that the US dollar is largely used by Japanese subsidiaries operating in all regions, whereas the European currencies are frequently used by subsidiaries operating in Europe.

We also conduct a logit estimation to investigate the determinants of invoice currency choice, mainly focusing on production subsidiaries operating in Asia. First, we find that conventional determinants such as exchange rate volatility and product differentiation have little impact on the subsidiaries' choice of invoice currency. Second, we demonstrate that in the production subsidiary's exports to Japan, intra-firm trade along its production chains facilitates yen-invoiced transactions, especially in the case of intermediate-goods exports. Third, exchange risk hedging instruments such as 'marry and netting' also promotes subsidiaries' yen-invoiced exports to Japan. Fourth, we find significantly negative impact of the group company's US dependence on subsidiaries' yen-invoiced exports. As long as the group company has a high dependence on the US market in terms of consolidated sales, Asia-based subsidiaries will have a lower (higher) tendency to choose the yen (US dollar) even for the subsidiaries' exports to Japan. Invoice currency choice in intra-firm trades may be determined by the final destination at the end of the production chains.

The remainder of this chapter is organized as follows. Section 6.2 describes the questionnaire survey. Section 6.3 presents the invoice currency choices of Japanese production subsidiaries by destination and source countries (regions) and section 6.4 reveals the invoice currency choice behaviour in intra-firm trade. Section 6.5 presents the result of the logit estimation to examine the determinants of invoicing decisions by Japanese production subsidiaries. Finally, section 6.6 concludes this chapter.

6.2   QUESTIONNAIRE SURVEYS: RIETI SURVEYS OF JAPANESE OVERSEAS SUBSIDIARIES IN 2010 AND 2014

In August 2010 and November 2014 we conducted a large-scale question-naire survey (henceforth, the 2010 Survey and the 2014 Survey) of Japanese firms' overseas subsidiaries. Conducting a large-scale questionnaire survey is quite expensive and we were fortunate to have financial support from the Research Institute of Economy, Trade and Industry (RIETI).[2] We sent questionnaires to 16 020 and 18 932 subsidiaries in August 2010 and November 2014 to collect firm-level information on FY2009 and FY2013, respectively. Surveyed subsidiaries were chosen from the Toyo Keizai's Overseas Japanese Companies database (henceforth, the OJC database). In the 2010 Survey, we chose subsidiaries of manufacturing, wholesale, or controlling offices that operated either in 21 Asia-Pacific countries (areas), three North-American countries (areas) or 37 European countries (areas). In the 2014 Survey, we added subsidiaries operating in South American countries to the sample. A total of 1479 and 1640 subsidiaries responded to the questionnaires in the 2010 and 2014 Surveys, respectively. We admit that the response rate of the questionnaire surveys is quite low. However, we collected very detailed information on invoice currency choices by Japanese overseas subsidiaries, which has not been obtained by previous studies.[3]

Table 6.1 compares the distribution of subsidiaries by industry between the 2010 and 2014 Surveys and the METI Survey, a well-known com-prehensive survey of Japanese overseas subsidiaries.[4] This comparison

---

[2]   We would like to thank RIETI for conducting the 2010 and 2014 Surveys, 'Questionnaire Survey on the Choice of Invoice Currency by Japanese Overseas Subsidiaries'. Questionnaires were sent out to manufacturing subsidiaries mainly owned by Japanese firms. If sales sub-sidiaries and controlling offices are not owned by Japanese manufacturing firms but by sales companies or financial institutions, they are excluded from the questionnaire survey.
[3]   Firms that responded to the 2010 and 2014 Surveys did not necessarily answer all questions, because our questions were very detailed. In the following sections, we tabulate the survey results, but the number of responses (answers) to each question often becomes smaller than the total number of responses.
[4]   We refer to the following two surveys: Ministry of Economy, Trade and Industry (METI), *The 40th Basic Survey on Overseas Business Activities* and *The 44th Basic Survey on Overseas Business Activities*.

Table 6.1 *Sample firms of the RIETI Survey*

Industry	2010 Survey				2014 Survey			
	RIETI			METI	RIETI			METI
	All 16020	Respondent 1479	Response Rate (%)	Respondent 12219	All 18932	Respondent 1640	Response Rate (%)	Respondent 19576
Manufacturing Industry Total	8990	784	8.7	7742	10247	806	7.9	9075
Foods	453	42	9.3	387	518	43	8.3	427
Textiles & Apparel	436	22	5.0	368	449	26	5.8	456
Pulp & Papers	78	12	15.4	129	79	7	8.9	140
Chemicals	1406	125	8.9	863	1574	140	8.9	984
Pharmaceuticals	150	16	10.7		199	14	7.0	
Petroleum and Coals	28	3	10.7	35	23	2	8.7	37
Rubber Products	249	16	6.4		290	23	7.9	
Glass & Ceramics	225	15	6.7	199	249	18	7.2	256
Steel Products	221	22	10.0	219	302	22	7.3	268
Nonferrous Metals	241	20	8.3	251	271	29	10.7	281
Metal Products	452	39	8.6	358	518	44	8.5	473
Machinery	1098	97	8.8	1007	1296	110	8.5	1273
Electrical Machinery	1812	150	8.3	1438	1968	157	8.0	1561
Transport Equipment	1383	136	9.8	1567	1646	121	7.4	1730
Precision Instruments	298	22	7.4		335	15	4.5	
Other Manufacturing	460	47	10.2	921	530	35	6.6	1189
Wholesale Industry Total	7030	695	10.3	4477	8685	834	9.6	10501

Source: 2010 and 2014 RIETI Survey; METI, *The 40th Basic Survey on Overseas Business Activities* and *The 44th Basic Survey on Overseas Business Activities.*

184

shows that the distribution of our 2010 and 2014 Surveys is similar to the corresponding METI Surveys. Although not presented in this chapter, Ito et al. (2015a) compared the simple arithmetic average of subsidiaries' sales amounts between the two surveys and confirmed their similarities.

While collecting these data on invoice currency use for both production and sales subsidiaries, this chapter focuses on the invoice currency decisions of production subsidiaries. Japanese firms have built global production and sales networks in which intra-firm trade plays an important role. In particular, regional production fragmentation in Asia has recently gained a great deal of attention. Against a backdrop of a growing body of literature on global value chains, we investigate the invoicing currency choice by overseas production subsidiaries that import intermediate inputs and export their products to various destination countries.[5]

6.3   OVERVIEW OF SUBSIDIARIES' TRADE AND INVOICING PATTERNS

Through the 2010 and 2014 Surveys, we obtained information on sales (export) and procurement (import) patterns of Japanese subsidiaries. Information on trading partner and choice of invoice currency for each transaction are also collected. Figure 6.1 presents a transaction map of one sample subsidiary (respondent) that operates in China. This manufacturing subsidiary imports or procures intermediate inputs from various source countries or the domestic market (shown by the dotted arrow) and exports products to various destination countries or sells products in the local market (shown by the solid arrow). For each transaction, we collect information on which currency is used for invoicing in exports and imports. We thus have two types of data on invoicing currency.

First, we calculate the *shares* of invoice currency for each subsidiary's exports and imports, which forms a basis of a firm-level invoicing currency data. Second, we tabulate data on the choice of invoice currency for each *product*. Since we have collected product-level information (that is, name of products traded and associated currency in invoice), we can distinguish

---

    5   Japanese sales subsidiaries tend to import final consumption goods and to sell them in local markets. Invoicing currency decisions in Japanese exports to overseas sales subsidiaries were investigated in Chapter 4 by using the data obtained from questionnaire surveys with Japanese head offices. However, it is worth analysing possible differences in invoicing currency choice between Japanese exports to production subsidiaries and those to sales subsidiaries using the data set obtained from questionnaire surveys with overseas subsidiaries as well, which is an issue to be investigated in our future studies.

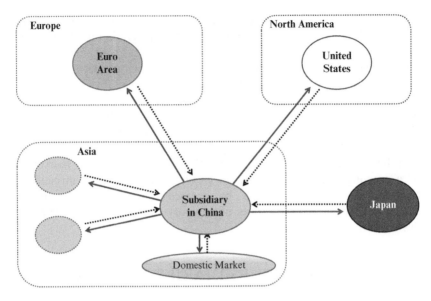

Note: Dotted arrows show the subsidiary's procurements (imports) of intermediate or finished goods from Japan. Solid arrows represent the subsidiary's sales (exports) of intermediate or finished goods to various destinations.

Figure 6.1   Sales and procurement patterns of overseas subsidiaries in China

between invoicing decisions for differentiated products and homogeneous products, as well as between final consumption goods and intermediate goods. We have also collected information on characteristics of a trading partner, for example a group company (including parent company) or other non-related company, for each product or intermediate input traded, which enables us to distinguish between invoicing currency choices for intra-firm trade and arm's length trade.

Before analysing the detailed data on the choice of invoice currency, let us check whether invoice currency is the same as settlement currency. Table 6.2 presents the regional breakdown data and shows that on average 88.6 per cent of sample firms (respondents) use the same currency for invoicing and settlement (column (1) of Table 6.2), and 8.1 per cent of firms generally use the same currency for invoicing and settlement with some exceptions (column (2)). The sum of these two shares amounts to 96.7 per cent, which means that most firms use the same currency for both stages of invoicing and settlement. Chapter 4 of this book also presented the result of how firms answer the same question through questionnaire surveys

Table 6.2   *Invoice currency and settlement currency*
                (Question) Is the same currency used for invoicing and settlement?

	Number of respondents	(1) Invoice currency is the same as settlement currency	(2) Invoice currency is generally the same as settlement currency, but there are some exceptions	(3) Invoice currency is typically different from settlement currency
Asia	743 (100.0)	646 (86.9)	60 (8.1)	37 (5.0)
Oceania	61 (100.0)	57 (93.4)	4 (6.6)	0 (0.0)
North America	339 (100.0)	313 (92.3)	23 (6.8)	3 (0.9)
South America	50 (100.0)	48 (96.0)	1 (2.0)	1 (2.0)
Euro Area	206 (100.0)	180 (87.4)	23 (11.2)	3 (1.5)
Other Europe	130 (100.0)	110 (84.6)	13 (10.0)	7 (5.4)
World	1529 (100.0)	1354 (88.6)	124 (8.1)	51 (3.3)

Note: Percentage share is in parenthesis.

Source: 2014 RIETI Survey.

with Japanese head offices, and obtained a very similar result.[6] Thus, we proceed to the following sections by assuming that invoice currency is the same as settlement currency.

6.3.1   Trade Patterns of Japanese Subsidiaries

Table 6.3 shows both import/procurement and export/sales information for manufacturing subsidiaries by source/destination country and by the

---

[6]   This finding is consistent with Friberg and Wilander (2008) who obtained similar data by a questionnaire survey conducted on Swedish exporters.

Table 6.3 Trade patterns of Japanese manufacturing subsidiaries

Source Country/Region Breakdown	2010				2014			
	Number of Respondents	(a) Imports from Japan (%)	(b) Local Procurements (%)	(c) Imports from Others (%)	Number of Respondents	(a) Imports from Japan (%)	(b) Local Procurements (%)	(c) Imports from Others (%)
Asia	**490**	**34.8**	**48.6**	**16.6**	**365**	**34.1**	**45.9**	**19.7**
• China	133	36.9	54.2	8.9	106	35.0	55.7	9.3
• **ASEAN-6**	**277**	**33.3**	**47.4**	**19.3**	**206**	**32.2**	**42.5**	**25.4**
North America	**178**	**30.5**	**60.0**	**9.6**	**137**	**25.6**	**60.0**	**13.7**
• United States	162	31.7	60.0	8.4	129	25.7	61.0	12.6
Europe	**108**	**26.4**	**47.5**	**25.1**	**85**	**23.8**	**49.4**	**26.6**
• Euro Area	65	27.1	53.1	18.2	47	21.8	57.2	21.0
• United Kingdom	15	29.9	44.6	25.5	17	32.9	36.4	30.1
Oceania	**18**	**12.9**	**66.8**	**20.2**	**15**	**13.9**	**62.7**	**23.4**
South America	n.a.	n.a.	n.a.	n.a.	**22**	**23.7**	**55.8**	**20.5**

Exports and Sales Destination	2010				2014			
	Number of Respondents	(a) Exports to Japan (%)	(b) Local Sales (%)	(c) Exports to Others (%)	Number of Respondents	(a) Exports to Japan (%)	(b) Local Sales (%)	(c) Exports to Others (%)
Asia	**492**	**28.0**	**47.9**	**24.1**	**342**	**26.0**	**50.3**	**23.7**
• China	135	36.4	49.1	14.5	96	31.7	52.6	15.7
• **ASEAN-6**	**276**	**25.4**	**44.7**	**29.9**	**197**	**26.0**	**46.1**	**27.9**
North America	**178**	**5.1**	**85.0**	**9.9**	**134**	**9.7**	**77.1**	**13.2**

• United States	162	4.6	86.8	8.6	127	8.6	78.3	13.1
Europe	**109**	**6.3**	**62.7**	**31.0**	**79**	**2.7**	**59.6**	**37.6**
• Euro Area	65	4.8	67.1	28.1	44	2.2	61.3	36.5
• United Kingdom	14	4.1	64.8	31.1	14	1.4	54.3	44.3
Oceania	**20**	**23.8**	**48.2**	**28.1**	**16**	**28.8**	**45.6**	**25.6**
South America	n.a.	n.a.	n.a.	n.a.	**17**	**3.6**	**74.7**	**21.7**

Notes: The upper panel shows intermediate input imports or procurements. The lower panel indicates exports or sales of production goods. ASEAN-6 includes Singapore, Malaysia, Indonesia, the Philippines, Thailand and Vietnam.

Source: 2010 and 2014 RIETI Survey.

Japanese subsidiary's location. As for the import/procurement patterns, local procurement accounts for the largest share in most countries or regions. However, Japanese subsidiaries in Asia tend to import more intermediate inputs from Japan compared with subsidiaries located in other countries/regions. In the 2014 Survey, Japanese subsidiaries in Asia imported 34.1 per cent of their intermediate inputs from Japan. This import/procurement pattern did not change markedly between the 2010 and 2014 Surveys.

Export/sales patterns differ markedly across regions. In North America, subsidiaries have a strong tendency to sell their products in the local market: 77.1 per cent of sales are directed toward local markets in the 2014 Survey. Japanese subsidiaries in Europe sell 59.6 per cent of their products in the local market in the 2014 Survey. The share of exports to other countries is 37.6 per cent, most of which are likely to be other European countries. In contrast, the share of local sales is 50.3 per cent in Asia, with 26.0 per cent of sales (exports) destined for Japan, while the share of exports to Japan is only 9.7 per cent and 2.7 per cent in North America and Europe, respectively. Thus, a percentage of exports to Japan in total exports is much higher in Asia than in North America and Europe. In addition, 23.7 per cent of Asian subsidiaries' exports are directed to other countries (excluding Japan), indicating that a notable feature of Asian subsidiaries' trade patterns is the strong tendency to export goods to foreign countries, including both Japan and other countries.

6.3.2   Invoice Currency Choice in Subsidiaries' Exports and Imports

Local sales and procurements
Using the *share* data obtained from the 2010 and 2014 Surveys, we discuss the subsidiaries' invoice currency choice in exports and imports. But, before observing the data for subsidiaries' exports and imports, let us summarize the subsidiaries' currency choice in their procurements from and sales in the local market, although we do not present any tables and figures about the local sales and procurements.[7] First, the local currency is mainly used in local procurements and sales by Japanese manufacturing subsidiaries. According to the 2014 Survey, for instance, 92.7 per cent of local procurements and 96.5 per cent of local sales in North America are priced in US dollars. In Europe, the euro and local currencies are generally used: 87.7 per cent of local procurements and 92.0 per cent of local sales are priced either in euros or local currencies.

---

[7]   See Ito et al. (2015b) and Sato and Shimizu (2016) for the choice of currency in subsidiaries' local procurements and sales.

Second, the US dollar and the yen are more often used in local procurements and sales in Asia. In local procurements of intermediate inputs in Asia, 40.7 per cent are priced in either yen or US dollars, and the US dollar is used more than the yen in local procurements: 28.9 per cent and 11.8 per cent are invoiced in US dollars and yen, respectively. While 71 per cent of local sales are priced in local currencies, the US dollar is used for 23.2 per cent of local sales in Asia, which is much higher than in Europe and other countries. The yen is used only for 3.2 per cent of local sales by Asia-based subsidiaries.

Subsidiaries' trade with Japan
Figure 6.2 shows the Japanese subsidiaries' invoice currency choice in imports from and exports to Japan. First, according to the 2014 Survey, 72.3 per cent of subsidiaries' imports of intermediate inputs from Japan are invoiced in US dollars in North America, while 87.3 per cent of

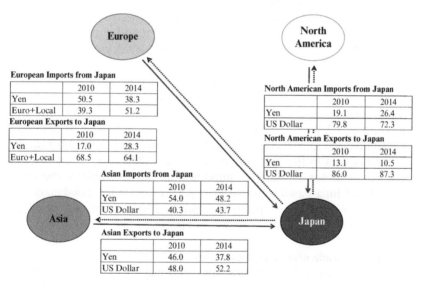

European Imports from Japan

	2010	2014
Yen	50.5	38.3
Euro+Local	39.3	51.2

European Exports to Japan

	2010	2014
Yen	17.0	28.3
Euro+Local	68.5	64.1

North American Imports from Japan

	2010	2014
Yen	19.1	26.4
US Dollar	79.8	72.3

North American Exports to Japan

	2010	2014
Yen	13.1	10.5
US Dollar	86.0	87.3

Asian Imports from Japan

	2010	2014
Yen	54.0	48.2
US Dollar	40.3	43.7

Asian Exports to Japan

	2010	2014
Yen	46.0	37.8
US Dollar	48.0	52.2

Notes: Dotted arrows show the subsidiaries' procurements (imports) of intermediate or finished goods from Japan. Solid arrows represent the subsidiaries' sales (exports) of intermediate or finished goods to various destinations. Invoice currency share obtained from 2010 and 2014 Surveys is presented. 'Euro+Local' denotes the sum of euro and other European currencies.

Source: 2010 and 2014 RIETI Survey.

Figure 6.2   Overseas subsidiaries invoice currency choice in imports from and exports to Japan (%)

subsidiaries' exports to Japan are invoiced in US dollars. The share of yen-invoiced transactions is far smaller: 26.4 per cent of North American imports from Japan and 10.5 per cent of its exports to Japan are invoiced in the yen.

Second, 51.2 per cent of imports from Japan are invoiced in the euro or other local currencies in Europe, while 64.1 per cent of exports from subsidiaries in Europe to Japan are invoiced in the euro or other European currencies. The share of the yen is higher in Europe than in North America: 38.3 per cent of European imports from Japan and 28.3 per cent of its exports to Japan are invoiced in the yen.

Third, in Asia, yen-invoiced imports are more common than US dollar-invoiced imports. According to the 2014 Survey, 48.2 per cent of imports from Japan are invoiced in yen, while the US dollar's invoicing share is 43.7 per cent (Figure 6.2). However, in exports from Asia-based subsidiaries to Japan, the US dollar tends to be used more than the yen: in 2014, 52.2 per cent of exports to Japan are invoiced in US dollars, while the yen accounts for just 37.8 per cent. Moreover, the share of yen-invoiced transactions declined from 2010 to 2014 in both Asian exports and imports. The share of US dollar transactions increased during that period, especially in Asian exports to Japan.

Fourth, Asian currencies are not frequently used in exports and imports by Japanese subsidiaries in Asia: other currencies including Asian currencies account for 10 per cent or less.[8] Although the data is not presented in this chapter, China-based subsidiaries increased their share of renminbi (RMB) invoiced imports from Japan from 3.8 per cent in the 2010 survey to 10.4 per cent in the 2014 Survey. However, RMB is not used at all in other countries for subsidiaries' imports from Japan. Similarly, the share of RMB in China-based subsidiaries' exports to Japan increased markedly from 0.8 per cent to 13.9 per cent, whereas RMB is not used at all by Japanese subsidiaries in other Asian countries.[9]

Subsidiaries' trade with foreign countries

Figure 6.3 presents the share of invoice currency in subsidiaries' imports from and exports to foreign countries except Japan. In both the 2010 and 2014 Surveys, 80 per cent or more of imports and exports are invoiced in US dollars by Japanese subsidiaries operating in North America. Japanese

---

[8] According to the 2014 Survey, Asian currencies are used only for 7.4 per cent of Asia-based subsidiaries' imports from Japan and for 9.5 per cent of their exports to Japan. See Ito et al. (2015b) and Sato and Shimizu (2016).

[9] See Sato and Shimizu (2016) for the use of RMB as invoice currency in subsidiaries' exports and imports.

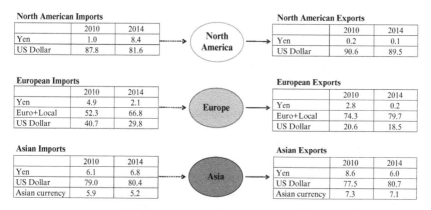

North American Imports

	2010	2014
Yen	1.0	8.4
US Dollar	87.8	81.6

North American Exports

	2010	2014
Yen	0.2	0.1
US Dollar	90.6	89.5

European Imports

	2010	2014
Yen	4.9	2.1
Euro+Local	52.3	66.8
US Dollar	40.7	29.8

European Exports

	2010	2014
Yen	2.8	0.2
Euro+Local	74.3	79.7
US Dollar	20.6	18.5

Asian Imports

	2010	2014
Yen	6.1	6.8
US Dollar	79.0	80.4
Asian currency	5.9	5.2

Asian Exports

	2010	2014
Yen	8.6	6.0
US Dollar	77.5	80.7
Asian currency	7.3	7.1

Notes: Tables on the left-hand side show the share of invoice currency in imports of Japanese subsidiaries located in North America, Europe or Asia. Tables on the right-hand side indicate the share of invoice currency in exports of Japanese subsidiaries located in North America, Europe or Asia. 'Euro+Local' denotes the sum of euro and other European currencies.

Source: 2010 and 2014 RIETI Survey.

Figure 6.3   *Overseas subsidiaries' invoice currency choice in imports from and exports to foreign countries except Japan (%)*

subsidiaries in Europe seldom use the yen for their imports from and exports to foreign countries excluding Japan. Only 2.1 per cent of imports from and 0.2 per cent of exports to foreign countries are invoiced in the yen. Almost all exports and imports of Europe-based subsidiaries are invoiced mainly in European currencies and partly in US dollars.

Our main interest is to what extent the yen is used for Asia-based subsidiaries' imports from and exports to foreign countries. Figure 6.3 shows that, according to the 2014 Survey, only 6.8 per cent of imports from and 6 per cent of exports to foreign countries are invoiced in yen, while 80 per cent or more of imports and exports are invoiced in US dollars. Although not presented in this chapter, Sato and Shimizu (2016) show that more than 80 per cent of Asia-based subsidiaries' exports to other Asian countries are invoiced in US dollars. Thus, the US dollar is largely used in Asia-based subsidiaries' trade with other countries, especially in intra-Asian trade.

Finally, Figure 6.3 indicates that Asia-based subsidiaries did not increase their use of Asian currencies. We do not present the detailed data on invoice currency choice of subsidiaries in each Asian country, but RMB-invoiced transactions increased only slightly in Asia-based subsidiaries' exports to foreign countries. Sato and Shimizu (2016) show that, according to the 2014 Survey, RMB is used in only 5.2 per cent of China-based subsidiaries' exports to foreign countries compared with approximately 80 per cent of exports being invoiced in US dollars. Only Taiwan uses RMB in exports to other countries, whereas Taiwan's RMB transactions are likely to be related to Taiwan's exports to China. Japanese subsidiaries operating in other Asian countries did not use RMB at all for their exports to foreign countries.[10]

6.3.3   Invoice Currency Choice by Industry

Let us next observe whether invoice currency choices differ across industries focusing on Asia-based subsidiaries. Tables 6.4a and 6.4b present the invoice currency share of Asia-based subsidiaries' imports from and exports to Japan, respectively. First, it is hard to find a clear pattern of invoice currency choice in Asia-based subsidiaries' imports from and exports to Japan. In imports from Japan (Table 6.4a), the share of the yen is somewhat higher than that of the US dollar. In the 2014 Survey, the share of the yen exceeds 50 per cent in three industries (Chemicals; Metal Products; Machinery). But, the yen invoice share also declined from 2010 to 2014 in three industries, including Metal Products, Machinery and Transport Equipment.

Second, Table 6.4b presents the invoice currency choice of Asia-based subsidiaries' exports to Japan. From 2010 to 2014, the US dollar increased its role of invoice currency, and the share of US dollar-invoiced exports appears to be larger than or at least almost the same as the share of yen-invoiced exports in 2014.

Third, and more importantly, it appears hard to find a clear pattern of invoice currency choice by industry. In the 2010 Survey, for instance, the share of yen-invoiced imports is 65.3 per cent and 70.8 per cent in Asia-based subsidiaries' imports of Machinery and Transport Equipment, respectively (Table 6.4a). However, the yen-invoiced share of these industries declined largely in the 2014 Survey, and the industry difference of invoice currency choice becomes smaller. This is the case even for Asia-based subsidiaries' exports to Japan (Table 6.4b).

Fourth, in the case of Asia-based subsidiaries' imports from and exports to foreign countries, the US dollar is mainly used and the share of the yen is very low, mostly 10 per cent or less in the 2014 Survey, in all industries (Tables 6.5a and 6.5b). Despite a difference in the share of invoice currency across industries, it appears hard to find a clear pattern of invoice currency choice, except that the Machinery and Metal Products exhibit the highest share of yen-invoiced imports and exports across industries.

---

[10]   See also Ito et al. (2015b) for further details of RMB transactions in Asian countries.

*Table 6.4   Asia-based subsidiaries' invoice currency choice by industry:
trade with Japan*

6.4a   Imports from Japan by selected industry

Asia-based subsidiaries (2014 Survey)	Number of Respondents	(a) Yen (%)	(b) US Dollar (%)	(c) Euro (%)	(d) Renminbi (%)	(e) Local Currency (%)	(f) Others (%)
Chemicals	43	57.7	41.6	0.0	0.7	0.0	0.0
Metal Products	24	55.8	32.1	0.0	7.9	0.4	3.8
Machinery	39	57.4	31.7	2.6	4.7	3.5	0.0
Electrical Machinery	58	41.9	45.9	0.0	5.1	7.0	0.1
Transport Equipment	38	49.9	39.7	0.0	2.5	7.9	0.0
(2010 Survey)							
Chemicals	60	51.6	41.0	0.4	0.0	6.2	0.8
Metal Products	25	62.7	26.0	0.0	4.0	7.3	0.0
Machinery	44	65.3	27.4	2.3	2.4	2.5	0.1
Electrical Machinery	98	40.2	56.3	0.0	0.8	1.6	1.0
Transport Equipment	55	70.8	24.7	0.0	0.0	4.5	0.0

6.4   INVOICE CURRENCY CHOICE IN INTRA-FIRM TRADE

In this section we investigate *product*-level data with regard to the choice of invoice currency, focusing particularly on production subsidiaries in Asia (all Asian countries). Tables 6.4 to 6.7 present the share of invoice currencies in 2010 and 2014. Through the questionnaires, we collected information on the main invoice currency for a particular product (or intermediate goods) in imports from or exports to a selected country. These are transaction-level data, and the volume or value of imports and exports are not collected by the questionnaire surveys. Thus, the share of invoice currency is calculated in terms of the number of transactions and the simple arithmetic average is used in this section.

6.4b   Exports to Japan by selected industry

Asia-based subsidiaries (2014 Survey)	Number of Respondents	(a) Yen (%)	(b) US Dollar (%)	(c) Euro (%)	(d) Renminbi (%)	(e) Local Currency (%)	(f) Others (%)
Chemicals	32	34.7	59.1	0.0	3.1	3.1	0.0
Metal Products	14	55.0	45.0	0.0	0.0	0.0	0.0
Machinery	30	46.8	39.5	0.0	3.3	10.3	0.0
Electrical Machinery	48	33.9	52.7	0.0	9.2	4.2	0.0
Transport Equipment	20	40.3	45.3	0.0	0.0	10.0	4.5
(2010 Survey)							
Chemicals	45	43.1	44.0	0.0	0.0	12.9	0.0
Metal Products	16	58.2	31.3	0.0	4.4	6.2	0.0
Machinery	37	49.3	39.3	0.7	0.0	10.7	0.0
Electrical Machinery	91	34.4	63.2	0.4	0.0	2.0	0.0
Transport Equipment	29	75.2	21.4	0.0	0.0	3.4	0.0

Source: 2010 and 2014 RIETI Survey.

6.4.1   Intra-firm Trade with Japan

Tables 6.6 and 6.7 show the share of invoice currency by trading partner in production subsidiaries' imports from and exports to Japan, respectively. The shares of 'Japanese Head Office' and 'Group Company' indicate invoice currency choices for intra-firm trade.

First, in US imports of intermediate inputs from Japan, Table 6.6 shows that the US dollar is the currency used most often in intra-firm imports. In 2014, 75.3 per cent of imports from Japanese head offices and 63.2 per cent of imports from group companies are invoiced in US dollars, while the rest of the imports are invoiced in the yen. A similar pattern of invoice currency choice can be observed in the euro area. In 2014, 65.7 per cent of imports from Japanese head offices are invoiced in the euro and 34.3 per cent are invoiced in the yen. In imports from group companies, however, the share of yen-invoiced imports is somewhat higher than that of euro-invoiced imports: the share of euro and yen is 41.2 per cent and 58.8 per cent, respectively.

Table 6.5   *Asia-based subsidiaries' invoice currency choice by industry:*
             trade with foreign countries except Japan

6.5a   *Imports from foreign countries (except Japan) by selected industry*

Asia-based subsidiaries (2014 Survey)		Number of Respondents	(a) Yen (%)	(b) US Dollar (%)	(c) Euro (%)	(d) Renminbi (%)	(e) Local Currency (%)	(f) Others (%)
	Chemicals	32	2.2	84.0	3.8	0.0	6.9	3.1
	Metal Products	17	4.4	84.2	0.6	0.0	0.0	10.8
	Machinery	27	10.4	76.8	6.7	0.0	5.2	1.0
	Electrical Machinery	35	8.0	83.8	2.5	3.4	2.1	0.1
	Transport Equipment	26	9.2	70.7	3.8	0.2	7.6	8.5
(2010 Survey)								
	Chemicals	44	1.7	84.0	6.6	0.1	6.0	1.7
	Metal Products	10	26.5	41.3	13.0	0.0	0.0	19.2
	Machinery	27	8.5	70.7	14.4	0.7	3.5	2.2
	Electrical Machinery	69	4.4	87.8	1.4	0.1	2.8	3.6
	Transport Equipment	27	12.4	61.8	13.6	0.0	11.6	0.7

Second, in US exports to Japan (Table 6.7), the US dollar is predominantly used. In 2014, 88.1 per cent of exports to Japanese head offices are invoiced in US dollars. In the euro area's exports to Japanese head offices, 77.8 per cent are invoiced in the euro in 2014. Thus, Japanese subsidiaries operating in advanced countries tend to choose not the yen but the exporter's currency in intra-firm exports to Japanese head offices (Table 6.7).[11]

Third, in Asian imports of intermediate inputs from Japan, the yen and the US dollar are largely used (Table 6.6). The share of the yen (54.4 per cent) is higher than that of the US dollar (39.7 per cent) in 2014 in imports from Japanese head offices, while the share of the US dollar (48.5 per cent) surpasses that of the yen (43.9 per cent) in imports from group companies.

---

[11] Our results are different from the finding of Friberg and Wilander (2008), which indicates that an importer's or customer's currency is used more often in intra-firm trade.

6.5b   Exports to foreign countries (except Japan) by selected industry

Asia-based subsidiaries (2014 Survey)	Number of Respondents	(a) Yen (%)	(b) US Dollar (%)	(c) Euro (%)	(d) Renminbi (%)	(e) Local Currency (%)	(f) Others (%)
Chemicals	38	4.5	84.1	1.1	2.4	5.6	2.4
Metal Products	15	10.0	90.0	0.0	0.0	0.0	0.0
Machinery	25	11.7	59.4	8.6	3.2	15.4	1.6
Electrical Machinery	43	4.6	84.5	3.7	2.3	2.3	2.6
Transport Equipment	26	5.8	72.1	0.0	0.0	12.1	10.0
(2010 Survey)							
Chemicals	53	2.1	74.9	3.3	1.4	14.9	3.4
Metal Products	18	16.9	64.9	5.6	4.4	0.0	8.1
Machinery	30	8.6	75.6	3.8	0.7	6.0	5.3
Electrical Machinery	73	8.1	83.2	3.1	0.0	3.4	2.2
Transport Equipment	38	15.9	65.3	5.4	1.2	11.3	0.8

Source: 2010 and 2014 RIETI Survey.

In contrast, in intra-firm exports from Asia to Japan, the US dollar-invoiced exports are more common than yen-invoiced exports (Table 6.7). According to the 2014 Survey, 60.4 per cent of Asian exports to Japanese head offices and 50 per cent of exports to group companies in Japan are invoiced in US dollars.[12]

Fourth, *Sogo Shosha* (general trading companies) play an important role in Asian imports from Japan: according to the 2014 Survey, about 22 per cent of Asia-based subsidiaries' imports from Japan were through *Sogo Shosha* in terms of the number of answers (transactions),[13] which is far larger than the corresponding imports of subsidiaries operating in other regions (Table 6.6). In Asia-based subsidiaries' imports through *Sogo Shosha*, the share of yen-invoiced imports (54.5 per cent) is larger than

[12]   Japanese subsidiaries operating in Asia also conduct a different pricing (invoicing) strategy from that observed by Friberg and Wilander (2008).
[13]   The share is calculated using the information on number of answers (transactions) reported in parenthesis in Table 6.6.

Table 6.6 Intra-firm imports from Japan

Imports from Japan (%)	Location of Subsidiaries													
	Asia		China		ASEAN-6		United States		Euro Area		Oceania		Latin America	
	2010	2014	2010	2014	2010	2014	2010	2014	2010	2014	2010	2014	2010	2014
1. Japanese Head Office														
1. JPY	58.8	54.4	53.0	43.8	57.5	58.6	20.9	24.7	50.7	34.3	44.4	55.6	n.a.	76.9
2. USD	38.0	39.7	45.5	44.8	37.7	38.5	79.1	75.3	8.5	0.0	22.2	33.3	n.a.	23.1
3. Euro	0.4	0.0	0.0	0.0	0.7	0.0	0.0	0.0	39.4	65.7	0.0	0.0	n.a.	0.0
4. Renminbi	0.2	3.6	0.8	11.5	0.0	0.0	0.0	0.0	0.0	0.0	0.0	0.0	n.a.	0.0
5. Local	2.2	2.3	0.0	0.0	3.7	3.0	0.0	0.0	0.0	0.0	33.3	11.1	n.a.	0.0
6. Others	0.4	0.0	0.8	0.0	0.4	0.0	0.0	0.0	1.4	0.0	0.0	0.0	n.a.	0.0
TOTAL	100.0	100.0	100.0	100.0	100.0	100.0	100.0	100.0	100.0	100.0	100.0	100.0	n.a.	100.0
(No. of answers)	(498)	(307)	(132)	(96)	(268)	(169)	(158)	(77)	(71)	(35)	(9)	(9)	(n.a.)	(13)
2. Group Company														
1. JPY	51.9	43.9	36.1	33.3	47.8	53.6	20.4	36.8	56.3	58.8	40.0	0.0	n.a.	33.3
2. USD	46.5	48.5	58.3	51.9	52.2	42.9	77.6	63.2	18.8	0.0	20.0	100.0	n.a.	66.7
3. Euro	0.0	0.0	0.0	0.0	0.0	0.0	2.0	0.0	25.0	41.2	0.0	0.0	n.a.	0.0
4. Renminbi	0.8	4.5	2.8	11.1	0.0	0.0	0.0	0.0	0.0	0.0	0.0	0.0	n.a.	0.0
5. Local	0.8	3.0	2.8	3.7	0.0	3.6	0.0	0.0	0.0	0.0	40.0	0.0	n.a.	0.0
6. Others	0.0	0.0	0.0	0.0	0.0	0.0	0.0	0.0	0.0	0.0	0.0	0.0	n.a.	0.0
TOTAL	100.0	100.0	100.0	100.0	100.0	100.0	100.0	100.0	100.0	100.0	100.0	100.0	n.a.	100.0
(No. of answers)	(129)	(66)	(36)	(27)	(69)	(28)	(49)	(19)	(16)	(17)	(5)	(1)	(n.a.)	(3)

Table 6.6 (continued)

Imports from Japan (%)	Location of Subsidiaries												
	Asia		China		ASEAN-6		United States		Euro Area		Oceania		Latin America	
	2010	2014	2010	2014	2010	2014	2010	2014	2010	2014	2010	2014	2010	2014
3. Japanese *Sogo Shosha*														
1. JPY	56.9	54.5	41.5	61.5	59.5	47.9	29.4	50.0	60.0	0.0	0.0	0.0	n.a.	25.0
2. USD	38.7	40.0	53.7	26.9	35.7	47.9	70.6	50.0	0.0	0.0	0.0	0.0	n.a.	75.0
3. Euro	0.0	0.0	0.0	0.0	0.0	0.0	0.0	0.0	40.0	0.0	0.0	0.0	n.a.	0.0
4. Renminbi	1.5	2.7	4.9	11.5	0.0	0.0	0.0	0.0	0.0	0.0	0.0	0.0	n.a.	0.0
5. Local	2.9	2.7	0.0	0.0	4.8	4.2	0.0	0.0	0.0	0.0	0.0	0.0	n.a.	0.0
6. Others	0.0	0.0	0.0	0.0	0.0	0.0	0.0	0.0	0.0	0.0	0.0	0.0	n.a.	0.0
TOTAL (No. of answers)	100.0 (137)	100.0 (110)	100.0 (41)	100.0 (26)	100.0 (84)	100.0 (71)	100.0 (17)	100.0 (12)	100.0 (5)	100.0 (0)	100.0 (0)	100.0 (0)	n.a. (n.a.)	100.0 (4)
4. Other Company														
1. JPY	53.4	52.0	44.4	0.0	52.5	55.6	47.1	58.3	33.3	33.3	100.0	0.0	n.a.	100.0
2. USD	32.8	44.0	33.3	100.0	35.0	44.4	47.1	41.7	0.0	33.3	0.0	0.0	n.a.	0.0
3. Euro	0.0	0.0	0.0	0.0	0.0	0.0	0.0	0.0	33.3	33.3	0.0	0.0	n.a.	0.0
4. Renminbi	3.4	0.0	22.2	0.0	0.0	0.0	0.0	0.0	0.0	0.0	0.0	0.0	n.a.	0.0
5. Local	6.9	4.0	0.0	0.0	7.5	0.0	0.0	0.0	0.0	0.0	0.0	0.0	n.a.	0.0
6. Others	3.4	0.0	0.0	0.0	5.0	0.0	5.9	0.0	33.3	0.0	0.0	0.0	n.a.	0.0
TOTAL (No. of answers)	100.0 (58)	100.0 (25)	100.0 (9)	100.0 (2)	100.0 (40)	100.0 (18)	100.0 (17)	100.0 (12)	100.0 (*9*)	100.0 (3)	100.0 (2)	100.0 (0)	n.a. (n.a.)	100.0 (2)

Notes: Figures in parenthesis (No. of answers) denote the number of transactions.

Source: 2010 and 2014 RIETI Survey.

Table 6.7 Intra-firm exports to Japan

Exports to Japan (%)	Location of Subsidiaries													
	Asia		China		ASEAN-6		United States		Euro Area		Oceania		Latin America	
	2010	2014	2010	2014	2010	2014	2010	2014	2010	2014	2010	2014	2010	2014
1. To Japanese Head Office														
1. JPY	46.3	31.3	51.8	30.9	42.4	25.9	8.3	11.9	6.3	22.2	25.0	0.0	n.a.	0.0
2. USD	45.8	60.4	46.4	53.1	45.5	69.6	91.7	88.1	6.3	0.0	37.5	75.0	n.a.	100.0
3. Euro	0.3	0.0	0.0	0.0	0.5	0.0	0.0	0.0	87.5	77.8	0.0	0.0	n.a.	0.0
4. Renminbi	0.5	5.7	1.8	16.0	0.0	0.0	0.0	0.0	0.0	0.0	0.0	0.0	n.a.	0.0
5. Local	6.8	2.6	0.0	0.0	11.1	4.5	0.0	0.0	0.0	0.0	25.0	25.0	n.a.	0.0
6. Others	0.3	0.0	0.0	0.0	0.5	0.0	0.0	0.0	0.0	0.0	12.5	0.0	n.a.	0.0
TOTAL (No. of answers)	100.0 (369)	100.0 (227)	100.0 (112)	100.0 (81)	100.0 (198)	100.0 (112)	100.0 (36)	100.0 (42)	100.0 (16)	100.0 (9)	100.0 (8)	100.0 (4)	n.a. (na.)	100.0 (3)
2. To Group Company														
1. JPY	50.8	38.1	45.5	41.2	44.7	37.5	13.3	0.0	0.0	50.0	0.0	0.0	n.a.	na.
2. USD	46.0	50.0	54.5	47.1	50.0	50.0	86.7	100.0	14.3	0.0	100.0	0.0	n.a.	na.
3. Euro	0.0	0.0	0.0	0.0	0.0	0.0	0.0	0.0	85.7	50.0	0.0	0.0	n.a.	na.
4. Renminbi	0.0	2.4	0.0	5.9	0.0	0.0	0.0	0.0	0.0	0.0	0.0	0.0	n.a.	na.
5. Local	1.6	9.5	0.0	5.9	2.6	12.5	0.0	0.0	0.0	0.0	0.0	100.0	n.a.	na.
6. Others	1.6	0.0	0.0	0.0	2.6	0.0	0.0	0.0	0.0	0.0	0.0	0.0	n.a.	na.
TOTAL (No. of answers)	100.0 (63)	100.0 (42)	100.0 (11)	100.0 (17)	100.0 (38)	100.0 (24)	100.0 (15)	100.0 (3)	100.0 (7)	100.0 (2)	100.0 (2)	100.0 (1)	n.a. (na.)	100.0 (0)

Table 6.7 (continued)

Exports to Japan (%)	Location of Subsidiaries													
	Asia		China		ASEAN-6		United States		Euro Area		Oceania		Latin America	
	2010	2014	2010	2014	2010	2014	2010	2014	2010	2014	2010	2014	2010	2014
3. To Japanese Sogo Shosha														
1. JPY	8.3	64.3	33.3	100.0	0.0	55.6	0.0	0.0	0.0	0.0	0.0	0.0	n.a.	0.0
2. USD	91.7	28.6	66.7	0.0	100.0	33.3	0.0	100.0	0.0	0.0	100.0	0.0	n.a.	100.0
3. Euro	0.0	0.0	0.0	0.0	0.0	0.0	0.0	0.0	0.0	0.0	0.0	0.0	n.a.	0.0
4. Renminbi	0.0	0.0	0.0	0.0	0.0	0.0	0.0	0.0	0.0	0.0	0.0	0.0	n.a.	0.0
5. Local	0.0	7.1	0.0	0.0	0.0	11.1	0.0	0.0	0.0	0.0	0.0	100.0	n.a.	0.0
6. Others	0.0	0.0	0.0	0.0	0.0	0.0	0.0	0.0	0.0	0.0	0.0	0.0	n.a.	0.0
TOTAL (No. of answers)	100.0 (12)	100.0 (14)	100.0 (3)	100.0 (3)	100.0 (7)	100.0 (9)	100.0 (0)	100.0 (1)	100.0 (0)	100.0 (0)	100.0 (1)	100.0 (2)	n.a. (na.)	100.0 (1)
4. To Others														
1. JPY	42.1	22.2	40.0	0.0	50.0	40.0	12.5	0.0	50.0	0.0	0.0	100.0	n.a.	n.a.
2. USD	42.1	55.6	60.0	100.0	33.3	20.0	87.5	0.0	25.0	0.0	100.0	0.0	n.a.	n.a.
3. Euro	0.0	0.0	0.0	0.0	0.0	0.0	0.0	0.0	25.0	0.0	0.0	0.0	n.a.	n.a.
4. Renminbi	0.0	0.0	0.0	0.0	0.0	0.0	0.0	0.0	0.0	0.0	0.0	0.0	n.a.	n.a.
5. Local	5.3	0.0	0.0	0.0	8.3	0.0	0.0	0.0	0.0	0.0	0.0	0.0	n.a.	n.a.
6. Others	10.5	22.2	0.0	0.0	8.3	40.0	0.0	0.0	0.0	0.0	0.0	0.0	n.a.	n.a.
TOTAL (No. of answers)	100.0 (19)	100.0 (9)	100.0 (5)	100.0 (4)	100.0 (12)	100.0 (5)	100.0 (8)	100.0 (0)	100.0 (4)	100.0 (0)	100.0 (1)	100.0 (1)	n.a. (na.)	100.0 (0)

Notes: Figures in parenthesis (No. of answers) denote the number of transactions.

Source: 2010 and 2014 RIETI Survey.

that of US dollar-invoiced imports (40.0 per cent) in 2014. In contrast, Japanese subsidiaries seldom export their products through *Sogo Shosha*. In terms of the number of transactions, less than 5 per cent of Asia-based subsidiaries' exports to Japan are through *Sogo Shosha* (Table 6.7).

6.4.2   Intra-firm Trade with Foreign Countries

Tables 6.8 and 6.9 present the share of each invoice currency used in a subsidiary's trade with foreign countries except Japan. First, in intra-firm imports from and exports to group companies operating in foreign countries, overseas subsidiaries tend to use the US dollar for trade invoicing. According to the 2014 Survey, 87.2 per cent of US imports from foreign companies (arm's-length trade) and 88.9 per cent of US imports from group companies (intra-firm trade) are invoiced in US dollars (Table 6.8). This is the case even for subsidiaries' exports to customers, group companies and distributors in foreign countries, except for the subsidiaries operating in Europe where euro-invoiced transactions are more common in exports to foreign customers (Table 6.9).

Second, Asia-based subsidiaries tend to use the US dollar in imports from both foreign companies (arm's-length trade) and group companies (intra-firm trade). The share of the US dollar is also high in Asia-based subsidiaries' exports to foreign countries, but the US dollar share appears to be somewhat higher in exports to customers and distributors (arm's-length trade: 86.0 per cent and 88.9 per cent) than in exports to group companies (intra-firm trade: 75.7 per cent).

In summary, Japanese subsidiaries operating in North America (United States) and Europe (euro area) tend to use the US dollar and euro, respectively, in their imports from and exports to foreign countries except Japan, where the use of the yen is typically less than 10 per cent in both imports and exports. In contrast, Asia-based subsidiaries tend to use both the yen and the US dollar in imports from and exports to Japan. In intra-firm imports from Japan, the share of yen-invoiced imports is slightly higher than that of US dollar-invoiced imports. However, in intra-firm exports to Japan, the share of the US dollar is higher than that of the yen. Thus, the choice of invoice currency depends on where Japanese production subsidiaries operate, and the US dollar is frequently used even in Asia-based subsidiaries' intra-firm trade with Japan.

Table 6.8 Intra-firm imports from foreign countries

Imports from Foreign Countries (%)	Location of Subsidiaries													
	Asia		China		ASEAN-6		United States		Euro Area		Oceania		Latin America	
	2010	2014	2010	2014	2010	2014	2010	2014	2010	2014	2010	2014	2010	2014
1. Foreign Company														
1. JPY	3.0	1.1	2.7	0.0	2.7	1.5	0.0	0.0	0.0	0.0	0.0	0.0	n.a.	0.0
2. USD	80.5	88.8	78.4	100.0	81.9	88.8	77.4	87.2	59.5	42.1	50.0	100.0	n.a.	72.7
3. Euro	8.7	6.1	16.2	0.0	8.7	6.0	15.1	8.5	35.1	57.9	25.0	0.0	n.a.	27.3
4. Renminbi	0.9	0.0	2.7	0.0	0.0	0.0	0.0	2.1	0.0	0.0	0.0	0.0	n.a.	0.0
5. Local	5.2	2.2	0.0	0.0	4.7	1.5	5.7	2.1	2.7	0.0	25.0	0.0	n.a.	0.0
6. Others	1.7	1.7	0.0	0.0	2.0	2.2	1.9	0.0	2.7	0.0	0.0	0.0	n.a.	0.0
TOTAL (No. of Answers)	100.0 (231)	100.0 (179)	100.0 (37)	100.0 (21)	100.0 (149)	100.0 (134)	100.0 (53)	100.0 (47)	100.0 (37)	100.0 (19)	100.0 (8)	100.0 (9)	n.a. (n.a.)	100.0 (11)
2. Group Company														
1. JPY	7.2	3.4	4.5	0.0	6.3	5.4	4.1	2.8	8.3	0.0	0.0	0.0	n.a.	6.3
2. USD	80.3	85.3	77.3	93.1	80.2	82.4	89.8	88.9	58.3	60.0	42.9	100.0	n.a.	93.8
3. Euro	2.6	4.3	9.1	3.4	1.0	5.4	6.1	2.8	25.0	30.0	28.6	0.0	n.a.	0.0
4. Renminbi	0.0	0.9	0.0	3.4	0.0	0.0	0.0	0.0	0.0	0.0	0.0	0.0	n.a.	0.0
5. Local	2.6	1.7	4.5	0.0	3.1	1.4	0.0	5.6	8.3	0.0	28.6	0.0	n.a.	0.0
6. Others	7.2	4.3	4.5	0.0	9.4	5.4	0.0	0.0	0.0	10.0	0.0	0.0	n.a.	0.0
TOTAL (No. of Answers)	100.0 (152)	100.0 (116)	100.0 (22)	100.0 (29)	100.0 (96)	100.0 (74)	100.0 (49)	100.0 (36)	100.0 (24)	100.0 (10)	100.0 (7)	100.0 (1)	n.a. (n.a.)	100.0 (16)

3. Others

1. JPY	2.4	2.3	0.0	16.7	3.2	0.0	0.0	0.0	0.0	0.0	0.0	0.0	n.a.	0.0
2. USD	80.0	88.6	83.3	33.3	79.4	96.8	100.0	83.3	25.0	25.0	0.0	20.0	n.a.	0.0
3. Euro	4.7	0.0	11.1	0.0	1.6	0.0	0.0	16.7	37.5	75.0	50.0	0.0	n.a.	0.0
4. Renminbi	0.0	6.8	0.0	50.0	0.0	0.0	0.0	0.0	0.0	0.0	0.0	0.0	n.a.	0.0
5. Local	4.7	0.0	0.0	0.0	6.3	0.0	0.0	0.0	0.0	0.0	0.0	60.0	n.a.	0.0
6. Others	8.2	2.3	5.6	0.0	9.5	3.2	0.0	0.0	37.5	0.0	50.0	20.0	n.a.	0.0
TOTAL (No. of Answers)	100.0 (85)	100.0 (44)	100.0 (18)	100.0 (6)	100.0 (63)	100.0 (31)	100.0 (2)	100.0 (6)	100.0 (8)	100.0 (4)	100.0 (2)	100.0 (5)	n.a. (n.a.)	100.0 (0)

Note: Figures in parenthesis (No. of answers) denote the number of transactions.

Source: 2010 and 2014 RIETI Survey.

Table 6.9 Intra-firm exports to foreign countries

Exports to Foreign Countries (%)	Location of Subsidiaries													
	Asia		China		ASEAN-6		United States		Euro Area		Oceania		Latin America	
	2010	2014	2010	2014	2010	2014	2010	2014	2010	2014	2010	2014	2010	2014
1. To Customers														
1. JPY	7.3	9.6	20.0	18.8	3.9	7.4	4.1	0.0	0.0	0.0	0.0	0.0	n.a.	0.0
2. USD	82.9	86.0	70.0	81.3	87.4	85.2	90.5	86.5	23.8	11.1	50.0	85.7	n.a.	66.7
3. Euro	1.6	0.0	0.0	0.0	2.4	0.0	2.7	5.8	76.2	88.9	12.5	0.0	n.a.	0.0
4. Renminbi	1.6	0.0	6.7	0.0	0.0	0.0	0.0	0.0	0.0	0.0	0.0	0.0	n.a.	0.0
5. Local	4.7	3.7	0.0	0.0	3.9	6.2	1.4	7.7	0.0	0.0	12.5	0.0	n.a.	33.3
6. Others	2.1	0.7	3.3	0.0	2.4	1.2	1.4	0.0	0.0	0.0	25.0	14.3	n.a.	0.0
TOTAL (No. of Answers)	100.0 (193)	100.0 (136)	100.0 (30)	100.0 (32)	100.0 (127)	100.0 (81)	100.0 (74)	100.0 (52)	100.0 (21)	100.0 (27)	100.0 (8)	100.0 (7)	n.a. (n.a.)	100.0 (3)
2. To Group Companies														
1. JPY	6.0	5.0	3.5	0.0	8.1	6.4	0.0	0.0	0.0	0.0	0.0	0.0	n.a.	0.0
2. USD	77.2	75.7	78.9	72.7	74.3	78.2	76.5	72.7	18.8	43.5	25.0	0.0	n.a.	57.1
3. Euro	4.3	5.7	5.3	11.4	4.1	3.8	17.6	9.1	78.1	47.8	0.0	0.0	n.a.	28.6
4. Renminbi	1.3	3.6	5.3	11.4	0.0	0.0	0.0	0.0	0.0	0.0	0.0	0.0	n.a.	0.0
5. Local	7.3	7.1	3.5	2.3	9.5	9.0	2.9	18.2	3.1	8.7	75.0	0.0	n.a.	14.3
6. Others	3.9	2.9	3.5	2.3	4.1	2.6	2.9	0.0	0.0	0.0	0.0	0.0	n.a.	0.0
TOTAL (No. of Answers)	100.0 (232)	100.0 (140)	100.0 (57)	100.0 (44)	100.0 (148)	100.0 (78)	100.0 (34)	100.0 (22)	100.0 (32)	100.0 (23)	100.0 (4)	100.0 (0)	n.a. (n.a.)	100.0 (7)

3. To Distributors

1. JPY	0.0	2.8	0.0	0.0	0.0	0.0	0.0	0.0	20.0	0.0	0.0	0.0	n.a.	0.0
2. USD	88.4	88.9	91.7	85.7	84.2	95.5	100.0	92.9	40.0	100.0	75.0	100.0	n.a.	100.0
3. Euro	0.0	2.8	0.0	0.0	0.0	4.5	0.0	7.1	20.0	0.0	0.0	0.0	n.a.	0.0
4. Renminbi	0.0	5.6	0.0	14.3	0.0	0.0	0.0	0.0	0.0	0.0	0.0	0.0	n.a.	0.0
5. Local	9.3	0.0	0.0	0.0	15.8	0.0	0.0	0.0	20.0	0.0	25.0	0.0	n.a.	0.0
6. Others	2.3	0.0	8.3	0.0	0.0	0.0	0.0	0.0	0.0	0.0	0.0	0.0	n.a.	0.0
TOTAL (No. of Answers)	100.0 (43)	100.0 (36)	100.0 (12)	100.0 (7)	100.0 (19)	100.0 (22)	100.0 (14)	100.0 (14)	100.0 (5)	100.0 (3)	100.0 (4)	100.0 (3)	n.a. (n.a.)	100.0 (8)

4. To Others

1. JPY	11.8	0.0	0.0	0.0	18.2	0.0	0.0	0.0	0.0	0.0	0.0	0.0	n.a.	0.0
2. USD	64.7	100.0	0.0	100.0	72.7	100.0	100.0	100.0	16.7	0.0	0.0	0.0	n.a	0.0
3. Euro	0.0	0.0	0.0	0.0	0.0	0.0	0.0	0.0	33.3	0.0	0.0	0.0	n.a.	0.0
4. Renminbi	0.0	0.0	0.0	0.0	0.0	0.0	0.0	0.0	0.0	0.0	0.0	0.0	n.a.	0.0
5. Local	0.0	0.0	0.0	0.0	0.0	0.0	0.0	0.0	0.0	0.0	0.0	0.0	n.a.	0.0
6. Others	23.5	0.0	0.0	0.0	9.1	0.0	0.0	0.0	50.0	0.0	0.0	0.0	n.a.	0.0
TOTAL (No. of Answers)	100.0 (17)	100.0 (7)	100.0 (0)	100.0 (1)	100.0 (11)	100.0 (6)	100.0 (3)	100.0 (2)	100.0 (6)	100.0 (3)	100.0 (0)	100.0 (0)	n.a. (n.a.)	100.0 (0)

Notes: Figures in parenthesis (No. of answers) denote the number of transactions.

Source: 2010 and 2014 RIETI Survey.

6.5 DETERMINANTS OF INVOICE CURRENCY CHOICE

6.5.1 Empirical Model and Data Description

We have so far observed the invoice currency choices made by Japanese production subsidiaries, using the two types of data on invoice currency obtained from our questionnaire surveys. In this section we empirically analyse product-level invoice currency decisions using the data obtained from the 2010 and 2014 Surveys. An advantage of the product-level data is to obtain information not only on identity of trading partners (intra-firm or arm's-length trade) but also on the choice of invoice currency for each transaction.

As discussed in Chapter 2, we have two puzzles of Japanese invoicing currency pattern, and the second puzzle is the large share of US dollar-invoiced trade between Japan and Asian countries despite growing intra-firm trade along production and supply chains. We hereafter focus on the invoice currency choice of Asia-based subsidiaries in their trade with Japan. Specifically, Asia-based subsidiaries have a stronger tendency to export their products to Japan, but the share of yen-invoiced trade appears to have declined, as discussed in section 6.3. We investigate what factor contributed to the decline in yen-invoiced trade using new explanatory variables related to production chains and intra-firm trade as well as conventional determinants.

We conduct a pooled logit estimation of the following equation:

$$
\begin{aligned}
(Invoice_{ijk}) = {} & \beta_0 + \beta_1 Exr\,Vol_k + \beta_2 D\,(Rauch)_i + \\
& + \beta_3 D\,(EXIntermediate)_i + \beta_4 D\,(EXIntrafirm)_i \\
& + \beta_5 IMIntrafirm_j + \beta_6 IMInvoiceShare_j \\
& + \beta_7 D\,(Netting)_j + \beta_8 USdependence_j \\
& + \beta_9 D\,(Year\,2014) + \beta_{10} D\,(Industry) + \varepsilon_{ijk}
\end{aligned}
\tag{6.1}
$$

where $Invoice_{ijk}$ is a binary variable that takes 1 if product i of subsidiary j located in country k is invoiced in yen (or US dollars) in exports to Japan and is otherwise 0.[14] $D()$ denotes the dummy variable, and ε_{ijk} indicates the error term.

The empirical model draws upon the partial equilibrium model of invoice currency choice discussed in Chapter 2 where the size of exchange

---

[14] This binary variable is reasonable, because, as shown in Figure 6.2, 90 per cent or more of Asia-based subsidiaries' exports to Japan are invoiced in either yen or US dollars.

rate variance as well as the degree of product differentiation are major determinants of invoice currency. As a proxy for exchange rate variance, we use exchange rate volatility (*ExrVol*) in equation (6.1). The two-year exchange rate volatility is calculated based on the standard deviation of the bilateral nominal exchange rate between the exporter's (Asian) currency and the importer's currency (the yen).[15]

To measure to what extent product differentiation affects invoice currency choice, we use a dummy variable for product differentiation in terms of Rauch (1999). As we have the names of traded products, we categorize these products according to Rauch (1999)'s index, where *D*(*Rauch*) takes 1 if the product is classified as a differentiated product and is otherwise 0. We also have information on whether export goods are intermediate goods or final consumption goods. We use a dummy for intermediate goods, *D*(*EXIntermediate*), which takes 1 if the product is intermediate goods and is otherwise 0.

In the exchange rate pass-through literature, production costs also affect a firm's pricing behaviour, and the price index of the producer country is typically used in the empirical model. Instead of using such cost variables, we include an invoice currency's share in a subsidiary's intermediate-input imports (*IMInvoiceShare*).

To analyse the effect of intra-firm transactions on invoice currency choices, we include a dummy for intra-firm exports, *D*(*EXIntrafirm*), and a share of invoice currency in imports of intermediate goods (*IMIntrafirm*).

We also include the ratio of consolidated sales in the US to total consolidated sales as a new explanatory variable (*USdependence*) to check whether export and sales dependency on the US market on a consolidated basis affects the choice of invoicing currency. If Asia-based subsidiaries are involved in value chains where the final export destination is the US, the US dollar is likely to be chosen as invoice currency in transactions along the value chains. The data on foreign sales in the US market and total consolidated sales of the company (head office) are obtained from Annual Securities Reports of respective companies.

We include a dummy variable for 'marry and netting' as well. The 2010

---

[15] As discussed in section 2.2, in exports of differentiated products, the lower the exchange rate variance between Asian currency and the yen is, the more likely the third currency (the US dollar) is to be used in Asian exports to Japan. In exports of homogeneous products, however, the importer's currency (the yen) is likely to be chosen. In addition, the larger the exchange rate variance between Asian currency and the yen is, the more likely the third currency (the US dollar) is to be used as the second-best currency in Asian exports to Japan.

and 2014 surveys collected information on whether subsidiaries use the 'marry and/or netting' techniques for exchange rate risk management. The dummy variable, $D(Netting)$, takes 1 if subsidiary j uses 'marry and netting' in trade transactions.

Since we conducted two rounds of questionnaire surveys, a panel regression may appear possible. However, the response rate of our questionnaire surveys is quite low, which results in an extremely unbalanced panel data. We tried to set up a panel data carefully and found that we could not conduct the panel data estimation with only a few overlapping observations. We thus decided to conduct the pooled cross-section estimation including a dummy variable, $D(Year2014)$. To check the difference in invoicing decisions across industries, we also include industry dummies in our empirical analysis.

6.5.2 Empirical Results

We empirically test a hypothesis with regard to determinants of firm's choice of an invoice currency. Table 6.10 presents the results of the logit estimation for subsidiaries' invoicing decisions for exports to Japan, where the dependent variable is a binary variable that takes 1 if the yen or US dollar is used as an invoice currency and 0 otherwise.

The estimation results for subsidiaries' exports to Japan using the US dollar and the yen as the invoice currency are presented in columns (1) to (4) and in columns (5) to (8), respectively. First, in columns (1) and (5), we include two conventional explanatory variables, the exchange rate volatility ($ExrVol$) and the product differentiation ($D(Rauch)$), but the estimated coefficients are not statistically significant except for the coefficient of $D(Rauch)$ in column (5). The exchange rate volatility variable does not have any significant effect in all estimations.[16]

Second, in columns (2) and (6), we include additional explanatory variables related to the type of export goods ($D(EXIntermediate)$) and trading partners ($D(EXIntrafirm)$), but the estimated coefficients are not statistically significant except for the positive and significant effect of intermediate-goods exports that are invoiced in the yen.

Third, explanatory variables related to imports of intermediated input goods are included in columns (3) and (7). The variables for intra-firm import share ($IMIntrafirm$) and yen-invoiced import share ($IMInvoiceShare$) have

---

[16]   For robustness check regarding the definition of exchange rate volatility, we try other exchange rate volatility variables and different time windows. For example, the three-year volatility (including the current year and the previous two years) was tried and we found very similar results.

Table 6.10 Results of logit estimation: invoicing currency decisions in Asia-based subsidiaries 'exports to Japan

Explanatory Variables	Dependent Variable							
	USD	USD	USD	USD	JPY	JPY	JPY	JPY
	(1)	(2)	(3)	(4)	(5)	(6)	(7)	(8)
EXR Volatility (Two-year)	−0.669 (0.916)	−0.712 (0.919)	0.039 (0.823)	−0.040 (0.813)	0.085 (0.882)	0.123 (0.885)	0.068 (0.809)	0.017 (0.813)
D_Product Diff. (Rauch Index)	−0.054 (0.053)	−0.055 (0.054)	−0.016 (0.048)	−0.019 (0.048)	0.104** (0.052)	0.105** (0.052)	0.057 (0.048)	0.071 (0.048)
D_Intermediate Export		−0.051 (0.042)	−0.018 (0.038)	−0.023 (0.037)		0.069* (0.041)	0.073* (0.038)	0.078** (0.037)
D_Intra-Firm Export		−0.044 (0.071)	−0.116* (0.060)	−0.125** (0.059)		0.055 (0.070)	0.100 (0.066)	0.101 (0.065)
Intra-Firm Import			−0.00009 (0.00050)	0.00015 (0.00051)			0.00152*** (0.00051)	0.00125** (0.00052)
USD-Invoice Import			0.0061*** (0.0002)	0.0059*** (0.0002)				
JPY-Invoice Import							0.0060*** (0.0003)	0.0059*** (0.0003)
D_Marry & Netting				−0.047 (0.039)				0.096** (0.039)
US Dependence				0.0034** (0.0013)				−0.0027* (0.0015)
US_Dependence*D_Year				0.0682*** (0.0255)				−0.0583* (0.0300)

211

D_Year	0.171***	0.175***	0.0368	0.0982**	−0.174***	−0.179***	−0.121***	−0.163***
	(0.046)	(0.046)	(0.047)	(0.047)	(0.045)	(0.045)	(0.046)	(0.045)
Constant	0.411	0.749	−0.526	−0.403	−0.640	−1.100**	−2.708***	−2.770***
	(0.387)	(0.491)	(0.638)	(0.641)	(0.396)	(0.508)	(0.676)	(0.687)
D_Industry	Yes	Yes	Yes	Yes	Yes	Yes	Yes	Yes
Num. of Observations	714	712	647	647	714	712	647	647
Pseudo R^2	0.057	0.059	0.297	0.310	0.071	0.075	0.279	0.291

Notes: Results of logit estimation are reported (benchmark: exports of finished goods in arm's-length exports of the chemical industry). 'D_' denotes a dummy variable. Estimation includes industry dummies. Marginal effects are reported. Figures in parenthesis are standard errors (*p<0.10, **p< 0.05, ***p< 0.01).

a significantly positive effect on yen-invoiced exports to Japan. In column (7), the dummy for intermediate goods exports also has a significantly positive effect on yen-invoiced exports to Japan. In column (3), the variable for US dollar-invoiced imports of intermediate inputs (*IMInvoiceShare*) has a positive and significant impact on US dollar-invoiced exports, while the dummy for intra-firm exports to Japan (*D(EXIntrafirm)*) has a negative and significant impact on US dollar-invoiced exports to Japan.

Fourth, we include a dummy for 'marry and netting' (*D(Netting)*) and a US dependence ratio (*USdependence*) in columns (4) and (8). The 'marry and netting' dummy has a significantly positive effect on yen-invoiced exports to Japan (column (8)), while the dummy has an insignificant effect on US dollar-invoiced exports to Japan (column (4)). This result suggests that Asia-based subsidiaries will increase yen-invoiced exports to Japan if they can utilize more efficient exchange risk-hedging instruments.

The US dependence ratio has a significantly negative impact on yen-invoiced exports to Japan (column (8)) and a significantly positive effect on US dollar-invoiced exports to Japan (column (4)). We also include the interaction term between the US dependence ratio and the year dummy, *D(Year2014)*, which also takes a statistically significantly negative coefficient in column (8) and a significantly positive coefficient in column (4). Thus, the higher the export and sales dependence on the US market in terms of the group company's consolidated sales, the lower (higher) is the tendency to choose the yen (US dollar) for export invoicing. This impact becomes greater in the 2014 Survey.

6.6 CONCLUSION

This chapter presents new findings about invoice currency choices of Japanese overseas subsidiaries. Utilizing data tabulated from the 2010 and 2014 Surveys, we explore which currency is used by overseas production subsidiaries, which has not been empirically investigated before. Analysis of the questionnaire survey responses shows that Japanese subsidiaries located in North America tend to choose US dollar invoicing, while the euro is often used by subsidiaries operating in Europe. In contrast, the share of yen invoicing is relatively high among Japanese subsidiaries operating in Asia, but US dollar invoicing is also common even in the Asian subsidiaries' trade with Japanese head offices and group companies. The question is why the US dollar as well as the yen is used as an invoice currency and why the share of the US dollar has increased in intra-firm trade between Asia and Japan.

By conducting a logit estimation, we have found that in production subsidiaries' exports to Japan, intra-firm trades along production chains tend to have more yen-invoiced transactions, especially in the case of intermediate-goods transactions. Utilizing efficient exchange risk hedging instruments such as 'marry and netting' is also likely to increase yen-invoiced transactions. A more interesting finding is the negative impact of the group company's US dependence on subsidiaries' yen-invoiced exports. As long as the group company has a high dependence on the US market in terms of consolidated sales, Asia-based subsidiaries will have a lower (higher) tendency to choose the yen (US dollar) even for the subsidiaries' exports to Japan, and this tendency becomes stronger in 2014.

Thus, the novel finding of this chapter provides an answer to the second puzzle presented in Chapter 2. Our empirical analysis has revealed that the choice of invoice currency in intra-firm trade will promote yen-invoiced exports to Japan from production subsidiaries operating in Asia. However, the more they export finished products to the US, the less they use the yen for trade among the group companies. Invoice currency choice in intra-firm trades may be determined by the final destination at the end of the production chains.

This chapter focuses mainly on the invoice currency choice and exchange risk management of overseas production subsidiaries. For further under-standing of Japanese firms' exchange risk management strategy, it is neces-sary to investigate the invoice currency choice of overseas sales subsidiaries as well. This question needs to be investigated in our future research.

7. Invoicing currency and yen internationalization

7.1 INTRODUCTION

The previous chapters of the book have analysed in detail how Japanese exporting companies are choosing invoice currencies with currency risk. Of course, they would prefer to pay for labour and imported inputs in yen as well as produce and sell their goods abroad invoiced in yen, if the trading partners allowed it. That would be an ideal environment for Japanese exporting firms. However, in reality, Japanese exporters face currency risk, because sometimes trading partners prefer invoicing and settlement in the US dollar. Doing business completely in yen would require the yen to become 'internationalized', that is, for the yen to become widely used in invoicing, transaction, settlement and saving *outside* Japan. The internationalization of a currency depends on volume of imports and exports, ease of capital flows, attractiveness of financial assets, and other financial and macroeconomic factors – most of them being beyond the control of individual firms.

The country in which the company happens to be established determines its fate when it comes to managing currency risk. American companies tend to benefit from the fact that the US dollar is the international currency, and many part suppliers and customers of products are happy to do business in the US dollar. A company in a small open economy with a floating exchange rate regime may have to deal with exports and imports in various trading partners' currencies. If the home currency has a high volatility, the trading partners may be reluctant to accept invoicing in the producer's currency, and exporters from the small open economy have to find ways to hedge currency risk.

In general, the government of a small open economy has an incentive to pursue the exchange rate regime that may be conducive to trade, especially resident exporters. If most of the exports of the small open economy go to the United States and countries that use the US dollar as an invoice currency, it is natural that exporters and importers of the small open economy will use the US dollar as an invoice currency. In addition, the government has an incentive to keep the exchange rate vis-à-vis the US dollar stable.

The best way to eliminate currency risk is to establish a single currency with major trading partners, so that the currency risk will be mutually eliminated. This is a solution aimed at by the Eurozone countries. A downside is that each member of the currency union has to give up sovereignty in monetary policy. Costs other than currency risk may become overwhelming if the currency union region does not satisfy conditions for an optimum currency area, *à la* Robert Mundell and Ronald McKinnon. An easier solution for a small open economy is to peg the currency unilaterally to the US dollar (or the euro) because your economy is very much integrated – high shares of imports, exports and investment – with the United States (or the euro area). However, the fixed exchange rate regime carries its own risk, which was demonstrated in the Asian currency crisis of 1997–98 and several episodes of financial crisis among the Latin American countries.

Japan is not exactly a *small* open economy. In terms of countries' economic size, Japan had been number 2 for decades, until China overtook Japan in 2010. In terms of economic size, the Japanese yen has been used for cross-border trade and investment. In the 1970s and 1980s, usage of the Japanese yen was as widespread as the Deutschmark and British pound, after the dominant US dollar. However, since the adoption of the Eurozone, the euro is much more widely used than the Japanese yen or the British pound. For decades, the US dollar, the euro, the Japanese yen and the British pound were considered to be the top four international currencies. They were the four composition currencies of the Special Drawing Rights (SDR), which is the accounting unit of the International Monetary Fund (IMF). In 2016, the Chinese yuan was added as the fifth SDR currency.

This chapter reviews the process of yen internationalization in detail, and explores reasons why the degree of internationalization did not go up as much as it had been hoped. Later in the chapter we make some observations on a recent push by the Chinese government to internationalize the Chinese Renminbi (RMB) in contrast to the Japanese experience.

7.2   INTERNATIONALIZATION OF A CURRENCY

In general, how can we determine a currency is *internationalized*? The literature usually defines the roles of an international currency as analogous to those of a domestic currency: unit of account, medium of exchange, and store of value. In addition, the roles are divided into use in the private sector versus use in the public sector. Thus, the role is categorized in a 3 by 2 matrix with three roles and two sectors. Table 7.1 shows such a matrix,

Table 7.1   Dimensions of an international currency

	Private Sector	Official Sector
Unit of account	Trade invoicing	Being pegged by other countries
	Denomination of financial products issued by companies and financial institutions of other countries	High weights in (official or de facto) currency baskets of foreign central banks
	Denomination of offshore financial products by domestic companies	(IMF) SDR composition currency
		Denomination of inter-national bonds issued by other governments or IFIs
Medium of exchange (Settlement)	Trade settlement	Intervention currency by other monetary authorities
	International financial transaction settlement	Government financial transactions (such as ODA)
		Central Bank swaps currency
		Currency circulation abroad (e.g., dollarization)
Store of value	Cross-border deposits	Foreign reserves (of other countries)
	Cross-border securities investment	Sovereign Wealth Funds (of other countries)

Source: Authors' creation, slightly modified from Ito (2011, 2017), which was based on the matrix first proposed by Kenen (1983) and Cohen (1971) .

where the left-hand column is for private sector use and the right-hand column is for public sector use.[1]

A currency can be called fully internationalized when the currency scores high in each of the six cells of the table. Let us examine whether the

---

[1]   The table was first proposed by Cohen (1971) in the context of the British pound vs. the US dollar; then it was popularized by Kenen (1983). This was then applied to the Chinese internationalization context by Ito (2011, 2017).

yen has become an international currency. Invoicing exports and imports in yen is the unit-of-account role in the private sector.

If invoicing in yen becomes widespread, it contributes to the degree of yen internationalization. Conversely, if aspects of yen internationalization in other cells become more heightened, then it provides grounds for the firms to use the yen as an invoice currency. In that sense, invoicing in yen, or lack thereof, is both a part of the definition and a consequence of other aspects of yen internationalization.

7.2.1 Private Sector, Unit of Account

Invoicing has been examined in the previous chapters of this book. In Chapter 2, section 2.3 presents a macro statistics of invoicing currencies based on customs data. As was discussed, the share of yen-invoiced exports to the world rose from 28.9 per cent in 1980 to 42.0 per cent in 1983. The increase can be attributed to the change in the Foreign Exchange and Foreign Trade Control Act (FEFTCA) of 1980. However, the share of exports invoiced in yen did not rise beyond the 1983 level, but declined to 33.4 per cent in 1987, even though further liberalization took place in 1984. It turned out that the yen invoicing ratio of exports to the world remained around 40 per cent from 1983 to the present.

The yen is used more in invoicing exports to Asian countries. The yen-invoiced ratio rose above 50 per cent in the early 2000s. However, the ratio has declined to just above 40 per cent in recent years. The yen-invoiced ratio is much lower for exports to the US, at around 10 per cent, and to Europe at around 30 per cent.

For imports to Japan, the share of yen invoicing is lower than the exports. It started at almost zero in 1980, but rose to 25 per cent by the mid-1990s. The share has been fluctuating between 25 per cent and 30 per cent to the present. The share of yen-invoiced imports is high among those from Europe, and has lately reached 60 per cent, up from 30 per cent in the late 1980s. The share of yen-invoiced imports from the US and Asia is around 20 per cent.

Often export invoicing and import invoicing are discussed separately when reasons for their stagnation are examined. However, they may be related, in the sense that a low import yen invoicing may be a cause as well as a consequence of low export invoicing. If trading partners of Japanese exporters also export to Japan, they may not mind invoicing and paying in yen. A typical trading pattern of Japan – importing resources and raw materials from the resource-rich Middle East and other developing countries and exporting manufactured goods to the US and European countries – was not suited to yen invoicing for exports or imports.

In sum, the shares of yen-invoiced exports and imports in the last twenty years have been stagnant following a steady rise in the 1980s and early 1990s. A lack of progress may point to a limit in yen invoicing when other factors are not helping exporters and importers to invoice their trades in yen. Other factors include both rational decisions of Japanese companies and other aspects (cells) of the yen internationalization matrix.

7.2.2 Private Sector, Medium of Exchange

Two indicators are commonly used to show which currencies are actually traded in the foreign exchange market and used for settlements among banks. The most comprehensive measure for foreign exchange transactions is a Triennial Survey conducted by the Bank for International Settlements (BIS). One of the measures for foreign exchange settlement is the SWIFT settlement data.

Every three years the BIS conducts a survey of all exchange rate transactions covering all banks and other financial institutions in almost all countries for the month of April. Central banks cooperate to obtain data from all types of banks and financial institutions. Table 7.2 shows the BIS ranking of the currency transactions in global transactions. Each foreign exchange transaction involves two currencies, and the total share of all currencies is 200 per cent. USD had a share of 87.6 per cent in 2016, which means that 87.6 per cent of all currency-pair transactions involved USD on one side. The euro was the second most traded currency, with a 31.3 per cent share. The Japanese yen, the third most traded currency, had a 21.6 per cent share, implying that one-fifth of all foreign exchange transactions involved the Japanese yen. The Chinese yuan was in eighth place with a 4 per cent share.

The SWIFT settlement data are based on the global interbank payment system, also called SWIFT. SWIFT publishes the settlement data by currency every month. The ranking shows the actual usage through the SWIFT settlement system. Figure 7.1 shows the currency ranking of the SWIFT settlement in June 2017. After the dominant US dollar (40.5 per cent) and the euro (32.9 per cent), the GBP is a distant third (7.3 per cent). The Japanese yen is in fourth place with 3.2 per cent. The Canadian dollar is in fifth with 2.04 per cent, and the Chinese yuan is in sixth with 1.98 per cent.

7.2.3 Private Sector, Store of Value

The currency is judged to be used as a store of value when the deposits and securities denominated by the yen are held by foreigners. Foreigners can

Table 7.2 BIS Triennial Surveys, 2001–16

Currency distribution of OTC foreign exchange turnover
Net-net basis,[1] percentage shares of average daily turnover in April[2]

Currency	2001 Share (%)	Rank	2004 Share (%)	Rank	2007 Share (%)	Rank	2010 Share (%)	Rank	2013 Share (%)	Rank	2016 Share (%)	Rank
USD	89.9	1	88.0	1	85.6	1	84.9	1	87.0	1	87.6	1
EUR	37.9	2	37.4	2	37.0	2	39.1	2	33.4	2	31.3	2
JPY	23.5	3	20.8	3	17.2	3	19.0	3	23.1	3	21.6	3
GBP	13.0	4	16.5	4	14.9	4	12.9	4	11.8	4	12.8	4
AUD	4.3	7	6.0	6	6.6	6	7.6	5	8.6	5	6.9	5
CAD	4.5	6	4.2	7	4.3	7	5.3	7	4.6	7	5.1	6
CHF	6.0	5	6.0	5	6.8	5	6.3	6	5.2	6	4.8	7
CNY[3]	0.0	35	0.1	29	0.5	20	0.9	17	2.2	9	4.0	8
SEK	2.5	8	2.2	8	2.7	9	2.2	9	1.8	11	2.2	9
MXN[3]	0.8	14	1.1	12	1.3	12	1.3	14	2.5	8	2.2	10
NZD[3]	0.6	16	1.1	13	1.9	11	1.6	10	2.0	10	2.1	11
SGD[3]	1.1	12	0.9	14	1.2	13	1.4	12	1.4	15	1.8	12
HKD[3]	2.2	9	1.8	9	2.7	8	2.4	8	1.4	13	1.7	13
NOK[3]	1.5	10	1.4	10	2.1	10	1.3	13	1.4	14	1.7	14
KRW[3]	0.8	15	1.1	11	1.2	14	1.5	11	1.2	17	1.6	15

Notes:
1. Adjusted for local and cross-border inter-dealer double-counting (i.e. 'net-net' basis).
2. Because two currencies are involved in each transaction, the sum of the percentage shares of individual currencies totals 200% instead of 100%.
3. Turnover for years prior to 2013 may be underestimated owing to incomplete reporting of offshore trading in previous surveys. Methodological changes in the 2013 survey ensured more complete coverage of activity in emerging market and other currencies.

Source: Bank of International Settlements, Triennial Survey, 2016.

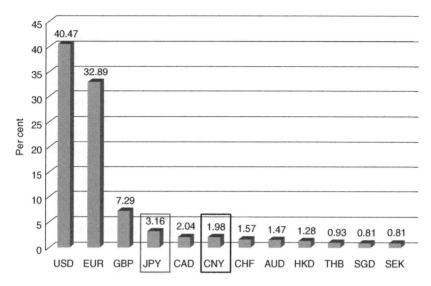

Source: SWIFT, RMT Tracker (July 2016).

Figure 7.1   SWIFT settlement, June 2017

hold those deposits onshore or offshore. In the case of the Japanese yen, almost all capital controls have been lifted, and many yen-denominated Japanese assets – bank deposits, government and private sector bonds and equities – are held by foreigners. However, among Japanese investors, yen-denominated assets issued by non-residents, such as Samurai bonds, are as popular as high-yield foreign-currency denominated securities. Issuing yen-denominated bonds by Japanese issuers outside Japan is not popular.

It would be easier for Japanese exporters to induce trading partners to accept invoicing and payment in yen if the trading partners have yen-denominated assets in their standard portfolios. This is one example showing how trade invoicing is related to other factors in the internationalization matrix.

7.2.4   Public Sector, Unit of Account

A unit of account in the public sector can be evaluated in several forms. First, if another country pegs its currency to the Japanese yen, then the yen is regarded as an internationalized currency. However, no country pegs its currency to the Japanese yen. If a country or a region of countries had chosen a fixed exchange rate for the yen, it would have been an easy job for Japanese exporters to invoice in yen and receive payments in yen. This is the same basic scenario that Germany enjoys as a member of the Eurozone. Conversely, if a group of countries traded with Japan as a top destination of exports and as a top source of imports, then the group of countries may have had an incentive to stabilize its exchange rate vis-à-vis the yen, if not peg it to the yen. In reality, this is not the case.

Second, if not a peg, a weight on the yen can be higher, so that the correlation between the yen and a currency of a trading partner can be high. Some Asian countries, most notably Singapore, have adopted a basket system, which means that they use monetary and exchange rate policy to keep the exchange rate close to a reference basket value of multiple exchange rates. If it were possible to engineer the stability of the real effective exchange rate, external shocks would be kept to a minimum. Ito (2017) showed that in the Asian region, it is the Chinese RMB, not the Japanese yen, that has a higher weight in the basket regressions of Asian currencies. For example, the Chinese RMB has the highest weight in the estimated Malaysian ringgit basket. Many Asian countries regard the Japanese yen as too volatile to follow.

There is one prominent public-sector unit of account which is not a currency for payment or store of value. Special Drawing Rights (SDR), created in 1969, were conceived as a unit of account at the IMF, although they were primarily aimed at supplementing the quota of shares by increasing liquidity from the IMF to member countries. The composition currencies of SDR had 16 currencies in the 1970s. However, the list was narrowed to 5 currencies in the 1980s: the US dollar, Deutschmark, French franc, Japanese yen and British pound. The Deutschmark and French franc were merged into the euro when the Eurozone was established. The SDR as a basket of four currencies continued from 1999 to 2016. The share of currencies in the SDR basket roughly reflects the economic power (GDP, exports, degree of currency internationalization) of each country. When the Chinese RMB was added as the fifth composition currency in 2016, the share in the SDR currency composition jumped ahead of the Japanese yen and British pound. The decision was based on a criterion of SDR basket shares which put a significant weight on the status of countries in exports in the world. The changes in the shares are summarized in Table 7.3. (See Ito (2017) for the process and examination of how IMF decided to include RMB into SDR valuation.)

Table 7.3   SDR composition currencies and shares

(a) Long-term changes (%)

	1980	1985	1990	1995	2000	2005	2010	2015
US Dollar	42	42	40	39	45	44	41.9	41.73
Euro					29	34	37.4	30.93
German Mark	19	19	21	21				
French Franc	13	12	11	11				
Japanese Yen	13	15	17	18	15	11	9.4	8.33
British Pound	13	12	11	11	11	11	11.3	8.09
Chinese Yuan								10.92

Source: International Monetary Fund.

(b) Details of changes from 2010 to 2015

SDR Basket		2010 standard	2015 Reform
(%)		Export 2/3; Foreign Reserves 1/3	Exports 50%; Foreign Reserves 16.7%; Foreign Exchange Transactions 16.7%; International Banking Liability and International Bond outstanding 16.7%
US dollar	USD	41.9	41.73
Euro	EUR	37.4	30.93
Renminbi	RMB		10.92
Japanese yen	JPY	9.4	8.33
British pound	GBP	11.3	8.09

Source: Adopted from Ito (2017).
Original Source: International Monetary Fund (2015).

7.2.5   Public Sector, Medium of Exchange

The public sector uses foreign currencies as a method of payment: when they engage in trade transactions or payment to international institutions, interventions in the foreign exchange market influence the exchange rate and lend/borrow to other governments. Advanced countries intervened quite frequently in the 1970s and 1980s in an attempt to stabilize the exchange rates among themselves. They have reduced frequencies of intervention, but when they do, they intervene in the four major currencies: USD, EUR, JPY and GBP. (See Ito (2007) for Japanese interventions.) Official lending for economic development or liquidity provision to avert a crisis can be done in any hard currencies. For example, some Japanese Official Development Assistance (ODA) – official lending – has been denominated and delivered in yen. If other countries accept the currency as a bilateral loan, then it is evidence of international use of medium of exchange. China is still a large borrower of development loans from the World Bank and Asian Development Bank. However, China has increased its own ODA to other developing countries, most notably to African countries. It is not clear whether Chinese ODAs are denominated in Chinese RMB or US dollars.

Central banks of G-10 countries have always maintained swap arrangements among themselves when liquidities were needed. The amount of bilateral swaps had dramatically increased, in some cases to the status of 'unlimited', during the Global Financial Crisis of 2008–2009. If the other side (counterpart country) requests or accepts the currency of a country, then it is a good sign that it has an international reserve currency status. The Federal Reserve extended swap lines to many advanced countries and some emerging market economies in 2008–10, as seen in the swap between the US dollar and the currency of the counterparty central bank. See Goldberg et al. (2011) for details of FRB swaps. The US dollar, as the international reserve currency, was demanded globally at the time of crisis.

In the Asian region, the currency swap agreement known as the Chiang Mai Initiative (CMI) was established in the wake of the Asian currency crisis of 1997–98. Initially, it was a web of bilateral swaps among the ten ASEAN countries plus Japan, China and Korea. Bilateral swaps were designed so that larger, more advanced countries would provide US dollars to a country in need of liquidity against the local currency. When the CMI progressed to a multilateral mechanism, known as CMI-M, participating countries earmarked foreign reserves in the US dollar for the reserve pooling. Again, the currency to be used was the US dollar.

After the Global Financial Crisis, China became very active in building bilateral local swap lines with other countries in promotion of the usage of RMB. For details of swaps initiated by the People's Bank of China, see Renmin University (2016).

7.2.6   Public Sector, Store of Value

The public sectors hold assets in foreign currencies for various reasons. One of these is foreign reserves, which are used in foreign exchange interventions. Almost all countries build up and hold foreign reserves (international reserves) as an asset. The currency composition of foreign reserves reveals how a country regards the importance of currencies. The extent to which other countries hold the currency can be a measure of internationalization. IMF COFER (Composition of Official Foreign Exchange Reserves) statistics show the currency composition of foreign reserves. Unfortunately, not all countries report currency compositions of their foreign reserves. Reserves are 'unallocated' for currencies, although they report the total amount of foreign reserves.

At the end of March 2017, the total reserves of all countries amounted to the equivalent of 10.9 trillion US dollars (see Table 7.4). Currency decompositions were reported for 'reporting countries', where reserves were valued at 8.8 billion US dollars. In the first quarter of 2017, the shares of major currencies among reporting countries are as follows: USD (64.52 per cent); EUR (19.28 per cent); JPY (4.55 per cent); GBP (4.28 per cent); CAD (1.93 per cent); AUD (1.84 per cent); CNY (1.00 per cent); CHF (0.16 per cent); and Others (2.43 per cent). The share of Japanese yen is still much higher than Chinese yuan (CNY). Recent changes are shown in Table 7.4.

7.3   HISTORY OF THE YEN'S INTERNATIONALIZATION

7.3.1   Liberalization and Deregulation of the Foreign Exchange Controls

In the chaotic years immediately after WWII, Japan experienced hyper-inflation, strict foreign exchange control, and multiple exchange rates under the occupation of the Allied Forces under US command. The exchange rate was unified at 360 yen per dollar in 1949, but many trade restrictions and tariffs were maintained, not to mention capital account transactions. Japan regained sovereignty, and became a member of the IMF in 1952, with Article 14 status. With a strong growth in exports, foreign exchange restrictions were gradually relaxed for imports and exports. Japan started in July 1960 to liberalize the yen-denominated transactions by non-residents. The Ministry of Finance authorized the residents to use the yen in the cross-border settlement of transactions and at the same time permitted foreign banks and non-residents to open the Non-resident Free Yen Accounts in Japan, through which they could

Table 7.4   Global foreign reserve, currency decomposition

		Q1 2016	Q2 2016	Q3 2016	Q4 2016	Q1 2017
Total Foreign Exchange Reserves		10925.78	10968.95	10994.11	10715.02	10899.37
Allocated Reserves		7779.73	8071.88	8366.85	8429.87	8848.95
Claims in US dollars		5095.69	5269.21	5417.21	5504.54	5709.50
	%	65.50%	65.28%	64.75%	65.30%	64.52%
Claims in euros		1517.93	1560.68	1640.83	1614.44	1706.44
	%	19.51%	19.33%	19.61%	19.15%	19.28%
Claims in Japanese yen		283.83	329.22	349.89	335.12	403.02
	%	3.65%	4.08%	4.18%	3.98%	4.55%
Claims in pounds sterling		361.16	367.22	367.82	365.52	378.71
	%	4.64%	4.55%	4.40%	4.34%	4.28%
Claims in Canadian dollars		140.36	147.76	159.91	165.15	171.06
	%	1.80%	1.83%	1.91%	1.96%	1.93%
Claims in Australian dollars		133.67	136.97	150.19	145.6	162.43
	%	1.72%	1.70%	1.80%	1.73%	1.84%
Claims in Chinese renminbi		NA	NA	NA	84.45	88.54
	%				1.00%	1.00%
Claims in Swiss francs		14.81	14.28	14.74	13.76	14.54
	%	0.19%	0.18%	0.18%	0.16%	0.16%
Claims in other currencies		232.27	246.54	266.26	201.3	214.71
	%	2.99%	3.05%	3.18%	2.39%	2.43%
Unallocated Reserves		3146.05	2897.07	2627.26	2285.16	2050.42

Source: International Monetary Fund, COFER.
(http://data.imf.org/?sk=E6A5F467-C14B-4AA8-9F6D-5A09EC4E62A4).

settle yen-denominated transactions. In 1964, Japan accepted the obligations under Article 8 of the Agreement which requires no restrictions on current transactions.

In 1960, only 0.1 per cent of Japanese exports and imports were denominated in yen. The share remained almost unchanged throughout the 1960s. Foreign exchange controls remained strict and it was costly for both residents and non-residents of Japan to conduct international transactions in yen. Moreover, no trading partners were willing to accept payments in yen. The world was under the fixed exchange rate regime, with only the dollar linked to gold, and there was no reason that exporters and importers would choose any currency other than the US dollar. The British pound was used internationally, especially among the Commonwealth countries (that is, former British colonies), as a nod to the legacy of the British pound's dominance prior to WWII.

In August 1971, the Bretton Woods system of global fixed exchange rates collapsed as the United States declared that the dollar was no longer convertible to gold and imposed an import surcharge. The persistent US trade deficits in the late 1960s were part of the reason that the US abandoned the Bretton Woods system. The regime change occurred after several years of US pressuring on Japan and Germany to curve exports to the US and revalue their currencies.

After a failed attempt to return to the fixed exchange rate with new exchange rates and a wider band, several major countries – Japan, Germany and the United Kingdom, among others – moved to a floating exchange rate in the spring of 1973. The yen appreciated most among the major currencies, from 360 yen/dollar before August 1971 to 308 yen/dollar in December 1971, to 270 in February 1973.

Following the collapse of the Bretton Woods regime, yen appreciation became a threat to Japanese exporters. Yen appreciation was overcome by efforts of Japanese exporters: raising productivities, cutting costs, moving higher on the technological ladder of manufacturing in pursuit of higher value added. In the process, the industrial structure evolved fast to catch up with the ever-appreciating value of the yen. The process of yen appreciation continued until the mid-1990s.

As the exchange rate fluctuated around the trend of steady appreciation, the Japanese Ministry of Finance deregulated various capital controls on the inflows and outflows. The range of Japanese assets that foreigners are allowed to invest in has been expanded with cautions not to exaggerate yen appreciation. Investment abroad by the Japanese residents was liberalized more enthusiastically in an attempt to slow down yen appreciation.

In Japan, the internationalization of the yen (that is, the wider use of the yen) has been repeatedly discussed as a policy goal in Japan since the 1980s. The major benefits were to reduce the currency risk of Japanese exporters. Many liberalization measures have been implemented to make the usage and holding of the yen easier for investors as well as exporters and importers. Capital controls were significantly removed in the 1980s and again in the mid-1990s. (See Table 7.5 for the chronology of liberalization steps.)

Table 7.5   Developments toward internationalization of the yen

Jul. 1960	Use of yen was permitted for overseas settlements. Introduction of non-residents' free-yen account.
Apr. 1964	Japan accepts the obligations under Article 8 of the IMF Agreements.
Dec. 1979	Foreign Exchange and Foreign Trade Control Act (New Foreign Exchange Act) amended on a broad range (to be implemented in Dec. 1980).
Apr. 1984	Abolition of real demand principle on which forward exchange transactions were permitted only when they were based on the real demands such as exports and imports.
May 1984	Ministry of Finance publishes the report of US–Japan yen–dollar committee titled 'Present Situation and the Future Developments for Financial Liberalization and Internationalization of the Yen'.
May 1997	Enactment of amended Foreign Exchange and Foreign Trade Act (to be implemented in April 1998) to liberalize outward and inward capital transactions, completely liberalize the foreign exchange business, etc.
Apr. 1998 Jul. 1998	Amended Exchange Act put into force. Ministry of Finance establishes Subcouncil on Internationalization of the yen under the Council on Foreign Exchange and Other Transactions.
Apr. 1999	Council on Foreign Exchange and Other Transactions releases recommendations titled 'Internationalization of the Yen for the 21st Century' that include improving financial and capital market environments and reviewing the yen's role in Asian countries' exchange system.
Jun. 2000	Study Group for the Promotion of the Internationalization of the Yen releases interim summarization of their discussion.

Source: Research paper and Policy Recommendation on 'Ways to promote foreign trade settlements denominated in local currencies in East Asia' commissioned by the ASEAN Secretariat. February 2010. Institute for International Monetary Affairs.

7.3.2   Amendment of Foreign Exchange and Foreign Trade Control Act of 1980

Following the rapid accumulation of balance of payment surpluses in the late 1970s, the Japanese government needed to respond to US pressure to reduce trade surpluses against the US. In early 1979 the Japanese government announced its intention to revise the foreign exchange-related laws and regulations from a positive list ('prohibition in principle') to a negative list ('permission in principle'), and implemented its comprehensive amendments in December 1979, effective December 1980. The main amendments included the following:

- Explicit stipulation of free principles of external transactions:
  – The Act explicitly stipulated that it is the basic principle that external transactions, including foreign exchange and foreign trade, can be made freely (without authorization).
- Liberalization of capital transactions and introduction of emergency regulation:
  – Capital account transactions became essentially liberalized under the prior notification system. Emergency regulations can be invoked on occasions such as when the maintenance of the equilibrium of the balance of payments is in jeopardy, when the capital flows incur volatile changes/fluctuations of the foreign exchange rate, and when massive movements of capital negatively affect the domestic money and capital markets.
  – Liberalization of services transactions and others.
  – Payments and receipts of payments were essentially liberalized.
  – Exports of means for payments were basically liberalized.

7.3.3   The US–Japan Yen–Dollar Committee of 1984

In the fall of 1983, Japan's increasing trade surplus against the US invited criticism from the US on the allegedly closed nature of Japanese financial and capital markets. It was built on the hypothesis that, if inward investment were allowed, the yen would appreciate to correct the trade imbalance. The US and Japanese governments negotiated how to open the Japanese financial market. Consequently, an agreement was reached in November 1983 between the two finance ministers of the US and Japan to establish the so-called 'Yen–Dollar Committee'. On the Japanese side, the Ministry of Finance prepared its policy report 'Current Situation on and Prospects for Financial Liberalization and the Internationalization of the Yen', to be released in April 1984. Accordingly, the report was released in May 1984 along with the release of the 'Report of US–Japan Yen Dollar Committee'.

The former report deliberated on such issues as the liberalization of deposit interest rates, deregulation of the banks' business hours and branch locations, creation of the yen-denominated BA (bankers' acceptance) market, and the entry of foreign banks into the Japanese trust business. It also proposed such measures as abolition of the *real demand principle* for foreign exchange transactions, liberalization of the use of yen abroad, an abolition of restrictions on the foreign exchange business, an abolition of the designated securities companies system, and creation of the Tokyo offshore market as a means for the internationalization of the yen.

The real demand principle was restriction on the forward transactions involving the yen to those customers who hold 'real demand' for such transactions. For example, foreigners who hold Japanese bonds that will mature in three months can have a contract with a bank with a fixed forward exchange rate. Similarly, Japanese exporters with receivables in the US dollar can have a six-month contract with a bank to convert the US dollar in the yen on the future date with a fixed forward exchange rate. However, with the real demand principle, those who would like to bet on yen appreciation or depreciation cannot transact forward contracts for investment purposes. By abolishing the real demand principle, those who would like to provide liquidity to the forward market can participate in the market, so that arbitrage – known as the covered interest rate parity – can hold with a small deviation. Costs became much lower too. Hedging and risk-taking foreign exchange transactions by Japanese firms and institutional investors became very active and the transaction volume of spot and forward transactions in Tokyo Market expanded rapidly.

7.3.4 The Amendment of Foreign Exchange and Foreign Trade Act (FEFTA) of 1998

The revised Foreign Exchange and Foreign Trade Law in April 1998 was the first major step toward the Japanese 'Big Bang'. The revised law deregulated domestic and foreign capital transactions and foreign exchange operations in principle and largely affected Japanese firms' exchange rate risk management. Here we examine the major changes related to trade settlement. The revisions included such comprehensive liberalization as:

- Liberalization of foreign exchange business: authorized foreign exchange banking system through which foreign exchange transactions were to be carried out and authorization and permission delivery was abolished and entry into and exit from foreign exchange business could be freely made by any market participants.
- Liberalization of capital and other transactions: prior authorization and/or notification requirements were essentially abolished so that capital transactions and their settlements could be freely made with the overseas counterparts.

- Upgrading of after-the-fact reporting system: efforts were made to upgrade the reporting system on an after-the-transaction basis in order to collect data on capital transactions for the compilation of payments statistics' balance as well as for the accurate monitoring of the market situation.

With the liberalization of settlements in foreign currencies, individuals were allowed to purchase products abroad and pay through a foreign bank account, as well as purchasing merchandise in Japan with dollars. Accordingly, Japanese firms were able to make trade settlements using foreign bank accounts. Nakakubo (1998) indicated that the following changes were worth noting for Japanese firms' exchange risk management, especially for trade settlement and foreign exchange risk management:

1. Companies and individuals with foreign currency deposits overseas were able to pay for imported goods in a foreign currency. Similarly, companies were able to perform trade settlements in foreign currencies, enabling more efficient foreign exchange management and greatly simplifying procedures.
2. The netting transactions, which enabled companies to settle accounts based on the net difference between exports and imports, instead of having to use gross account settlements in which exports and imports are treated separately, became available.
3. For large trading companies and manufacturing firms, a global treasury centre or so-called 'in-house bank' was created in a company's finance department or at an affiliated company, through which internal and external foreign currency settlements could be unified so that foreign exchange risks and costs could be efficiently managed.

Related to (3), we introduce the case of SONY. SONY Global Treasury Services Plc (SGTS) was established in London in December 2000 with the purpose of being a global centre for the entire SONY Group's foreign exchange management and fund management/raising operations. SGTS is positioned as a shared service centre which integrates foreign exchange and cash management operations across the SONY Group, while also coordinating financial risk management services for SONY Group companies worldwide. Recently, SGTS established SGTS Hong Kong in the Hong Kong Special Administrative Region and commenced operations in April 2011 with the aim of managing financial operations for the SONY Group's businesses in China and coordinating financial risk management services relating to SONY's major ODM (Original Design Manufacturing)/OEM (Original Equipment Manufacturing) businesses. SGTS Hong Kong also aims to enhance the SONY Group's RMB currency management by adopting RMB as the import/export currency for transactions across many of its subsidiaries in China and consolidating RMB at SGTS Hong Kong.[2]

7.4   WHY DID THE LIBERALIZATION FAIL TO PROMOTE YEN INVOICING?

In section 7.2 the dimensions of internationalization of a currency were explained and some statistics were presented. As an international currency, the Japanese yen is either number three or four in several rankings of currencies. The US dollar is a dominant international currency, followed by the euro. The Japanese yen and the British pound are the two currencies that are a distant third. After these four currencies, the Canadian dollar, the Australian dollar and the Swiss Franc form a group. In some measures, the Chinese yuan is significant, such as in the SDR composition share; in some other measures, however, it is still not relevant, such as the share in foreign reserves of other countries.

Section 7.3 explained that a series of measures were taken to help the yen's internationalization, although that was not a sole purpose. Most capital controls were abolished in the 1980s and any remaining controls were abolished in 1997, the so-called Japanese version of the Big Bang. However, these measures did not seem to help the degree of yen internationalization measured in six cells of the internationalization matrix, explained in section 7.2. In particular, yen invoicing of trades, explained in Chapter 2, and summarized in subsection 7.2.1, has not improved at all in the 1990s through to the present.

We will now pose several explanations for the failure in advancement in yen invoicing and, more generally, yen internationalization as a whole. The first set of explanations are based on our careful surveys of Japanese corporate behaviour studies in Chapters 3–6 in this book. First, Japanese firms behave rationally in choosing invoicing currency. Which currency exports (or imports) are invoiced is determined through negotiations between the two parties. Japanese firms that export to non-affiliated (such as subsidiaries) foreign firms insist on invoicing in the yen only when the Japanese firms have a competitive edge in the export destination market. The trading partners will absorb the currency risk. Second, when trading

---

[2]   Similar to SONY, Panasonic established their Panasonic Global Treasury Center as an overseas intra-group financial subsidiary in the Netherlands in 2006, which enhances the efficiency of group-wide treasury transactions by introducing a new round-the-clock global treasury system.

partners are group firms, the currency of the destination market or even the third currency may be chosen as an invoice currency. For example, subsidiaries in Asia to assemble finished goods from parts exported from Japan and then for export to the US would prefer the US dollar as an invoice currency. Another example is exports from Japan to sales subsidiaries in the US and in Europe. The headquarters in Japan can manage the multiple currency risk better than individual subsidiaries. Thus, the headquarters lets the invoice currency be that of the destination market.

The second set of explanations for the failure to advance yen invoicing of exports is the reinforcing mechanism between invoicing currency and the other five cells of the internationalization matrix. Foreign importers hesitate to invoice and pay in the yen, because they do not hold the yen in other parts of their business. They are not yen-earning exporters to Japan; they are not active portfolio investors in diverse currency denominations. Costs of foreign exchange transactions for yen-related cross-currency pairs, that is, those other than USD/JPY and EUR/JPY, are still high. For example, transactions costs, measured in the bid–ask spread, of the yen/baht are typically the sum of costs of the yen/dollar and the dollar/baht. There is no merit in trading directly in the yen for Asian trading partners.

Although the Japanese government and the Bank of Japan have pushed yen internationalization since the mid-1990s, almost no active policy interventions were adopted to promote the use of the yen. The basic stance was to remove institutional and taxation hurdles to using the yen if private sectors wanted to do so. Examples include the case of exempting foreigners from withholding tax on government securities.

In sum, stagnation of yen invoicing is both a cause and a consequence of stagnation of internationalization in the five other cells in the internationalization matrix.

7.5   THE INTERNATIONALIZATION OF THE RMB

7.5.1   Overview of the RMB Internationalization

Since 2009, the Chinese government has been pushing RMB internationalization. Ito (2017) reviews the progress of RMB internationalization in each of the six cells of the internationalization matrix. Renmin University (2017) also lists many statistics that are relevant in measuring the progress in RMB internationalization.[3]

---

[3]   Earlier papers on the internationalization of the RMB include Aizenman (2015), Eichengreen and Kawai (2014), Genberg (2009), Ito (2011), Park and Shin (2009) and Prasad

China seems to have a natural advantage in having its currency used widely in the global financial markets, as it overtook Japan in economic size in 2010. However, Japan had been in the number two position from the 1980s to 2010. Nevertheless, the yen internationalization did not proceed as well as some expected. Could RMB internationalization succeed more than yen internationalization?

There are two distinct differences between the processes of yen internationalization and that of the RMB internationalization.

A political drive for RMB internationalization was started by Zhou (2009), as argued by Ito (2017). Two measures are particularly interesting. First, the People's Bank of China (PBoC) pushed a currency swap agreement with many central banks. By the end of 2009, China concluded Currency Swap Agreements with the Republic of Korea, Hong Kong, Malaysia, Belarus, Indonesia and Argentina to provide RMB liquidity for trade and direct investment. Renmin University (2017) reports that by the end of 2016, the PBoC had signed 36 bilateral swap agreements with monetary authorities.

What is the purpose of these swaps? Since none of these countries, or financial institutions within them, had significant RMB liabilities, receiving RMB could not relieve a liquidity problem. But by extending these swaps, the PBoC could boast that it was doing its part to help countries in crisis. Moreover, the swaps promoted trade even if they were irrelevant as liquidity support. The announcement of the swaps was accompanied by a statement explaining that the arrangement was 'for the purpose of promoting bilateral trade and investment and strengthening financial cooperation'. China's goal was to encourage targeted countries to buy Chinese exports with RMB credit.

When the RMB is fully internationalized, the Chinese implementing currency swaps will provide a safety net that may rival the International Monetary Fund. Even when a country cannot borrow in the international market, or from the IMF, China can help. The magnitude of assistance that may be limited by the agreement and possible moral hazard will be an issue.

The swap agreements are initiatives pushed by China in conjunction with opening the RMB clearing in a financial centre or as a part of trade agreements.

Those countries that would like to establish an offshore RMB market were happy to accept a swap agreement. Those developing countries which had substantial trade relationships were happy to have a swap agreement, which may be useful in trade financing.

(2015) to name a few. However, reality moves quite fast. Below is the comprehensive state of RMB internationalization as of summer 2016.

An inclusion of RMB into the SDR basket was not automatic. Ito (2017) describes the criteria for inclusion and discussions at IMF. There were broadly two criteria: currency of a country with a large volume of exports and freely usable currency. The last piece of evidence for RMB as freely usable currency was that RMB was in the foreign reserves of other countries. IMF conducted a special, highly confidential survey among central banks to find out whether RMB was held as foreign reserves, because IMF's regular survey, COFER, did not detect RMB in foreign reserves of reporting countries. The survey was conducted in April–May 2015 in preparation for the decision later in the year. Since 2016:Q4, RMB appears as one of the reserve currencies in the COFER data.

China has also promoted direct RMB trading with non-US dollar currencies, which can eliminate the need for foreign counterparties to first buy and sell dollars in order to move between non-US dollar currencies and the RMB. Direct RMB trading has started with Malaysia (August 2010), the Russian Federation (November 2010), Japan (June 2012) and Australia (April 2013). In June 2014, the China Foreign Exchange Trade System (CFETS) announced the launch of direct trading between RMB and Great Britain's pound (GBP).

Chinese capital account controls are still reasonably strict, although the authorities are attempting a managed liberalization. Onshore yuan traded in Shanghai (CNY) and offshore yuan traded in Hong Kong (CNH) are technically two different currencies. Only domestically authorized participants could make transactions in CFETS in Shanghai. Non-residents can trade RMB in Hong Kong where the offshore rate, CNH, is determined, or any financial centres where China designates its clearing banks.

There are three different stock exchanges, depending on access and currency denomination. In Shanghai and Shenzhen, 'A shares', denominated in Chinese yuan, are traded, while in Hong Kong, 'H shares', denominated in Hong Kong dollars, are traded. Since participants cannot freely arbitrage between Hong Kong and Mainland (Shanghai and Shenzhen), the prices of the same company may deviate between Hong Kong and, for instance, Shanghai.

Ito (2017) showed that the currency premium between CNY and CNH and equity price premium between A shares and H shares have strong correlations. The pressure for capital inflow (or outflow) will show up as an onshore–offshore deviation both in the currency and equities markets. These deviations have not disappeared even after a series of capital account liberalization measures.

7.5.2 RMB Trade Settlement

The Japanese yen has been freely floating since 1973 and there have been no restrictions on the usage of the yen as payment and settlement of trade. China has just started the process of allowing the usage of its currency for trade settlement. In July 2009, the Chinese government launched a pilot scheme that allowed use of the RMB in settlement of trade with the ASEAN countries, Hong Kong, China, Macau and in five mainland cities. Since then, authorization of the RMB settled trade has been extended nationwide and essentially all trade with China can now be done in this way.

The RMB settled trade has also been promoted. Eichengreen and Kawai (2014) indicated that the share of the RMB trade settlement rose to 16.5 per cent of the Chinese total foreign trade in 2013:Q2 from below 1 per cent in 2010:Q1. However, more recent data shown in RMB internationalization report 2017 by Renmin University of China indicated a decline from 29.4 per cent in 2015 to 18.6 per cent in 2016.[4] The report explained that it was because the market was expecting the RMB to depreciate due to the Fed rate hike.

7.6   QUESTIONNAIRE SURVEY ON RMB USAGE BY JAPANESE FIRMS

From Questionnaire Survey on the Choice of Invoice Currency by Japanese Overseas Subsidiaries conducted in the August to September 2010 (hereafter, the 2010 Survey) and November 2014 to January 2015 (hereafter, the 2014 Survey), we investigate to what extent the use of RMB has been growing in trade of Japanese MNCs along the production chain.[5] We obtained useful information on what impedes the use of RMB and other Asian currencies for trade invoicing and whether the firms have a plan to increase the use of RMB and other Asian currencies in the future. Although those firms that responded to questionnaires are not necessarily the same between the 2010 and 2014 surveys, we can check the difference in results between the two surveys to discuss a possible increase in the use of Asian currencies.

Table 7.6 presents the 2010 and 2014 survey results obtained from Japanese overseas subsidiaries concerning the difficulties in using respective

---

[4]   According to Eichengreen and Kawai (2014), more than 80 per cent of these trade settlements have been with Hong Kong.
[5]   These questionnaire surveys were conducted by the Research Institute of Economy, Trade and Industry (RIETI).

Table 7.6 Problems in using respective currencies for trade invoicing

7.6a Results from the 2010 Survey

Answers in 2010 (Multiple answers are allowed)

(A) Name of currency	(B) Currency firms use for trade transactions	(C) Currency firms have difficulty in using for trade	(D) Problems					
			(D1) Foreign exchange controls/ regulations prevent non-residents' transactions of the currency	(D2) Foreign exchange controls/ regulations prevent operational hedging (marry and netting)	(D3) Capital controls/ restrictions prevent investment and fund-raising in that currency	(D4) High transaction costs involved with currency hedging	(D5) High foreign exchange volatility	(D6) Others
US Dollar	1224 (86.0)	714 (58.3)	31 [4.3]		40 [5.6]	84 [11.8]	**608** [85.2]	39 [5.5]
Euro	484 (34.0)	236 (48.8)	7 [3.0]		6 [2.5]	28 [11.9]	**210** [89.0]	11 [4.7]
Japanese yen	920 (64.6)	654 (71.1)	29 [4.4]		21 [3.2]	84 [12.8]	**593** [90.7]	25 [3.8]
Chinese Renminbi	149 (10.5)	76 (51.0)	**32** [42.1]		28 [36.8]	8 [10.5]	20 [26.3]	2 [2.6]
Hong Kong Dollar	83 (5.8)	18 (21.7)	2 [11.1]		1 [5.6]	2 [11.1]	**14** [77.8]	2 [11.1]

Table 7.6   (continued)

7.6a   Results from the 2010 Survey

(A) Name of currency	(B) Currency firms use for trade transactions	(C) Currency firms have difficulty in using for trade	Answers in 2010 (Multiple answers are allowed) (D) Problems					
			(D1) Foreign exchange controls/ regulations prevent non-residents' transactions of the currency	(D2) Foreign exchange controls/ regulations prevent operational hedging (marry and netting)	(D3) Capital controls/ restrictions prevent investment and fund-raising in that currency	(D4) High transaction costs involved with currency hedging	(D5) High foreign exchange volatility	(D6) Others
Taiwan Dollar	44 (3.1)	14 (31.8)	1 [7.1]		2 [14.3]	2 [14.3]	**12** [85.7]	0 [0.0]
Korean Won	22 (1.5)	10 (45.5)	0 [0.0]		0 [0.0]	1 [10.0]	**9** [90.0]	0 [0.0]
Singapore Dollar	143 (10.0)	45 (31.5)	2 [4.4]		4 [8.9]	8 [17.8]	**36** [80.0]	2 [4.4]
Malaysian Ringgit	55 (3.9)	24 (43.6)	6 [25.0]		4 [16.7]	1 [4.2]	**14** [58.3]	0 [0.0]
Indonesia Rupiah	41 (2.9)	26 (63.4)	1 [3.8]		0 [0.0]	3 [11.5]	**22** [84.6]	3 [11.5]

	(B)	(C)	(D1)	(D2)	(D3)	(D4)	(D5)	(D6)
Thai Baht	137 (9.6)	49 (35.8)	3 [6.1]		6 [12.2]	5 [10.2]	38 [77.6]	5 [10.2]
Philippines Peso	23 (1.6)	10 (43.5)	2 [20.0]		0 [0.0]	1 [10.0]	7 [70.0]	1 [10.0]
India Rupee	13 (0.9)	6 (46.2)	2 [33.3]		2 [33.3]	1 [16.7]	2 [33.3]	1 [16.7]

Notes: The total number of respondents (firms) is 1424. Figures in parenthesis in column (B) denote percentage figures based on the ratio of (B) to the total respondents (1424). Figures in parenthesis in column (C) denote percentage figures based on the ratio of (C) to (B). Figures in square brackets denote percentage figures based on the ratio of (D) to (C).

7.6b Results from the 2014 Survey

Answers in 2014 (Multiple answers are allowed)

(A) Name of currency	(B) Currency firms use for trade transactions	(C) Currency firms have difficulty in using for trade	(D) Problems					
			(D1) Foreign exchange controls/regulations prevent non-residents' transactions of the currency	(D2) Foreign exchange controls/regulations prevent operational hedging (marry and netting)	(D3) Capital controls/restrictions prevent investment and fund-raising in that currency	(D4) High transaction costs involved with currency hedging	(D5) High foreign exchange volatility	(D6) Others
US Dollar	1266 (83.9)	311 (46.6)	22 [7.1]	18 [6.2]	18 [6.2]	53 [18.3]	247 [85.2]	13 (4.5)

Table 7.6 (continued)

7.6b Results from the 2014 Survey

Answers in 2014 (Multiple answers are allowed)

(A) Name of currency	(B) Currency firms use for trade transactions	(C) Currency firms have difficulty in using for trade	(D) Problems					
			(D1) Foreign exchange controls/ regulations prevent non-residents' transactions of the currency	(D2) Foreign exchange controls/ regulations prevent operational hedging (marry and netting)	(D3) Capital controls/ restrictions prevent investment and fund-raising in that currency	(D4) High transaction costs involved with currency hedging	(D5) High foreign exchange volatility	(D6) Others
Euro	527 (34.9)	87 (13.0)	5 [5.7]	3 [3.8]	4 [5.0]	11 [13.8]	**70** [87.5]	3 (3.8)
Japanese yen	924 (60.4)	377 (40.8)	15 [4.0]	14 [3.7]	15 [4.0]	51 [13.5]	**357** [94.7]	8 (2.1)
Chinese Renminbi	147 (9.6)	41 (27.9)	12 [29.3]	14 [34.1]	16 [39.0]	10 [24.4]	**26** [63.4]	1 (2.4)
Hong Kong Dollar	63 (4.1)	4 (6.3)	0 [0.0]	0 [0.0]	0 [0.0]	1 [25.0]	**3** [75.0]	0 [0.0]
Taiwan Dollar	36 (2.4)	4 (11.1)	1 [25.0]	1 [25.0]	0 [0.0]	**2** [50.0]	0 [0.0]	1 (25.0)

Korean Won	25 (1.6)	3 (12.0)	0 [0.0]	0 [0.0]	0 [0.0]	1 [33.3]	3 [100.0]	0 [0.0]
Singapore Dollar	106 (6.9)	9 (8.5)	0 [0.0]	1 [11.1]	0 [0.0]	2 [22.2]	7 [77.8]	1 (11.1)
Malaysian Ringgit	56 (3.7)	12 (21.4)	3 [25.0]	2 [16.7]	2 [16.7]	3 [25.0]	8 [66.7]	1 (8.3)
Indonesia Rupiah	53 (3.5)	34 (64.2)	5 [14.7]	0 [0.0]	1 [2.9]	5 [14.7]	31 [91.2]	0 [0.0]
Thai Baht	127 (8.3)	23 (18.1)	0 [0.0]	1 [4.3]	2 [8.7]	3 [13.0]	18 [78.3]	1 (4.3)
Philippines Peso	18 (1.2)	5 (27.8)	0 [0.0]	0 [0.0]	1 [20.0]	0 [0.0]	4 [80.0]	0 [0.0]
India Rupee	28 (1.8)	10 (35.7)	0 [0.0]	1 [10.0]	1 [10.0]	2 [20.0]	6 [60.0]	1 [10.0]

Notes: The total number of respondents (firms) is 1529. Figures in parenthesis in column (B) denote percentage figures based on the ratio of (B) to the total respondents (1529). Figures in parenthesis in column (C) denote percentage figures based on the ratio of (C) to (B). Figures in square brackets denote percentage figures based on the ratio of (D) to (C).

Table 7.7 *Plan to increase RMB transactions in the future*

	2010				2014			
	Number of respondents	Yes	No	Others	Number of respondents	Yes	No	Others
Asia	755 (100.0)	160 (21.2)	572 (75.8)	23 (3.0)	623 (100.0)	99 (15.9)	501 (80.4)	23 (3.7)
Oceania	43 (100.0)	0 (0.0)	43 (100.0)	0 (0.0)	44 (100.0)	0 (0.0)	43 (97.7)	1 (2.3)
North America	273 (100.0)	6 (2.2)	262 (96.0)	5 (1.8)	204 (100.0)	3 (1.5)	196 (96.1)	5 (2.5)
South America					20 (100.0)	0 (0.0)	20 (100.0)	0 (0.0)
Europe (Euro area)	109 (100.0)	3 (2.8)	104 (95.4)	2 (1.8)	121 (100.0)	7 (5.8)	112 (92.6)	2 (1.7)
Europe (non-Euro area)	70 (100.0)	0 (0.0)	70 (100.0)	0 (0.0)	70 (100.0)	1 (1.4)	66 (94.3)	3 (4.3)
All	1250 (100.0)	169 (13.5)	1051 (84.1)	30 (2.4)	1082 (100.0)	110 (10.2)	938 (86.7)	34 (3.1)

Note: Figures in parenthesis denote percentage figures based on the ratio to the total respondents of respective regions.

Source: RIETI Questionnaire Survey 2010 and 2014.

Table 7.8 Plan to increase RMB transactions in the future (2014 Survey)

	(A) Number of respondents	(B) Do you have any plan to expand RMB transactions in the future?			(C) If 'Yes', what is the reason? (Multiple answers are allowed)			
		(B1) Yes	(B2) No	(B3) Others	(C1) Amount of RMB received has been increasing	(C2) Payment in RMB becomes more acceptable	(C3) RMB has become more easily used due to the progress of China's currency reform	(C4) Others
All Countries	1082	110 (10.2)	938 (86.7)	34 (3.1)	66	41	21	16
China	151	80 (53.0)	63 (41.7)	8 (5.3)	52	24	11	13
Hong Kong	39	10 (25.6)	26 (66.7)	3 (7.7)	6	7	3	0
Taiwan	46	2 (4.3)	42 (91.3)	2 (4.3)	0	0	1	1
Korea	22	0 (0.0)	21 (95.5)	1 (4.5)	0	0	0	0
Singapore	62	3 (4.8)	56 (90.3)	3 (4.8)	1	1	2	1

Table 7.8 (continued)

	(A) Number of respondents	(B) Do you have any plan to expand RMB transactions in the future?			(C) If 'Yes', what is the reason? (Multiple answers are allowed)			
		(B1) Yes	(B2) No	(B3) Others	(C1) Amount of RMB received has been increasing	(C2) Payment in RMB becomes more acceptable	(C3) RMB has become more easily used due to the progress of China's currency reform	(C4) Others
Malaysia	65	1 (1.5)	64 (98.5)	0 (0.0)	0	1	0	0
Thailand	85	0 (0.0)	82 (96.5)	3 (3.5)	0	0	0	0
Indonesia	73	0 (0.0)	72 (98.6)	1 (1.4)	0	0	0	0
Philippines	17	1 (5.9)	16 (94.1)	0 (0.0)	0	1	0	0
Vietnam	29	2 (6.9)	26 (89.7)	1 (3.4)	2	1	1	0
India	29	0 (0.0)	28 (96.6)	1 (3.4)	0	0	0	0

Note: Figures in parenthesis denote percentage figures based on the ratio of (B) to (A).

Source: RIETI Questionnaire Survey 2014.

Table 7.9   Experiences of RMB transactions (2014 Survey)

	Number of respondents	Yes			No
			If 'yes', which RMB?		
			CNY (Onshore RMB)	CNH (Offshore RMB)	
Asia	643 (100.0)	125 (19.4)	102 [85.0]	18 [15.0]	518 (80.6)
Oceania	43 (100.0)	1 (2.3)	1 [100.0]	0 [0.0]	42 (97.7)
North America	206 (100.0)	7 (3.4)	4 [57.1]	3 [42.9]	199 (96.6)
South America	20 (100.0)	0 (0.0)	0 [0.0]	0 [0.0]	20 (100.0)
Europe (Euro area)	123 (100.0)	5 (4.1)	4 [100.0]	0 [0.0]	118 (95.9)
Europe (Non-Euro area)	70 (100.0)	2 (2.9)	2 [100.0]	0 [0.0]	68 (97.1)
All	1105 (100.0)	140 (12.7)	113 [84.3]	21 [15.7]	965 (87.3)

Notes: Figures in parenthesis denote percentage figures based on the ratio to the total number of respondents. Figures in square brackets denote the ratio to the number of respondents that answered 'yes'. It must be noted that not all respondents who answered 'yes' answered the question, 'If "yes", which RMB?'

Source: RIETI Questionnaire Survey 2014.

currencies as invoice currency. First, as the usage of the currencies (column B) shows, the US dollar was the most used as an invoice currency: 86 per cent and 83.9 per cent of firms (respondents) used US dollars in 2010 and 2014 surveys, respectively, while the yen was the second most used currency and the euro the third. The RMB was the fourth most used currency: about 10 per cent of respondent firms used the RMB for trade invoicing. The ranking and the share of respective currencies do not change much between the 2010 and 2014 surveys.

Second, in an answer to the question: 'What is the problem when using respective currencies for trade invoicing?', '(D5) high foreign exchange rate volatility' accounts for the largest share in most currencies in both the

Table 7.10 The information on CNH usage for trade settlement (2014 Survey)

	Number of respondents	CNH is useful in hedging CNY transactions	Basically, we do not use CNH. But, in some cases, we use CNH due to the regulation on CNY transactions	We do not use CNH because only CNY can be used for trade settlement	Others
Asia	96 (100.0)	21 (21.9)	5 (5.2)	63 (65.6)	7 (7.3)
Oceania	1 (100.0)	0 (0.0)	0 (0.0)	1 (100.0)	0 (0.0)
North America	5 (100.0)	0 (0.0)	0 (0.0)	3 (60.0)	2 (40.0)
South America	0 (0.0)	0 (0.0)	0 (0.0)	0 (0.0)	0 (0.0)
Europe (Euro area)	3 (100.0)	0 (0.0)	0 (0.0)	3 (100.0)	0 (0.0)
Europe (Non-Euro area)	2 (100.0)	0 (0.0)	0 (0.0)	1 (50.0)	1 (50.0)
All	107 (100.0)	21 (19.6)	5 (4.7)	71 (66.4)	10 (9.3)

Note: Figures in parenthesis denote percentage figures based on the ratio to the total number of respondents.

Source: RIETI Questionnaire Survey 2014.

2010 and 2014 surveys. For RMB invoicing, the Japanese subsidiaries had difficulty using RMB due to '(D1) foreign exchange controls/regulations' in the 2010 survey. But, in the 2014 survey, 63.4 per cent of subsidiaries cited '(D5) high foreign exchange rate volatility' as a reason for the difficulty.

Third, Japanese subsidiaries had less difficulty in using RMB for trade transactions, as expressed in the 2014 survey compared to in the 2010 survey. In the third column of Table 7.6 ('(D3) currency firms have difficulty in using for trade'), the share of RMB declines from 51 per cent to 27.9 per cent. This is consistent with the improvement of the RMB foreign exchange transactions discussed above and also with a gradual shift of the RMB's exchange rate regime toward a more flexible one.

Table 7.7 presents the survey results of the question: 'Do you have any plans to increase RMB transactions in the future?'. Basically, few respondents answered 'yes' in either the 2010 or the 2014 survey, except for subsidiaries located in Asia. In the 2010 survey, only 21.2 per cent of respondents in Asia answered 'yes'. However, the share of respondents that answered 'yes' declined from 21.2 per cent to 15.9 per cent in the 2014 survey.

Table 7.8 presents the results of questionnaire surveys to Asian countries. According to the 2014 survey, more than half of the subsidiaries located in China and one quarter of subsidiaries located in Hong Kong plan to increase RMB transactions in the future, reflecting the growing use of RMB in China as suggested by columns (C1) and (C2) in Table 7.8. In contrast, only a few subsidiaries located in other Asian countries consider further use of RMB for their international transactions.

In the 2014 survey we obtained the information on the use of onshore RMB (CNY) and offshore RMB (CNH). Table 7.9 shows that only a few subsidiaries have engaged in RMB transactions, except in Asia. In Asia, 19.4 per cent of respondents use RMB for their transactions, 85 per cent of which use not CNH but CNY. This suggests that Japanese subsidiaries mainly use CNY for their operations in China.

Table 7.10 presents the information on why CNH is not used. Only 21.9 per cent of subsidiaries consider CNH useful in hedging CNY transactions, and two-thirds or more of subsidiaries do not use CNH because CNH cannot be used for trade settlements. Thus, we may conclude that only one-fifth of Japanese subsidiaries use CNH for hedging purpose, and the rest of subsidiaries are reluctant to use CNH for RMB transactions.

The above results indicate that RMB cross-border transactions are not increasing among Japanese multinational firms at the moment, despite the fact that the RMB internationalization has started from trade-related transactions. As the first step of RMB internationalization, the Chinese government focused on promoting the use of RMB for trade settlement without full convertibility of RMB. In addition, the Chinese government promoted the use of the offshore RMB (CNH) for cross-border transactions including trade settlements, deposit and direct investment. However, our survey results suggest, at least among the Japanese overseas subsidiaries, there is a limit for the usage of RMB as trade settlements without full liberalization in capital accounts.

In comparison with RMB internationalization, there are three marked differences from the yen internationalization. First, the Japanese government deregulated, albeit gradually, the foreign exchange and capital controls to make the yen fully convertible, in parallel with, if not ahead of, any policy measures toward internationalization of the yen. In that sense, yen internationalization was clearly market-driven. As suggested by Eichengreen and Kawai (2014), Japan was reluctant to internationalize the yen for trade settlement in the 1980s and the first half of the 1990s. In contrast, the Chinese monetary authorities (the government and the People's Bank of China) are using political pressure to increase the degree of RMB internationalization. The process is in part government-driven.

Second, the Chinese government promotes the internationalization of the currency, but on the other hand it wants to retain control over capital inflows and outflows to minimize the volatility and misalignment of the RMB. After the years of preventing too rapid an appreciation, the PBoC reversed this course and started to limit the extent of depreciation in 2015. Capital controls over outflows were strengthened.

Third, the initial success with RMB internationalization, especially the increase in RMB deposits in Hong Kong, seems to be stalling or being reversed recently. From the peak of 1 trillion RMB in December 2014, the RMB deposits in Hong Kong declined almost by half, to 507 billion in March 2017. The initial success may be in part to avoid capital controls, as argued by Zhang and Zhang (2017), or simply a speculative demand with appreciation expectation of the RMB. Once the pressure shifted from capital inflows to capital outflows, RMB deposits in Hong Kong started to decline. As argued above, Ito (2017) also documented and calculated various indicators, such as the onshore–offshore premiums in equities and in currencies, which indicate inward and outward pressure of capital flows. The indicators changed sign after mid-2015, suggesting pressures changed from inward to outward. Whether RMB internationalization will keep the flexible exchange rate regime remains to be seen.

As explained above, the Chinese government has been pursuing a rather conflicting approach to RMB internationalization, namely promoting the use of RMB while capital controls were maintained, if not strengthened. Japanese overseas subsidiaries are still reluctant to use the offshore RMB for their cross-border trade settlements. Japan in the past made an effort to promote the international use of the yen by removing capital controls and restrictions on yen transactions. In contrast, China has facilitated the RMB internationalization and developed the offshore RMB markets, while keeping strict capital controls on the international use of the onshore RMB. As long as capital controls exist, Japanese firms do not assume that the RMB is an international currency. One of the above survey results suggests that there is a dilemma: unless capital controls are lifted, firms will be reluctant to use RMB due to the restrictions; but if capital controls are lifted, the exchange rate volatility will rise, which makes the firms avoid the use of that currency.

7.7   CONCLUSION

This chapter shows that trade invoicing, which is a main theme of this book, is closely related to the degree of currency internationalization. Japanese firms benefit from the internationalized status – maybe number three or four in ranking – of the yen, but still suffer from not being able to get rid of the currency risk completely. The yen is not really a dominant currency like the US dollar, and there is no area comparable to the euro area for Germany that uses the yen. Hence, there is a limit to how much Japanese firms can use the yen as invoice currency. They have to accept the situation and manage risk. Even so, the Japanese government may have to promote the usage of the yen so that the base for its usage does not erode.

References

Aizenman, Joshua, 2015. 'Internationalization of the RMB, Capital Market Openness and Financial Reforms in China', *Pacific Economic Review*, **20**(3), pp. 444–60.

Allayannis, George, Jane Ihrig and James P. Weston, 2001. 'Exchange-Rate Hedging: Financial vs. Operational Strategies', *American Economic Review Papers & Proceedings*, **91**(2), pp. 391–5.

Bacchetta, Philippe and Eric van Wincoop, 2003. 'Why Do Consumer Prices React Less Than Import Prices to Exchange Rates?', *Journal of European Economic Association*, **1**(2–3), pp. 662–70.

Bacchetta, Philippe and Eric van Wincoop, 2005. 'A Theory of the Currency Denomination of International Trade', *Journal of International Economics*, **67**(2), pp. 295–319.

Bartram, Söhnke M., Gregory W. Brown and Bernadette A. Minton, 2010. 'Resolving the Exposure Puzzle: The Many Facets of Exchange Rate Exposure', *Journal of Financial Economics*, **95**, pp. 148–73.

Burstein, Ariel, Joao Neves and Sergio Rebelo, 2003. 'Distribution Costs and Real Exchange Rate Dynamics During Exchange Rate Based Stabilizations', *Journal of Monetary Economics*, **50**, pp. 1189–214.

Campa, Jose and Linda Goldberg, 2006. 'Distribution Margins, Imported Inputs, and the Sensitivity of the CPI to Exchange Rates', NBER Working Paper No. 12121 (March).

Campa, Jose and Linda Goldberg, 2008. 'Pass-Through of Exchange Rates to Consumption Prices: What Has Changed and Why?', in Takatoshi Ito and Andrew K. Rose, eds, *International Finance Issues in the Pacific Rim: Global Imbalances, Financial Liberalization, and Exchange Rate Policy*, NBER East Asian Seminar on Economics, Vol. 17, pp. 139–70.

Cao, Shuntao, Wei Dong and Ben Tomlin, 2015. 'Pricing-to-Market, Currency Invoicing and Exchange Rate Pass-Through to Producer Prices', *Journal of International Money and Finance*, **58**, pp. 128–49.

Carter, David, Christos Pantzalis and Betty J. Simkins, 2001. 'Firmwide Risk Management of Foreign Exchange Exposure by U.S. Multinational Corporations', Working Paper Series, *Risk Management* eJournal 01/2001, DOI:10.2139/ssrn.255891.

Chiand, Min-Hsien and Jia-Hui Lin, 2007. 'The Relationship between

Corporate Governance and Firm Productivity: Evidence from Taiwan's Manufacturing Firms', *Corporate Governance: An International Review*, **15**(5), pp. 768–79.

Choudhri, Ehsan U., Hamid Faruqee and Dalia S. Hakura, 2005. 'Explaining the Exchange Rate Pass-Through in Different Prices', *Journal of International Economics*, **65**, pp. 349–74.

Chung, Wanyu, 2016. 'Imported Inputs and Invoicing Currency Choice: Theory and Evidence from UK Transaction Data', *Journal of International Economics*, **99**, pp. 237–50.

Cohen, Benjamin J. 1971. *The Future of Sterling as an International Currency*, London: Macmillan.

Deutsche Bundesbank, 1991. 'The Significance of the Deutsche Mark as an Invoicing Currency in Foreign Trade', *Monthly Report of the Deutsche Bundesbank*, November, pp. 40–44.

Devereux, Michael B., Wei Dong and Ben Tomlin, 2017. 'Importers and Exporters in Exchange Rate Pass-Through and Currency Invoicing', *Journal of International Economics*, **105**, pp. 187–204.

Döhring, Björn, 2008. 'Hedging and Invoicing Strategies to Reduce Exchange Rate Exposure: A Euro-Area Perspective', Economic Papers No. 299, European Commission.

Donnenfeld, Shabtai and Alfred Haug, 2003. 'Currency Invoicing in International Trade: an Empirical Investigation', *Review of International Economics*, **11**(2), pp. 332–45.

Donnenfeld, Shabtai and Alfred Haug, 2008. 'Currency Invoicing of US Imports', *International Journal of Finance and Economics*, **13**(2), pp. 184–98.

Donnenfeld, Shabtai and Itzhak Zilcha, 1991. 'Pricing of Exports and Exchange Rate Uncertainty', *Review of International Economics*, **32**, pp. 1009–22.

Eichengreen, Barry and Masahiro Kawai, 2014. 'Issues for Renminbi Internationalization: An Overview', ADBI Working Paper Series No. 454.

Engle, Charles, 2006. 'Equivalence Results for Optimal Pass-Through, Optimal Indexing to Exchange Rates, and Optimal Choice of Currency for Exporting Price', *Journal of European Economic Association*, **4**(6), pp. 1249–60.

Fitzgerald, Doireann and Stefanie Haller, 2014. 'Pricing-to-Market: Evidence from Plant-Level Prices', *Review of Economic Studies*, **81**(2), pp. 761–86.

Friberg, Richard, 1998. 'In Which Currency Should Exporters Set their Prices?', *Journal of International Economics*, **45**(1), pp. 59–76.

Friberg, Richard and Fredrik Wilander, 2008. 'The Currency Denomination of Exports: A Questionnaire Study', *Journal of International Economics*, **75**(1), pp. 54–69.

Fukuda, Shin-ichi and Cong Ji, 1994. 'On the Choice of Invoice Currency by Japanese Exporters: The PTM Approach', *Journal of the Japanese and International Economies*, **8**, pp. 511–29.

Genberg, Hans, 2009. 'Currency Internationalisation: Analytical and Policy Issues', in Bank of International Settlements, BoK-BIS Seminar on Currency Internationalisation: Lessons from the Global Financial Crisis and Prospects for the Future in Asia and the Pacific, 19–20 March 2009, available at http://www.bis.org/arp/conf_0903.htm.

Giovannini, Alberto, 1988. 'Exchange Rates and Traded Goods Prices', *Journal of International Economics*, **24**, pp. 45–68.

Goldberg, Linda S. and Cédric Tille, 2008. 'Vehicle Currency Use in International Trade', *Journal of International Economics*, **76**(2), pp. 177–92.

Goldberg, Linda S. and Cédric Tille, 2016. 'Micro, Macro, and Strategic Forces in International Trade Invoicing: Synthesis and Novel Patterns', *Journal of International Economics*, **102**, pp. 173–87.

Goldberg, Linda S., Craig Kennedy and Jason Miu, 2011. 'Central Bank Dollar Swap Lines and Overseas Dollar Funding Costs', FRBNY Economic Policy Review, May, pp. 3–20.

Goldberg, Pinelopi Koujianou and Michael M. Knetter, 1997. 'Goods Prices and Exchange Rates: What Have We Learned?', *Journal of Economic Literature*, **35**(3), pp. 1243–72.

Gopinath, Gita and Roberto Rigobon, 2008. 'Sticky Borders', *Quarterly Journal of Economics*, **123**(2), pp. 531–75.

Gopinath, Gita, Oleg Itskhoki and Roberto Rigobon, 2010. 'Currency Choice and Exchange Rate Pass-Through', *American Economic Review*, **100**(1), pp. 301–36.

Gopinath, Gita, Pierre-Oliver Gourinchas, Chang-Tai Hsieh and Nicholas Li, 2011. 'International Prices, Costs, and Markup Differences', *American Economic Review*, **101**(6), pp. 2450–86.

Grassman, Sven, 1973. 'A Fundamental Symmetry in International Payments', *Journal of International Economics*, **3**, pp. 105–16.

Grassman, Sven, 1976. 'Currency Distribution and Forward Cover in Foreign Trade', *Journal of International Economics*, **6**, pp. 215–21.

Hakala, Jürgen and Uwe Wystup, 2002. *Foreign Exchange Risk: Models, Instruments, and Strategies*, London: Risk Books.

Hanagaki, Takashi and Masahiro Hori, 2015. 'The Exchange Rate and the Performance of Japanese Firms: a Preliminary Analysis Using Firm-level Panel Data', Economic and Social Research Institute, Cabinet Office, Japan, ESRI International Conference, 31 July, available at http://www.esri.go.jp/jp/workshop/150731/Session4_hori.pdf.

Hommel, Ulrich, 2003. 'Financial Versus Operative Hedging of Currency Risk', Global Finance Journal, **14**(1), pp. 1–18.

International Monetary Fund, 2015. 'Press Release: IMF Executive Board Completes the 2015 Review of SDR Valuation', 1 December, available at https://www.imf.org/external/np/sec/pr/2015/pr15543.htm.

Ito, Hiro and Masahiro Kawai, 2016. 'Trade Invoicing in Major Currencies in 1970s–1990s: Lessons for Renminbi Internationalization', *Journal of the Japanese and International Economies*, **42**, pp. 123–45.

Ito, Takatoshi, 1993. 'The Yen and the International Monetary System', in C.F. Bergsten and M. Noland, eds, *Pacific Dynamism and the International Economic System*, Washington, DC: Institute of International Economics, pp. 299–322.

Ito, Takatoshi, 2007. 'Myths and Reality of Foreign Exchange Interventions: An Application to Japan', *International Journal of Finance & Economics*, **12**(2), pp. 133–54.

Ito, Takatoshi, 2011. 'The Internationalization of the RMB: Opportunities and Pitfalls', Council on Foreign Relations, CGS-IIGG Working Paper No. 15, November 2011, available at: http://www.cfr.org/china/internationalization-rmb-opportunities-pitfalls/p26287.

Ito, Takatoshi, 2017. 'A New Financial Order in Asia: Will a RMB Bloc Emerge?', *Journal of International Money and Finance*, **74**, pp. 232–57.

Ito, Takatoshi and Kiyotaka Sato, 2008. 'Exchange Rate Changes and Inflation in Post-Crisis Asian Economies: VAR Analysis of the Exchange Rate Pass-Through', *Journal of Money, Credit and Banking*, **40**(7), pp. 1407–38.

Ito, Takatoshi, Satoshi Koibuchi, Kiyotaka Sato and Junko Shimizu, 2010a. 'Exchange Rate Risk Management and Choice of Invoice Currency of Japanese Firms – from the 2009 RIETI Questionnaire Survey Results', RIETI Discussion Paper Series 10-J-032 [in Japanese].

Ito, Takatoshi, Satoshi Koibuchi, Kiyotaka Sato and Junko Shimizu, 2010b. 'Why Has the Yen Failed to Become a Dominant Invoice Currency in Asia? A Firm-Level Analysis of Japanese Exporters' Invoicing Behaviour', NBER Working Paper No. 16231.

Ito, Takatoshi, Satoshi Koibuchi, Kiyotaka Sato and Junko Shimizu, 2012. 'The Choice of an Invoicing Currency by Globally Operating Firms: A Firm-Level Analysis of Japanese Exporters', *International Journal of Finance and Economics*, **17**(4), pp. 305–20.

Ito, Takatoshi, Satoshi Koibuchi, Kiyotaka Sato and Junko Shimizu, 2013. 'Choice of Invoicing Currency: New Evidence from a Questionnaire Survey of Japanese Export Firms', *RIETI Discussion Paper Series*, 13-E-034, April.

Ito, Takatoshi, Satoshi Koibuchi, Kiyotaka Sato and Junko Shimizu, 2015a.

'Choice of Invoice Currency in Global Production and Sales Networks: The Case of Japanese Overseas Subsidiaries', RIETI Discussion Paper Series, 15-E-084.

Ito, Takatoshi, Satoshi Koibuchi, Kiyotaka Sato and Junko Shimizu, 2015b. 'Exchange Risk Management and the Choice of Invoice Currency: 2014 Questionnaire Survey of Japanese Overseas Subsidiaries', RIETI Discussion Paper Series, 15-J-054 [in Japanese].

Ito, Takatoshi, Satoshi Koibuchi, Kiyotaka Sato and Junko Shimizu, 2016a. 'Choice of Invoicing Currency in Japanese Trade: Industry and Commodity Level Analysis', RIETI Discussion Paper Series 16-E-031.

Ito, Takatoshi, Satoshi Koibuchi, Kiyotaka Sato and Junko Shimizu, 2016b. 'Exchange Rate Exposure and Exchange Rate Risk Management: The Case of Japanese Exporting Firms', *Journal of the Japanese and International Economies*, **41**, pp. 17–29.

Jayasinghe, Prabhath and Albert K. Tsui, 2008. 'Exchange Rate Exposure of Sectoral Returns and Volatilities: Evidence From Japanese Industrial Sectors', *Japan and the World Economy*, **20**(4), pp. 639–60.

Johnson, Martin and Daniel Pick, 1997. 'Currency Quandary: The Choice of Invoicing Currency under Exchange-Rate Uncertainty', *Review of International Economics*, **5**(1), pp. 118–28.

Kamps, Annette, 2006. 'The Euro as Invoicing Currency in International Trade', ECB Working Paper No. 665, European Central Bank.

Kawai, Masahiro, 1996. 'The Japanese Yen as an International Currency: Performance and Prospects', in Ryuzo Sato, Rama Ramachandran and Hajime Hori, eds, *Organization, Performance, and Equity: Perspectives on the Japanese Economy*, Boston, MA: Kluwer Academic Publishers, pp. 305–55.

Kenen, Peter, 1983. 'The Role of the Dollar as an International Currency', Group of Thirty Occasional Papers, No. 13, New York.

Kim, Young Sang, Ike Mathur and Jouahn Nam, 2006. 'Is Operational Hedging a Substitute for or a Complement to Financial Hedging?', *Journal of Corporate Finance*, **12**(4), pp. 834–53.

Knetter, Michael M., 1989. 'Price Discrimination by U.S. and German Exporters', *American Economic Review*, **79**(1), pp. 198–210.

Knetter, Michael M., 1993. 'International Comparison of Pricing-to-Market Behavior', *American Economic Review*, **83**, pp. 473–86.

Krugman, Paul, 1980. 'Vehicle Currencies and the Structure of International Exchange', *Journal of Money, Credit and Banking*, **12**, pp. 513–26.

Krugman, Paul, 1984. 'The International Role of the Dollar: Theory and Prospect', in John Bilson and Richard Marston, eds, *Exchange Rate Theory and Practice*, Chicago, IL: University of Chicago Press, pp. 261–78.

Krugman, Paul R., 1987. 'Pricing to Market When the Exchange Rate Changes', in Sven W. Arndt and J. David Richardson, eds, *Real-Financial Linkage Among the Open Economies*, Cambridge, MA: MIT Press, pp. 49–70.

Leibtag, Ephraim, Alice Nakamura, Emi Nakamura and Dawit Zerom, 2007. 'Cost Pass-Through in the U.S. Coffee Industry', Economic Research Report No. 38, United States Department of Agriculture.

Ligthart, Jenny and Jorge A. da Silva, 2007. 'Currency Invoicing in International Trade: A Panel Data Approach', Tilburg University Discussion Paper No. 2007-25.

Marston, Richard C., 1990. 'Pricing to Market in Japanese Manufacturing', *Journal of International Economics*, **29**, pp. 217–36.

McKinnon, Ronald, I., 1979. *Money in International Exchange: The Convertible Currency System*, New York and Oxford: Oxford University Press.

Nakakubo, Fumio, 1998. 'Revision of the Foreign Exchange Law and the Possibility of Capital Outflow', NLI Research, no. 117, NLI Research Institute, available at: http://www.nli-research.co.jp/english/econom ics/1998/eco9808a.pdf.

Nakamura, Emi, 2008. 'Pass-Through in Retail and Wholesale', *American Economic Review: Papers & Proceedings*, **98**(2), pp. 430–37.

Nakamura, Emi and Dawit Zerom, 2010. 'Accounting for Incomplete Pass-Through', *Review of Economic Studies*, **77**(3), pp. 1192–230.

Neiman, Brent, 2007. 'Multinationals, Intrafirm Trades, and International Macro Dynamics', Working Paper, Harvard University.

Neiman, Brent, 2010. 'Stickiness, Synchronization, and Passthrough in Intrafirm Trade Prices', *Journal of Monetary Economics*, **57**(3), pp. 295–308.

Oi, Hiroyuki, Akira Otani and Toyoichiro Shirota, 2004. 'The Choice of Invoice Currency in International Trade: Implications for the Internationalization of the Yen', *Monetary and Economic Studies*, Institute for Monetary and Economic Studies, Bank of Japan, March, pp. 27–64.

Page, S.A.B., 1977. 'Currency of Invoicing in Merchandise Trade', *National Institute Economic Review*, **33**, pp. 1241–64.

Page, S.A.B., 1981. 'The Choice of Invoicing Currency in Merchandise Trade', *National Institute Economic Review*, **85**, pp. 60–72.

Pantzalis, Christos, Betty J. Simkins and Paul A. Laux, 2001. 'Operational Hedges and the Foreign Exchange Exposure of US Multinational Corporations', *Journal of International Business Studies*, **32**(44), pp. 793–813.

Park, Yung Chul and Kwanho Shin, 2009. 'Internationalization of Currency in East Asia: Implications for Regional Monetary and

Financial Cooperation', in Bank of International Settlements, BoK-BIS
Seminar on Currency Internationalization: Lessons from the Global
Financial Crisis and Prospects for the Future in Asia and the Pacific,
19–20 March 2009, available at: http://www.bis.org/arp/conf_0903.htm.
Parsons, Craig and Kiyotaka Sato, 2008. 'New Estimates of Exchange Rate
Pass-Through in Japanese Exports', *International Journal of Finance and
Economics*, **13**(2), pp. 174–83.
Pramborg, Bengt, 2005. 'Foreign Exchange Risk-Management Practices
Between Swedish and Korean Firms', *Pacific-Basin Finance Journal*, **13**,
pp. 343–66.
Prasad, Eswar S., 2015. 'The Renminbi's Ascendance in International
Finance', in R. Glick and M. Spiegel, eds, *Policy Challenge in a
Diverging Global Economy*, Asia Economic Policy Conference, Federal
Reserve Bank of San Francisco, November, pp. 207–56.
Rauch, James E., 1999. 'Networks Versus Markets in International Trade',
Journal of International Economics, **48**(1), pp. 7–35.
Renmin University of China, International Monetary Institute, 2016.
'Currency Internationalization and Macro Risk Management', RMB
Internationalization Report 2016, Beijing, 24 July, available at: http://
www.imi.org.cn/report/19770.
Renmin University of China, International Monetary Institute, 2017.
'Strengthen the Financial Transaction Function of RMB', RMB
Internationalization Report 2017, Beijing, 15 July, available at: http://www.
imi.org.cn/en/wp-content/uploads/2017/07/%E3%80%90IMI-Research-
Report-No.-1702.EN%E3%80%91RMB-Internationalization-Report-
2017-Press-Release.pdf.
Sato, Kiyotaka, 1999. 'The International Use of the Japanese Yen: The Case
of Japan's Trade with East Asia', *The World Economy*, **22**(4), pp. 547–84.
Sato, Kiyotaka, 2003. 'Currency Invoicing in Japanese Exports to East
Asia: Implications for the Yen Internationalization', *Asian Economic
Journal*, **17**(2), pp. 129–54.
Sato, Kiyotaka and Junko Shimizu, 2016. 'The International Use of
Renminbi: Evidence from Japanese Firm-Level Data', RIETI Discussion
Paper Series, 16-E-033.
Shapiro, Alan C., 1996. *Multinational Financial Management*, 5th edn,
Hoboken, NJ: Wiley.
Takagi, Shinji and Yushi Yoshida, 2001. 'Exchange Rate Movements and
Tradable Goods Prices in East Asia: An Analysis Based on Japanese
Customs Data, 1988–1999', *IMF Staff Papers*, **48**(2), pp. 266–89.
Tavlas, George S., 1997. 'The International Use of the US Dollar: An
Optimum Currency Area Perspective', *The World Economy*, **20**(6), pp.
709–47.

Tavlas, George S. and Yuzuru Ozeki, 1992. 'The Internationalization of Currencies: An Appraisal of the Japanese Yen', Occasional Paper No. 90, Washington, DC: International Monetary Fund.

Zhang, Ming and Bin Zhang, 2017. 'The Boom and Bust of the RMB's Internationalization: A Perspective from Cross-Border Arbitrage', *Asian Economic Policy Review*, **12**(2), pp. 237–53.

Zhou, Xiaochuan, 2009. 'Reform the International Monetary System', 23 March 2009, accessed on 1 September 2016 at: http://www.pbc.gov.cn/english/130724/2842945/index.html.

Index

Printed and bound by CPI Group (UK) Ltd, Croydon, CR0 4YY

23/04/2025

14660958-0005